An education to give your child the freedom to flourish

John Tranmer, chair of the Independent Association of Prep Schools (IAPS), highlights the rich diversity a prep school education offers and how it enables your child to flourish

Welcome to the 2016 edition of *John Catt's Preparatory Schools* guide.

It is my pleasure and privilege to be asked to contribute the foreword to such an important publication, and one which will hopefully help you choose the correct school to guide your child through the most important, early years of their education.

By attending a prep school, a child is guaranteed an education like no other; a curriculum that is not dictated by government but is broad, balanced and tailored to their needs, a favourable staff to pupil ratio and a focus on traditional values like courtesy and respect both inside and outside of the classroom.

Independent schools offer outstanding education that embraces both innovation, technology and important traditions that are tried and tested. A wealth of extra-curricular opportunities will also fall at your child's feet, and these typically embrace performing arts and skills as well as the many sports clubs and tournaments you may have come to expect.

Staying in the sporting world for example, we at IAPS now arrange competitions in areas such as sailing and martial arts in addition to the many traditional sports, including netball, rugby, hockey, cricket, football, swimming and tennis. Prep schools will help your child to discover and develop their talents, interests and skills which will stay with them for the rest of their life.

Indeed, choosing a school is a lifelong decision. The choice you make will directly impact the way your child sees the world, and will profoundly shape the way they grow into adulthood. With the opportunities and teaching methods employed at independent schools, my extensive experience suggests that preparatory education ensures your child is given the best possible start, one which will help to equip him or her with the knowledge, skills and attributes to create a happy and purposeful future.

Yet the independent sector is no longer exclusive in the sense that only those from affluent families have access to private schools. The vast majority of prep schools offer fee support (often referred to as 'bursaries') and at IAPS we encourage our member schools to be inclusive. Schemes like iTrust, a charity set up and supported by IAPS, have helped contribute to the many millions of pounds worth of discounts parents have been offered to help them fund their child's education. These schemes are usually means-tested to ensure that appropriate support is offered to the most deserving families.

I am sure you are reading this with many important questions running through your head. Which prep school is right for my child? What do I need to think about when making the choice? Do I really need all the information enclosed in this book? Yes, you probably do, but there are key areas you should definitely think about.

Factors like location will come into the equation, as will the choice between single-sex and co-educational. If you are contemplating boarding, a popular option typically for children aged 8+, travel times may not be an important factor but for many the length of commute to school is very relevant. Some children cope well with lengthy journeys, others do not. Think carefully about what suits your child. Likewise, some children will thrive in virtually any school whereas others may benefit from particular features such as single-sex education. Having taught in single-sex and co-educational schools as well as those

> Independent schools offer outstanding education that embraces both innovation, technology and important traditions that are tried and tested.

JOHN CATT'S

Preparatory Schools 2016

19th Edition
Editor: Samantha Wilkins

JOHN
CATT
EDUCATIONAL
LIMITED

Published in 2016 by
John Catt Educational Ltd,
12 Deben Mill Business Centre,
Woodbridge, Suffolk IP12 1BL UK
Tel: 01394 389850   Fax: 01394 386893
Email: enquiries@johncatt.com
Website: www.johncatt.com
© 2016 John Catt Educational Ltd

**A CIP catalogue record for this book is available from the
British Library.**

ISBN: 978 1 908717 72 5

Contacts
Editor
Samantha Wilkins

Advertising & School Profiles
Tel: +44 (0) 1394 389850
Email: sales@johncatt.com

Distribution/Book Sales
Tel: +44 (0) 1394 389863
Email: booksales@johncatt.com

Contents

GDST schools. Where girls can.

Choosing your daughter's school is one of the biggest decisions you, as parents, will make. At the GDST we put girls first, ensuring that everything in their school lives is calibrated and designed to meet their educational and pastoral needs.

The GDST has always been a pioneer of girls' education in the UK. Our network of 26 schools and academies provides unmatched opportunities, connections and resources for girls between the ages of three and 18.

GDST schools in London

Blackheath High School
Bromley High School
Croydon High School
Kensington Prep School
Northwood College for Girls
Notting Hill & Ealing High School

Putney High School
South Hampstead High School
Streatham & Clapham High School
Sutton High School
Sydenham High School
Wimbledon High School

GDST schools and academies outside London

The Belvedere Academy, Liverpool
Birkenhead High School Academy
Brighton & Hove High School
Howell's School, Llandaff
Ipswich High School for Girls
Newcastle High School for Girls
Northampton High School

Norwich High School for Girls
Nottingham Girls' High School
Oxford High School
Portsmouth High School
The Royal High School, Bath
Sheffield High School
Shrewsbury High School

 gdst Girls' Day School Trust

A network of Confident, Composed, Courageous, Committed girls.

See www.gdst.net to find your closest GDST school or academy, and arrange a visit.

with boarding, I know that the variety of provision within the independent sector is one of its greatest strengths.

Please look carefully at the details of the prep schools relevant for you and consider how best you feel they can help your child's education and development into a young adult. This guide will help enormously and you should cross-reference it by looking at individual websites and, most importantly, by arranging to visit possible schools. Such visits are tremendously important as you will not experience the full potential of a school without meeting the children and staff who make each community individual and special. The time and effort you put into your research will be very worthwhile. When you visit, I suggest you pay particular attention to the following:

- Atmosphere – is it a happy, purposeful place? Do the staff and children seem relaxed? Is the school full of energy and life yet well organised and structured?

- Facilities – Good classrooms are at the heart of excellent schools. Are the classrooms well-resourced for teaching and learning? Is there evidence of academic progress and creativity? Are there spaces for sport and play?

- Relationships – How do the children interact with the staff and each other? Is there consistency in the way that children behave? If you do not know any of the children or families currently associated with the school, ask if you might be able to arrange a conversation with someone suitable. Such an insider's point of view is often invaluable.

Do not let the hard work at this stage put you off. Simply by picking up this book, you have in your hands one of the best possible tools in helping you make the decision right for you. Visit the websites of organisations like the ISC (www.isc.co.uk) and IAPS (iaps.uk), and do not hesitate to contact schools if the information you require is not readily available.

I am confident that you will be impressed when you visit any of the schools detailed in this guide. Choosing a prep school is a difficult task, but the outcome is hugely rewarding. This is the first step on a tremendously exciting ladder.

I wish you every success in making the right choice, and wish you and your child all the best for the future.

John Tranmer was formerly Headmaster of The Froebelian School (1991-2015)
John was appointed as Chairman of IAPS from 2015 -2018
For more information about IAPS, see page 27

How to use this guidebook

Are you looking for...

Help and advice?

If so, take a look at our editorial section (pages 5 to 33). Here you will find articles written by experts in their field covering issues you may well come across when choosing a school for your child.

A school or college in a certain geographical region?

Then you need to go to the map on D88 to find the directory page reference to a particular region. We suggest that you look first in the directory for basic information about all the schools in each region, complete with contact details, so that you will be better informed about the choices available to you. From this section you will be directed to more detailed information in the profile section, where this is available.

A certain type of school or college in a particular area?

Look in the directories for the area you want (again, you can find a directory page reference from the regional map on D88). Underneath each school listed you will find icons that denote different types of schools or qualifications that they offer. You can find a key to these icons on the following page; this key is repeated at the front of each section of the directory.

A specific school or college?

If you know the name of the school or college but are unsure of its location, simply go to the index at the back of the guide where you will find all the schools listed alphabetically. You will find that some page numbers are prefixed with the letter D, this denotes that the school appears in the directory section. Page numbers not prefixed by the letter D denote schools that have chosen to include a fuller school profile, which will provide you with much more extensive information.

More information on relevant educational organisations and examinations?

In the editorial section you will find 'Initial advice', a helpful explanation of the various educational organisations relevant to preparatory schools. There are articles from the Boarding Schools Association (BSA), Girls' Schools Association (GSA), Headmasters' and Headmistresses' Conference (HMC), Independent Association of Preparatory Schools (IAPS), Independent Schools Association (ISA), Independent Schools Council (ISC) and the Society of Heads.

Keys to directory information

The diagrams below explain what the different icons used in the directory mean, and indicate the type of information given for each school in the directory.

Key to directory

County	**Wherefordshire**
Name of school or college	**College Academy**
Indicates that this school has a profile	*For further details see p. 00*
Address and contact number	Which Street, Whosville, Wherefordshire AB12 3CD
	Tel: 01000 000000
Head's name	**Head Master:** Dr A Person
Age range	**Age range:** 11–18
Number of pupils. B = boys G = girls	**No. of pupils:** 660 B330 G330
Fees per annum.	**Fees:** Day £11,000 WB £16,000 FB £20,000
Day = fees for day pupils.	
WB = fees for weekly boarders.	
FB = fees for full boarders.	

Key to directory icons (abridged)

Key to symbols:
- Boys' school
- Girls' school
- International school
- (IAPS) Member of IAPS
- (GSA) Member of GSA

- (ISA) Member of ISA
- (HMC) Member of HMC
- (BSA) Member of BSA
- Member of Society of Heads

Schools offering:
- Boarding accommodation
- Bursaries
- A levels
- International Baccalaureate
- Learning support

Choosing a school – the key questions

However much a school may appeal at first sight, you still need sound information to form your judgement.

Schools attract pupils by their reputations, so most go to considerable lengths to ensure that parents are presented with an attractive image. Modern marketing techniques try to promote good points and play down (without totally obscuring) bad ones. But every Head knows that, however good the school prospectus is, it only serves to attract parents through the school gates. Thereafter the decision depends on what they see and hear. Research we have carried out over the years suggests that in many cases the most important factor in choosing a school is the impression given by the Head. As well as finding out what goes on in a school, parents need to be reassured by the aura of confidence that they expect from a Head. How they judge the latter may help them form their opinion of the former. In other words, how a Head answers questions is important in itself and, to get you started, we have drawn up a list of points that you may like to consider. Some can be posed as questions and some are points you'll only want to check in your mind. They are not listed in any particular order and their significance will vary from family to family, but they should be useful in helping you to form an opinion.

Before visiting and asking questions, **check the facts** – such as which association the school belongs to, how big it is, how many staff *etc*. Is there any form of financial pie chart showing how the school's resources are used? The answers to questions like these should be in the promotional material you've been sent. If they aren't, you've already got a good question to ask!

Check the website. Is it up-to-date? Almost certainly not 100% because that's just about impossible, but it shouldn't be obsolete. And that first impression is very important.

When you get to the school you will want to judge the overall atmosphere and decide whether it will suit you and your child. Are any other members of the family going to help to pay the fees? If so, their views are important and the school's attitude towards them may be instructive.

When you make it to the inner sanctum, **what do you make of the Head as a person?** Age? Family? Staying? Moving on? Retiring? Busted flush? Accessible to children, parents and staff? If you never get to see the Head, but deal with an admissions person of some sort, it may not mean you should rule the school out, but it certainly tells you something about the school's view of pupil recruitment.

Academic priorities – attitude towards league tables? This is a forked question. If the answer is 'We're most concerned with doing the best for the child', you pitch them a late-developer; if the answer is, 'Well, frankly, we have a very high entry threshold', then you say 'So we have to give you a foolproof academic winner, do we?'

Supplementary questions:

- What is the ratio of teachers to pupils?
- What are the professional qualifications of the teaching staff?
- What is the school's retention rate? In prep schools this means how many pupils do they lose at 11 when the school goes on to 13.
- How long is the school day – and week?
- What are the school's exam results?
- What are the criteria for presenting them?
- Were they consistent over the years?
- Is progress accelerated for the academically bright?
- How does the school cope with pupils who do not work?
- Where do pupils go when they leave?
- How important and well resourced are sports, extracurricular and after school activities, music and drama?
- What cultural or other visits are arranged away from the school?

Other topics to cover:

- What is the school's mission?
- What is its attitude to religion?
- How well is the school integrated into the local community?
- How have they responded to the Charities Act initiatives?
- What are the responsibilities and obligations at weekends for parents, pupils and the school?
- Does the school keep a watching brief or reserve the option to get involved after a weekend incident?
- What is the school's attitude to discipline?
- Have there been problems with drugs, drink or sex? How have they been dealt with?
- What is the school's policy on bullying?
- How does the school cope with pupils' problems?
- What sort of academic and pastoral advice is available?
- What positive steps are taken to encourage good manners, behaviour and sportsmanship?
- What is the uniform?
- What steps are taken to ensure that pupils take pride in their personal appearance?
- How often does the school communicate with parents through reports, parent/teacher meetings or other visits?
- What level of parental involvement is encouraged both in terms of keeping in touch with staff about your own child and more generally, eg a Parents' Association?
- Is it possible to have the names and addresses of parents with children at the school to approach them for an opinion?

And finally – and perhaps most importantly – what does your child make of the school, the adults met, the other children met, pupils at the school in other contexts, and the website?

The breakfast club

Katie Gedye shares Moor Park's approach to energising students in the morning, whilst also allowing them to discover valuable lessons

Take a snapshot of most prep schools across the country at 7 am and you would find a very familiar picture: matrons and prefects would be bustling around, opening curtains and trying to rouse sleepy children, who, as children, want to roll over and pull the duvet back over their head!

However, at Moor Park Prep School in Shropshire, the boarding team pride themselves on trying to do things a little differently and the morning routine is no exception. At 7 am every morning of the summer term, the boarders don their trainers and running kit, tear out of the front door and embark on 'The breakfast club'.

The children respond each year to challenges set by Deputy Head, Simon Gedye, who tasks them, with collectively attempting to run miles, climb mountains and tour the world (metaphorically, of course!)! Although each year has a slightly different theme, the challenge remains the same; to get up and run two laps of the school every morning that you board. If children achieve the feat, Mr Gedye offers the elixir of prizes: breakfast in bed served by the Headmaster and his wife!

The boarders are invited to run at least 1km before breakfast. But Moor Park pupils rarely stick to the bare minimum in anything they do: many boarders clock up over 3km each and every morning. The turn out on Saturday mornings was regularly 100% with over 100 boarders running. However, this may have had more to do with the children being allowed to run in their pajamas and occasionally in fancy dress.

Often the theme requires a 'water leg', for example when they were 'crossing the North Sea' on their tour around Britain. Undeterred, and always up for anything, the children swapped their trainers for a swimsuit and dashed to the pool to swim lengths.

Parents and grandparents will now be having flashbacks to their own school days. To freezing cold, outdoor pools and harsh running punishments dealt out by stern school masters. But you only have to look at the faces of the children here to work out how they feel about this adventure. Each and every child who takes part loves it. Despite not always finding it easy to get out from under the duvet, the sense of achievement by the end is always worth it.

The breakfast club is voluntary. There are no consequences for not running, except perhaps a feeling of 'having missed out' when the champions of the day are cheered at breakfast. Taking inspiration from the Tour

de France, the top runners were presented with yellow jerseys to wear whilst running – the ambassadors, if you like, inspiring those around them to speed up too. Each week they, in turn, nominated the next two and so on, until by the end over a dozen children were all proudly running in their yellow breakfast club t shirts.

For the Year 8 girls, who have, in previous years, competed at both county and national level, fitness was always going to be their driving force. Teenagers, however, are not renowned for their enthusiasm early in the mornings. Even during their common entrance exams, when staff thought they would relish a few extra moments under the duvet, the children ran, finding that a little exercise first thing in the morning was a great way to start the day.

As a Prep School, Moor Park tries to do just that – prepare the children for the next step. And yet, we often go out of our way to make things easy for the children – we are desperate for them not to fail. The breakfast club teaches them about commitment, determination and so much more. Firstly, to make an independent choice – they run or they don't. They have to organise themselves without reminders; if their kit isn't ready up in their dorms by bedtime, they can't run. Time keeping is crucial; laps have to be completed and the children showered and

dressed and at breakfast by 7.30 am or the laps don't count – no excuses. It is not unheard of for runners vying for the top spot to have had laps deducted for leaving their bed unmade in their haste to get downstairs.

Through the breakfast club, the boarding staff are teaching skills for life and that the most worthwhile achievements don't come easy; they require effort and commitment. The children, year on year, surprise themselves and their parents with what they are capable of.

On completion, the champion runners always look forward to their breakfast in bed with great relish – often trying to order seconds from the Headmaster before their luck runs out. However, for most of the children it isn't about the reward or a huge prize; many only receive applause in recognition of their efforts. So what is it that gets them out of bed each morning – even on the chilly wet ones? I think it is this – Moor Park children love a challenge, want to be outdoors more than indoors and are intrinsically competitive. Not in a 'win at all costs' kind of a way but in a 'come on, everyone, we can do this' kind of a way.

Every Prep School seeks to find their unique selling point, their 'something special' to tell the parents as they tour around the school. Moor Park's unique selling point is not the breakfast club, but the children running it.

Katie Gedye is Head of Lower School and Houseparent at Moor Park Prep School
For more information, see page 79
www.moorpark.org.uk

It is, increasingly, a woman's world

Angela Drew, Headmistress of Bromley High School, explains the advantages of a single-sex education for both girls and boys

Twenty years ago there was no great difference between the success of boys and girls in examinations. Now girls outperform boys in examinations at all levels and in virtually all subjects – even in formally male preserves such as physical education, maths and physics. Girls are now 35% more likely to go to university than boys and by 2025, 70% of university students are destined to be female.

Certainly, we need to turn our attention to the education of boys, to solving the conundrum of how to motivate boys to achieve their best. Having spent ten years as the governor of a small boys' only Prep School, I was always struck by the eagerness and enthusiasm of young boys' in the classroom, the prevalence of laughter in their learning and also the competitive spirit which drove lessons along. Equally striking is the politeness of boys in the single-sex Prep School environment. In an all boys' environment there is often a palpable emphasis on old fashioned courtesy – on shaking hands, making eye contact and initiating polite conversation.

A single-sex environment frees boys and girls to be themselves – the best version of themselves that they can be. My own school is one of those increasingly rare institutions: a school which is single-sex right through from 4-18 - no co-educational Sixth Form or Kindergarten tacked on at the beginning or end for us. Once, single-sex education might have been perceived as the safe, traditional option but, for me, it has come to represent a distinctive and even radical choice. To choose a girls' education is to opt for an infrastructure which promotes resilience and supports girls in selecting the riskier, harder and more aspirational path in life – and it is also the source of much joy, friendship and fun.

It is wonderful to see mud splattered girls of 7 or 8 revelling in their first encounters with rugby or learning to win and lose in hockey and netball; girls entertaining the elderly with songs from their panto; girls participating wildly in the actions of 'The Twelve Days of Christmas'. There is a sense of joyful abandon, a happiness at being part of the group. But there is an equal sense of enjoyment in the academic satisfaction of working together and that is true from the earliest years.

Each child is unique: no two girls learn in exactly

the same way and every boy has his individual traits and preferences. Yet, while we tend to shy away from simple generalisations about boys' and girls' ways of learning, certain observable differences are seen in the behaviour of boys and girls in the playground and in the classroom. Boys tend to play different kinds of games from girls. Boys are typically more hierarchical; girls more collaborative. As they grow older, girls tend to be better at articulating their feelings, but boys tend to answer more often in class discussion.

Crucially for Junior Schools and Prep Schools, girls tend to develop communication skills more quickly than boys. They start to talk earlier and more fluently. By the age of 3 99% of girls can talk, whereas it takes almost an additional year for boys to reach this level. By the age of 7, only 20% of girls display difficulties in reading, compared with 33% of boys.

Girls also write at an earlier stage. Thus in the early years of Junior School, boys tend to be more active in the classroom but slower to develop the fine motor control necessary for writing.

All this means that the learning environment in a girls' only Junior School can be much more language rich from the very beginning (and correspondingly, boys' only junior schools can develop boys' self-esteem and self-confidence through a curriculum which engages their enthusiasm and inculcates a love of learning).

At the 4-11 Junior section of Bromley High School, the learning in the classroom is enriched through an immersion in language - through storytelling, creative writing and drama. As part of the co-curricular programme, girls work with a professional storyteller to learn the lost art of telling folk tales. Words and ideas are at the heart of all we do to stimulate the girls' curiosity and imagination through diverse programme of visits, activities and festivities. Dressing up is a visual expression of girls' vivid imaginations at work – as is richly evident in the saris and sunflower dresses on India day and 'swinging 60s' day or the costuming of the huge range of plays, concerts and productions each year.

But perhaps even more importantly in a Junior School is that an all girls' school sets out to encourage risk-taking and resilience from the earliest years. If women are to flourish in the workplaces that now welcome them in, they must learn to tackle new challenges and to live with failures when they come.

So girls schools will challenge the stereotypes outside the classroom too: there will be choirs and orchestras but also rock groups. Girls will always be encouraged to leave their comfort zone and try something new. Chess, circus skills, fencing, computing clubs are just as popular as ballet and gymnastics in an all girls' environment.

Let's celebrate our single sex Junior Schools – and in girls' only Junior Schools let confidence grow and creativity flourish.

For more information about Bromley High School, see page 50
www.bromleyhigh.gdst.net

Education where the grass really is greener

Neil Shaw, Headmaster of Westonbirt Prep School, says a move from the city to the country has much to offer both parents and students

Whilst representing Westonbirt Prep at the recent Independent Schools' Show in Battersea, and listening to their excellent series of lectures, I was struck by the intense pressure and competition faced by parents living in London to get their children into the best maintained schools or to take advantage of the excellent independent schools that are on offer.

I listened to advice given to city parents regarding issues such as public transport for getting their children to school (up to an hour a day on the underground or bus) and how city schools manage the requirement for PE and sport in the curriculum when they lack adequate outdoor space. These are very real worries and anxieties for parents, which I have no doubt will filter down to their children; living and being educated in a frenetic, competitive, fast-paced and stressful urban environment is a concern, particularly in a climate where pupil

'wellbeing' is a hot topic.

Across the shires of the beautiful West Country, just 90 minutes from London, we have the perfect solution. Independent Prep and Senior Schools in rural settings which offer a contemporary and rich educational experience located within beautiful estates, parklands and even forests – putting the real 'forest' back into forest school.

I am often amazed (and a little envious) of my peers from university who chose to focus their careers in London and have subsequently benefitted from the staggering house price inflation over the last 15 years. It is apparent to me that couples who have been fortunate to profit from property ownership in the capital could easily afford to sell-up, buy a good sized family home with a large garden in Gloucestershire and still afford to pay independent school fees for multiple children.

If work commitments preclude either parent from leaving the city entirely, it is perfectly possible to commute from Kemble Station to Paddington and, making good use of the cost-effective wrap-around child care at the beginning and end of each school day at Westonbirt Prep from 7.45 am to 6 pm, still drop off the children at school and collect them at the end of the day.

The benefits include a high educational expectation but low pressure ethos for your child. Abundant fresh air and open spaces for sports and outdoor education; forest school in a real forest. A broad curriculum with small class sizes and a large family home with outdoor space to explore and entertain. All just 90 minutes from London with excellent transport links for parents to commute to the office and maintain social lives.

The educational and health benefits alone justify a move from the city. They say the grass is always greener, but in rural Gloucestershire, if you are able to combine buying a home in the country with investing in a first class education at the same time, it seems to me the grass really is greener.

The benefits include a high educational expectation but low pressure ethos for your child. Abundant fresh air and open spaces for sports and outdoor education; forest school in a real forest.

For more information about Westonbirt Prep School, see page 41
www.westonbirt.org

Looking at schooling differently: re-thinking the transition at 13+

Andrew Marshall-Taylor says that by reducing their Common Entrance timetable, the school has created a dynamic curriculum that allows pupils to thrive academically, socially and emotionally

Over-testing, hothousing, extra tutoring: these are all themes which appear with alarming regularity in the media nowadays. For some time, the Common Entrance exam has been under fire as an overly pressurised and outdated way of gaining entry to independent senior schools. Criticism often focuses on the fact that 12 and 13-year-olds are having to go through a rigorous regime of past papers and preparation when time could be better spent developing a love of learning and acquiring the necessary educational skills and tools that will enable them to flourish when they make the transition to the senior school environment.

At Monkton Prep School, it was over five years ago that we started to recognise that whilst our Year 7 and 8 pupils were achieving very good grades at Common Entrance, they weren't necessarily developing their ability to learn well independently or in a group context. We wanted our pupils to really embrace this phase of their life, to feel the

satisfaction and sense of achievement that comes from growing as an independent learner. We wanted pupils to be both inspired and challenged in equal measure rather than subject them to the pressures and stresses that Common Entrance in all subjects inevitably brings.

Out of this realisation a new Year 7 and 8 curriculum at Monkton Prep was born. Our aim was to create a Sixth Form environment for the oldest pupils in the school in which they would be able to thrive on all levels - academically, socially and emotionally. Academic rigour wouldn't fall by the wayside; we envisaged it as the natural by-product of guiding pupils in how to be reflective, resilient enquirers who could communicate their ideas and come up with original, creative solutions to tricky problems. Equally important for us was to provide opportunities for learning, both within the curriculum and as part of our extracurricular offering.

The Common Entrance subjects to be examined

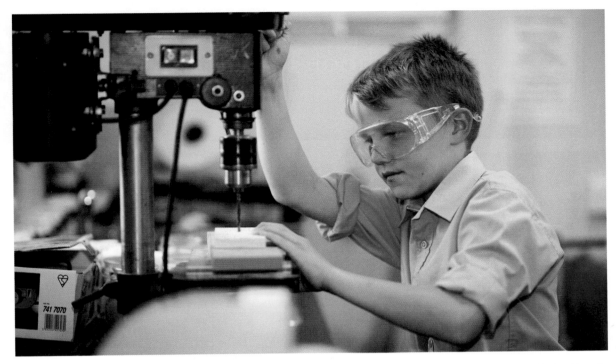

were reduced to a core group: English, maths, science, French and Latin. In geography, history and religious studies, the exam was replaced by an extended project. Across the three subjects pupils would have to do at least one extended written project and one oral presentation. These three subjects would then be assessed using a skills matrix, adapted from the International Baccalaureate model of skills and knowledge acquisition.

Art, design and technology and music were kept alongside these core subjects but new subjects were also added. On a carousel basis, our pupils have been introduced to Mandarin, thinking skills, current affairs, performing arts and outdoor education. We have also added in study periods so that pupils begin to learn how to manage their own work effectively and independently. A teacher is always on hand during these periods to advise and to guide if need be.

Underpinning it all has been the emphasis on learning to lead, to coach, to take responsibility and to make a contribution to the community. Our pupils have had training seminars on all of these and it is fantastic to see the way they engage with our younger pupils as they coach and mentor throughout the school. When they team up with the younger pupils, it is more than just a friendly conversation – the pupils learn to listen well, to guide and give encouragement and to pass on any concerns to staff if these arise and they feel it is necessary. The Year 7 and 8 pupils have responded well to being given these new challenges. Whether it is leading discussions on the school and eco councils, planning and running a whole school fete, being involved in the interview processes for new staff or acting as ambassadors of the school as they meet parents and visitors, we are enormously proud of them as they grow in confidence and self-belief. We have found, too, that the increase in self-esteem translates into more confidence in the learning environment - the confidence to enquire, investigate, state opinions and try new things.

Reducing our Common Entrance timetable has opened up the way to a more creative and dynamic curriculum. It is has been a very welcome change amongst the pupils, the staff and the parents. And, with a yearly average of over 20 of our pupils winning scholarships to top independent schools, it seems that senior schools like it too!

Andrew Marshall-Taylor is Headmaster of Monkton Prep School
For more information about Monkton Prep School, see page 40
www.monktonprep.com

Supporting international schools

UK Independent Schools have a world class reputation and therefore attract students from all over the world, but supporting and integrating international students has its own challenges

The number of overseas students attending UK independent schools has risen dramatically in recent years, with schools benefitting from the political changes which have released students from behind the iron or bamboo curtains thereby bringing significant financial benefits to independent schools. However, attracting and supporting international students, particularly at Prep School age brings about its own logistical as well as pastoral challenges.

Hilary Moriarty, National Director of the Boarding Schools' Association 2006 - 2014, has seen that a school's academic performance is often the principal focus for overseas families when identifying a school: "There is no doubt that international students have become very important customers of boarding schools in Britain. But the competition for such students has also increased: American, Canadian, Australian and New Zealand schools all see the value of these high-net-worth children, mostly with highly developed mathematical skills and often highly trained musicians even before they reach us. In today's world, international students need colloquial and assured fluency in English, almost a by-product of studying in an English-speaking country, as much as they need the good grades to access the very best higher education. But the schools also need the students, who are likely to be highly motivated and very hard working, as well as bright to begin with. Their high grades helping enhance any school's league table position".

The market has widened, rather than just Hong Kong, China and Russia are now very important markets for the British boarding model, as well as the growing wealth of countries such as Nigeria. Many schools now regularly spend time marketing in Asia, Africa and Europe particularly and Education Fairs and Shows are highly attended by both schools and families. The Independent Schools Show, which originally took place just in London, now has a Dubai and Geneva show, enabling schools to meet overseas based families directly.

Having overseas students is not a new thing for schools after all, boarding schools were set up for all the overseas based families of diplomats and military serving personnel. It is the numbers of such students, particularly those that do not speak English as their first language that has increased so significantly.

Many schools that are keen to appeal to the international market, have a dedicated EAL (English as an Additional Language) team, to help international students achieve their academic potential and additional tailored support is often available to any students who would like it. These lessons are given on a one-to-one basis, and can often be outside the main timetabled lessons, as well as some support during lessons. As a result, international students can expect the same academic success as those who speak English as their first language.

Schools also make a lot of effort to ensure that the students are encouraged to speak English at all times through discussion of news events, pronunciation work and paired reading. Many schools have noticed how this

> Moving and living in a new country is a daunting experience for anybody, particularly Prep School children, but guardian agencies and schools have developed various offers to help make the process easier.

PREP SCHOOL

Reflecting the best in the prep and junior school world.

Published each term and available in print, e-zine and our Prep School app.

Subscriptions available from www.johncattbookshop.com

www.prepschoolmag.co.uk

has benefitted the whole school community, as English children go and visit their friends abroad and significantly improve their foreign language skills.

Moving and living in a new country is a daunting experience for anybody, particularly Prep School children, but guardian agencies and schools have developed various offers to help make the process easier. Gabbitas, a leading education consultancy, offers a support package to new students, an Elite Start service. Debbie Cowley, Director of Student Support Services & Guardianship at Gabbitas explains, "As part of our service we ask students to arrive in the UK between two and five days before they start school, giving them time to recover from jetlag, become acclimatised to our weather and food, and practice their English before joining the school 'environment'. They are then shown the local area, including places to eat and shop, and can be helped with the purchase of any school items (uniform, sports equipment etc). We will also accompany them to school on their first day to help them settle in".

It is not just the Guardians that help the children settle in, some schools offer international clubs which help students to integrate into the school and develop their understanding of British culture – as well as share their own cultures. As we live in an increasingly global society this can be of great benefit to all students.

Modern technology has also changed the way in which schools can support their international students. Skype and Facetime calls to families enable students to make eye contact whilst speaking. At Ludgrove, Sophie Barber tries to always ensure that calls take place either in the morning or at lunchtime rather than the end of the day when the boys are tired: "This makes a big difference

to a boy whose parents are in Hong Kong or elsewhere and who will not see his parents at matches etc like many of the others".

At Ludgrove, as with most other schools who invite applications from students living abroad, they have a dedicated member of office staff for all the overseas boys, who liaises with parents for travel arrangements, checking unaccompanied minor forms, and booking taxi pick-up and drop-offs at the airports. Sophie Barber explains, "The school tries to book the same taxi driver for a boy so that he can build up a rapport and trust with him and the taxi driver will always stay with the boy until the airline and flight attendants take over responsibility. Whilst we do not help families choose guardians but leave that entirely to them, we do stipulate that anyone living abroad must have a recognised guardian or family member in the UK who can be contacted and even be able to have the boy to stay at short notice in emergency."

Pastoral support is very important and schools have to ensure that the whole team understands how to provide support, from the matrons, to the resident nurse and the boarding houseparents and other staff whether in a tutorial role as 'Division Master' or just as a good 'listening ear'. This can involve helping a child adjust to a new diet/menu or working closely with parents and the school doctor to understand foreign medicines and alternative therapies or simply helping the child to pack-up at the end of term, working out what can stay at school and what needs to go home with them. Our experience at School Trunk tells us that the sheer volume of belongings accumulated at school seems to grow annually and storage is becoming an increasing problem for schools, especially as the number of international students increases.

International students matter to boarding schools not only here, but also in the Americas and in the Antipodes. While it was heartening in 2015 to see numbers of British boarders rising, international students constitute more than a third of boarders in British independent schools, and schools have never been more alert to their needs and interests if they want to keep these students choosing British schools. Providing a complete support package to international students will help to ensure that this continues to be a supportive market for the UK independent school sector.

School Trunk is a dedicated provider to the Independent Schools sector providing holiday storage and uniform care services helping schools support their overseas students.

Chelsea Hayes is the Director of School Trunk
For more information, see page 20
www.schooltrunk.org

Initial advice

Educational institutions often belong to organisations that encourage high standards. Here we give a brief guide to what some of the initials mean.

BSA

The Boarding Schools' Association

Since its foundation in 1966, the Boarding Schools' Association (BSA) has had the twin objectives of the promotion of boarding education and the development of quality boarding through high standards of pastoral care and boarding accommodation. Parents and prospective pupils choosing a boarding school can, therefore, be assured that the 500 schools in membership of the BSA are committed to providing the best possible boarding environment for their pupils.

A school can only join the BSA if it is in membership of one of the ISC (Independent Schools Council) constituent associations or in membership of SBSA (State Boarding Schools' Association). These two bodies require member schools to be regularly inspected by the Independent Schools' Inspectorate (ISI) or Ofsted. Between April 2007 and August 2011, all boarding inspections, in both independent and state schools, were carried out by Ofsted, whose reports can be found on their website. Boarding inspection of independent schools has been conducted by ISI since September 2012. Ofsted retains responsibility for the inspection of boarding in state schools. Boarding inspections must be conducted every three years. Boarding is judged against the National Minimum Standards for Boarding Schools (revised 2011) with considerable input from the BSA.

Relationship with government

The BSA is in regular communication with the Department for Education (DfE) on all boarding matters. The Children Act (1989) and the Care Standards Act (2001) require boarding schools to conform to national legislation and the promotion of this legislation and the training required to carry it out are matters on which the DfE and the BSA work closely. The key area is in training.

Boarding training

The programme of training for boarding staff whose schools are in membership of the BSA has been supported and sponsored in the past by the DfE. The BSA maintains the high standards expected as a consequence of that support. The Utting Report on the Safeguards for Children Living Away from Home highlighted the importance of the development of 'policy, practice and training for services for children who live away from home'. It focuses on the right of parents to expect that staff looking after children

are competent to do so, and points out the responsibility of central government to secure consistent national standards in promoting the welfare of children away from home. The Singleton Review (March 2009) reiterated the importance of rigorous safeguarding of such children.

In addition the BSA organises five conferences and more than 50 seminars a year for governors, Heads, deputies, housemasters and housemistresses, and matrons and medical staff where further training takes place in formal sessions and in sharing good practice. The BSA provides the following range of training and information:

- Professional qualifications for both teaching and non-teaching staff in boarding schools. The BSA has been responsible for the development of courses leading to university validated Certificates of Professional Practice in Boarding Education. These certificates, the result of at least two years' study, are awarded by the University of Roehampton.

- A rolling programme of day seminars on current boarding legislation and good practice.

State Boarding Schools Association

The BSA issues information on the 38 state boarding schools in England and Wales and the BSA should be contacted for details of these schools. In these schools parents pay for boarding but not for education, so fees are substantially lower than in an independent boarding school.

National Director: Robin Fletcher MBA, MPhil, FRSA
Director of Training: Alex Thomson OBE, BSc(Hons), PGCE, DipEd, FCIPD
Boarding Schools' Association
4th Floor
134-136 Buckingham Palace Road
London SWIW 9SA
Tel: 020 7798 1580
Fax: 020 7798 1581
Email: bsa@boarding.org.uk
Website: www.boarding.org.uk

BOARDING SCHOOLS'
ASSOCIATION

GSA

The Girls' Schools Association, to which Heads of leading girls' schools belong

The Girls' Schools Association represents the heads of many of the top performing day and boarding schools in the UK independent schools sector and is a member of the Independent Schools Council.

Many of the schools in GSA membership were founded in the 19th century when a national movement to provide better education for girls and women gathered momentum. Campaigners founded new schools in which girls studied similar subjects to boys – a far cry from the superficial curriculum they had previously been given.

Today, 21st century girls' schools come in many different shapes and sizes. Some cater for 100% girls, others provide a predominantly girls-only environment with boys in the nursery and/or sixth form. Some follow a diamond model, with equal numbers of boys but separate classrooms between the ages of 11 to 16. Educational provision across the Association offers a choice of day, boarding, weekly, and flexi-boarding education. Schools range in type from large urban schools of 1000 pupils to small rural schools of around 200. Many schools have junior and pre-prep departments, and can offer a complete education from three/four to 18. A significant proportion of schools also have religious affiliations. Heads of schools in the Girls' Day School Trust (GDST) are members of the GSA.

The GSA encourages high standards of education for girls and promotes the benefits of being taught in a largely girls-only environment. As a whole, GSA schools punch well above their weight when it comes to academic achievement; analysis of A Level statistics shows they are more likely to study and do well in STEM (science, technology, engineering, maths) subjects than girls in other schools. Approximately 94% go on to higher education.

The Association aims to inform and influence national educational debate and is a powerful and well-respected voice within the educational establishment, advising and lobbying educational policy makers on core education issues as well as those relating to girls' schools and the education of girls. The Association liaises with the Department for Education, the Office for Standards in Education, the Qualifications and Curriculum Authority and other bodies.

The GSA also provides its members and their staff with professional development courses, conferences, advice and opportunities to debate and share best practice, ensuring that they have every opportunity to remain fully up-to-date with all aspects of their profession.

As the GSA is one of the constituent bodies of the Independent Schools' Council (ISC), its schools are required to undergo a regular cycle of inspections to ensure that these rigorous standards are being maintained. GSA schools must also belong to the Association of Governing Bodies of Independent Schools, and Heads must be in membership of the Association of School and College Leaders (ASCL).

The Association's secretariat is based in Leicester.

Suite 105, 108 New Walk, Leicester LE1 7EA
Tel: 0116 254 1619
Email: office@gsa.uk.com
Website: www.gsa.uk.com
Twitter: @GSAUK

President 2015: Caroline Jones, Headington
Vice President: Alun Jones, St Gabriel's (Newbury)
Executive Director: Charlotte Vere

HMC

The Headmasters' and Headmistresses' Conference, to which the Heads of leading independent schools belong

Founded in 1869 the HMC exists to enable members to discuss matters of common interest and to influence important developments in education. It looks after the professional interests of members, central to which is their wish to provide the best possible educational opportunities for their pupils.

The Heads of some 269 leading independent schools are members of The Headmasters' and Headmistresses' Conference, whose membership now includes Heads of boys', girls' and coeducational schools. International membership includes the Heads of around 60 schools throughout the world.

The great variety of these schools is one of the strengths of HMC but all must exhibit high quality in the education provided. While day schools are the largest group, about a quarter of HMC schools consist mainly of boarders and others have a smaller boarding element including weekly and flexible boarders.

All schools are noted for their academic excellence and achieve good results, including those with pupils from a broad ability band. Members believe that good education consists of more than academic results and schools provide pupils with a wide range of educational co-curricular activities and with strong pastoral support.

Only those schools that meet with the rigorous membership criteria are admitted and this helps ensure that HMC is synonymous with high quality in education. There is a set of membership requirements and a Code of Practice to which members must subscribe. Those who want the intimate atmosphere of a small school will find some with around 350 pupils. Others who want a wide range of facilities and specialisations will find these offered in large day or boarding schools. Many have over 1000 pupils. About 50 schools are for boys only, others are coeducational throughout or only in the sixth form. The first girls-only schools joined HMC in 2006. There are now about 20 girls-only schools.

Within HMC there are schools with continuous histories as long as any in the world and many others trace their origins to Tudor times, but HMC continues to admit to membership recently-founded schools that have achieved great success. The facilities in all HMC schools will be good but some have magnificent buildings and grounds that are the result of the generosity of benefactors over many years. Some have attractive rural settings, others are sited in the centres of cities.

Pupils come from all sorts of backgrounds. Bursaries and scholarships provided by the schools give about a third of the 215,000 pupils in HMC schools help with their fees. These average about £30,000 per annum for boarding schools and £12,000 for day schools. About 170,000 are day pupils and 43,000 are boarders.

Entry into some schools is highly selective but others are well-suited to a wide ability range. Senior boarding schools usually admit pupils after the Common Entrance examination taken when they are 13.

Most day schools select their pupils by 11+ examination. Many HMC schools have junior schools, some with nursery and pre-prep departments. The growing number of boarders from overseas is evidence of the high reputation of the schools worldwide.

The independent sector has always been fortunate in attracting very good teachers. Higher salary scales, excellent conditions of employment, exciting educational opportunities and good pupil/teacher ratios bring rewards commensurate with the demanding expectations. Schools expect teachers to have a good education culminating in a good honours degree and a professional qualification, though some do not insist on the latter especially if relevant experience is offered. Willingness to participate in the whole life of the school is essential.

Parents expect the school to provide not only good teaching that helps their children achieve the best possible examination results, but also the dedicated pastoral care and valuable educational experiences outside the classroom in music, drama, games, outdoor pursuits and community service. Over 90% of pupils go on to higher education, many of them winning places on the most highly-subscribed university courses.

All members attend the Annual Conference, usually held in a large conference centre in September/October. There are ten divisions covering England, Wales, Scotland and Ireland where members meet once a term on a regional basis, and a distinctive international division.

The chairman and committee, with the advice of the general secretary and membership secretary, make decisions on matters referred by membership-led sub-committees, steering groups and working parties. Close links are maintained with other professional associations in membership of the Independent Schools Council and with the Association of School and College Leaders.

Membership Secretary: Ian Power.
Tel: 01858 465260
General Secretary: Dr William Richardson.
Tel: 01858 469059
12 The Point
Rockingham Road
Market Harborough
Leicestershire LE16 7QU
Email: gensec@hmc.org.uk
Website: www.hmc.org.uk

Leading
Independent
Schools

IAPS

The Independent Association of Preparatory Schools (IAPS) is a membership association representing leading headteachers and their prep schools in the UK and overseas

With more than 600 members, IAPS schools represent a multi-billion pound enterprise, educating more than 160,000 children and employing more than 20,000 staff.

Schools are spread throughout cities, towns and the countryside and offer pupils the choice of day, boarding, weekly and flexible boarding, in both single-sex and coeducational settings. Sizes vary from 100 to more than 800 per school, with the majority between 150 and 400. Most schools are charitable trusts, some are limited companies and a few are proprietary. There are also junior schools attached to senior schools, choir schools, those with a particular religious affiliation and those that offer specialist provision as well as some schools with an age range extending to age 16 or above.

IAPS only accredits those schools that can demonstrate that they provide the highest standards of education and care. Member schools offer an all-round, values-led, broad education, which produces confident, adaptable, motivated children with a lifelong passion for learning. In order to be elected to membership, a Head must be suitably qualified and schools must be accredited through a satisfactory inspection. IAPS offers its members and their staff a comprehensive and up-to-date programme of professional development courses to ensure that high professional standards are maintained.

Pupils are offered a rich and varied school life. The targets of the National Curriculum are regarded as a basic foundation, which is greatly extended by the wider programmes of study offered. Specialist subject teaching begins at an early age and pupils are offered a range of cultural and sporting opportunities. Together with more than 30 recreational games, music, art and drama form part of curricular and extracurricular activities. In addition, IAPS organises holiday and term-time sporting competitions for pupils to take part in, including skiing, sailing, judo, swimming, golf, fencing and squash, amongst many others.

IAPS has well-established links with senior independent schools, and experience in methods of transfer and entry to them. As the voice of independent prep school education, it has national influence and actively defends and promotes the interests of its members. It lobbies the government on their behalf and promotes prep school issues on a national and international stage. IAPS works directly with ministers and national policy advisers to ensure that the needs of the prep school sector are met.

IAPS
11 Waterloo Place, Leamington Spa,
Warwickshire CV32 5LA
Tel: 01926 887833
Fax: 01926 888014
Email: iaps@iaps.uk
Website: www.iaps.org.uk

Excellence in Education
The Independent Association
of Prep Schools

ISA

The Independent Schools Association, with membership across all types of school

The Independent Schools Association (ISA), established in 1879, is one of the oldest of the Headteachers' associations of independent schools that make up the Independent Schools' Council (ISC). It began life as the Association of Principals of Private Schools, which was created to encourage high standards and foster friendliness and cooperation among Heads who had previously worked in isolation. In 1895 it was incorporated as The Private Schools Association and in 1927 the word 'private' was replaced by 'independent'. The recently published history of the association, *Pro Liberis*, demonstrates the strong links ISA has with proprietorial schools, which is still the case today, even though boards of governors now run the majority of schools.

Membership is open to any independent school Head or proprietor provided they meet the necessary criteria, which includes the accreditation standards of the Independent Schools Inspectorate (ISI). ISA's executive council is elected by members and supports all developments of the Association through its committee structure and the strong regional network of co-ordinators and area committees. Each of ISA's seven areas in turn supports members through regular training events and meetings.

ISA celebrates a wide ranging membership, not confined to any one type of school, but including all: nursery, pre-preparatory, junior and senior, all-through schools, coeducational, single-sex, boarding, day and performing arts and special schools.

Promoting best practice and fellowship remains at the core of the ISA, as it did when it began 130 years ago. The association is growing, and its 367 members and their schools enjoy high quality national conferences and courses that foster excellence in independent education. ISA's central office also supports members and provides advice, and represents the views of its membership at national and governmental levels. Pupils in ISA schools enjoy a wide variety of competitions, in particular the wealth of sporting, artistic and academic activities at area and national level.

President : Lord Lexden

Chief Executive: Neil Roskilly, BA PGCE NPQH FRSA FRGS

ISA, 1 Boys' British School
East Street, Saffron Walden,
Essex CB10 1LS
Tel: 01799 523619
Fax: 01799 524892
Email: isa@isaschools.org.uk
Website: www.isaschools.org.uk

The Society of Heads

The Society of Heads represents the interests of the smaller independent secondary schools.

The Society of Heads represents the interests of the smaller, independent, secondary schools. The Society celebrated its 50th Anniversary in 2011. The Society has as its members over 110 Heads of well-established secondary schools, many with a boarding element, meeting a wide range of educational needs. All member schools provide education up to 18, with sixth forms offering both A and AS levels and/or the International Baccalaureate. Also some offer vocational courses. Many have junior schools attached to their foundation. A number cater for pupils with special educational needs, whilst others offer places to gifted dancers and musicians. All the schools provide education appropriate to their pupils' individual requirements together with the best in pastoral care.

The average size of the schools is about 350, and all aim to provide small classes ensuring favourable pupil:teacher ratios. The majority are coeducational and offer facilities for both boarding and day pupils. Many of the schools are non-denominational, whilst others have specific religious foundations.

The Society believes that independent schools are an important part of Britain's national education system. Given their independence, the schools can either introduce new developments ahead of the maintained sector or offer certain courses specifically appropriate to the pupils in their schools. They are able to respond quickly to the needs of parents and pupils alike.

Schools are admitted to membership of the Society only after a strict inspection procedure carried out by the Independent Schools Inspectorate. Regular inspection visits thereafter ensure that standards are maintained.

The Society is a constituent member of the Independent Schools Council and every full member in the Society has been accredited to it. All the Society's Heads belong to the Association of School and College Leaders (ASCL) (or another recognised union for school leaders) and their schools are members of AGBIS.

The Society's policy is: to maintain high standards of education, acting as a guarantee of quality to parents who choose a Society school for their children; to ensure the genuine independence of member schools; to provide an opportunity for Heads to share ideas and common concerns for the benefit of the children in their care; to provide training opportunities for Heads and staff in order to keep them abreast of new educational initiatives; to promote links with higher and further education and the professions, so that pupils leaving the Society's schools are given the best advice and opportunities for their future careers; and to help Heads strengthen relations with their local communities.

The Society of Heads' Office,
12 The Point, Rockingham Road,
Market Harborough,
Leicestershire LE16 7QU
Tel: 01858 433760
Fax: 01858 461413
Email: gensec@thesocietyofheads.org.uk
Website: www.thesocietyofheads.org.uk

The Independent Schools Council

The Independent Schools Council (ISC) works with its members to promote and preserve the quality, diversity and excellence of UK independent education both at home and abroad

What is the ISC?

ISC brings eight associations together to represent over 1,250 independent schools in the UK. These schools are ranked among the best in the world and educate more than half a million children each year, around 80% of independently educated pupils. ISC also represents 130 British International schools in more than 50 countries worldwide.

ISC schools

ISC schools are at the forefront of educational achievement in every way and offer great choice to parents looking for the right school to suit their child. There are schools to suit every need, whether you want a day or boarding school, single-sex or co-education, a large or a small school, or schools offering specialisms, such as in the Arts. They are the most academically successful schools, offering excellent teaching and pastoral care, an astonishing breadth of co-curricular activities and outstanding facilities.

Our schools are very diverse: some of our schools are selective and highly academic, offering a chance to stretch the bright child. Others have very strong drama or music departments full of creative opportunities in plays, orchestras and choirs. For children with special needs such as dyslexia or autism there are many outstanding independent schools that offer the best provision in the country.

And of course, our schools have very strong track records of high achievement at sport, offering superb facilities, excellent coaches and a full fixture list. Independent schools excel at the traditional sports like football and rugby, but also offer more unusual sports like rowing, fencing and even rock climbing.

There is also a wealth of co-curricular opportunity available. Whether your child is into debating, sailing, the Model United Nations or is interested in army training in the Combined Cadet Force, most schools offer numerous clubs and activities. It all adds up to an exciting, broad and stimulating all-round education.

Academic results

ISC schools achieve excellent academic results. At A level, 51% of entries from pupils at ISC schools were awarded at least an A grade, compared to over 26% nationally. Independent schools account for 14% of A level entries, but 27% of A/A* grades and 32% of A* grades. Just over 8% of GCSE entries come from ISC schools, but pupils achieve 29% of A* grades. ISC schools continue to be strong in traditional subject areas such as maths, science and modern foreign languages.

Fee Assistance

ISC schools are sympathetic to the financial challenges facing many parents and the number of bursaries and scholarships available has grown to reflect this, with £660 million available in fee assistance. Over one third of ISC pupils receive help with their fees.

ISC associations

There are eight member associations of ISC each with its own distinctive ethos reflected in their entrance criteria and quality assurance:

Girls' Schools Association (GSA) – see page 25

Headmasters' and Headmistresses' Conference (HMC) – see page 25

Independent Association of Prep Schools (IAPS) – see page 27

Independent Schools Association (ISA) – see page 27

The Society of Heads – see page 28

Association of Governing Bodies of Independent Schools (AGBIS)
www.agbis.org

Independent Schools' Bursars Association (ISBA)
www.theisba.org.uk

Council of British International Schools (COBIS)
www.cobis.org.uk

Two further organisations are affiliated to ISC: **Boarding Schools Association (BSA)** and **Scottish Council of Independent Schools (SCIS)**

The Independent Schools Council can be contacted at:
First Floor,
27 Queen Anne's Gate,
London,
SW1H 9BU
Telephone: 020 7766 7070
Fax: 020 7766 7071
Website: www.isc.co.uk

independent
schools
council

Help in finding the fees

Chris Procter, joint managing director of SFIA, outlines a planned approach to funding your child's school fees

Every year the Independent Schools Council (ISC) carries out a survey, which is completed by all 1267 schools in UK membership.

This year the census, which was carried out in January 2015, showed that school fees increased by an average of 3.6% . There are now 517,113 pupils at the 1267 ISC member schools, up slightly from 511,928 in 2013.

The share of girls and boys at ISC schools is very nearly equal, with girls representing 48.9% of all pupils.

The overall average boarding fee is £9,596 and the average day fee is £4,241. However, fees charged by schools vary by region: the average boarding fee ranges from £8,902 per term in Wales to £114,291 in Greater London; the average day fee ranges from £3,466 per term in the North to £5,173 in Greater London.

The overall cost (including university fees) might seem daunting: the cost of educating one child privately could well be very similar to that of buying a house but, as with house buying, the school fee commitment for the majority of parents can be made possible by spreading it over a long period rather than funding it all from current resources.

It is vital that parents do their financial homework, plan ahead, start to save early and regularly. Grandparents who have access to capital could be beneficial; by contributing to school fees they could help to reduce any inheritance tax liability.

Parents would be well-advised to consult a specialist financial adviser as early as possible, since a long-term plan for the payment of fees – possibly university as well as school – can prove very attractive from a financial point of view and thus offer greater peace of mind.

Funding fees is neither science, nor magic, nor is there any panacea. It is quite simply a question of planning and using whatever resources are available, such as income, capital, or tax reduction opportunities.

The fundamental point to recognise is that you, your circumstances and your wishes, or ambitions, for your children, or grandchildren are unique. They might well be similar to those of other people but they will still be uniquely different.

There will be no single solution to your problem. Indeed, after a review of all your circumstances, there might not be a problem at all.

So, what are the reasons for seeking advice about educational expenses?

- To reduce the overall cost?
- To get some tax benefit?
- To reduce your cash outflow?
- To invest capital to ensure that future fees are paid?
- To set aside money now for future fees?
- To provide protection for school fees?
- Or just to make sure that, as well as educating your children, you can still have a life!

Any, some, or all of the above – or others not listed – could be on your agenda. The important thing is to develop a strategy.

At this stage, it really does not help to get hung up on which financial product is the most suitable. The composition of a school fee plan will differ for each individual depending on a number of factors. That is why there is no one school fee plan on offer.

The simplest strategy and, in most cases, the most expensive option, is to write out a cheque for the whole bill when it arrives and post it back. Like most simple plans, that works very well, if you have the money.

Even if you do have the money, is that really the best way of doing things? Do you know that to fund £1,000 of school fees as a higher rate taxpayer paying 40% income tax, you currently need to earn £1,667, this rises to £2,000 if you are an additional rate taxpayer where the rate is 50%?

How then do you start to develop your strategy? As with most things in life, if you can define your objective, then you will know what you are aiming at. Your objective in this case will be:

(a) to determine how much money is needed and

(b) when it will be required.

You need to draw up a school fees schedule or what others would term a cash flow forecast.

So: How many children?

Which schools? (or use an average school fee)

When?

Any special needs?

Inflation guesstimate?

Include university costs?

With this basic information, the school fees schedule/cash flow forecast can be calculated and you will have defined what it is you are trying to achieve.

Remember though, that senior school fees are typically more than prep school fees – this needs to be factored in. Also be aware that the cost of university is not restricted to the fees alone; there is a lot of maintenance and other costs involved: accommodation, books, food, to name a few.

You now have one side of an equation, the relatively simple side. The other side is you and your resources. This also needs to be defined, but this is a much more difficult exercise. The reason that it is more difficult, of course, is that school fees are not the only drain on your resources. You probably have a mortgage, you want to have holidays, you need to buy food and clothes, you may be concerned that you should be funding a pension.

This is the key area of expertise, since your financial commitments are unique. A specialist in the area of school fees planning knows how to get at these commitments, to record them and help you to distribute your resources according to priority.

The options open to you as parents depend completely upon your adviser's knowledge of these complex personal financial issues. (Did I forget to mention your tax position, capital gains tax allowance, other tax allowances including those of your children and a lower or zero rate tax paying spouse or partner? These could well be used to your advantage.)

A typical school fees plan can incorporate many elements to fund short, medium and long-term fees. Each plan is designed according to individual circumstances and usually there is a special emphasis on what parents are looking to achieve, for example, to maximise overall savings and to minimise the outflow of cash.

Additionally it is possible to protect the payment of the fees in the event of unforeseen circumstances that could lead to a significant or total loss of earnings.

Short-term fees

Short-term fees are typically the termly amounts needed within five years: these are usually funded from such things as guaranteed investments, liquid capital, loan plans (if no savings are available) or maturing insurance policies, investments *etc.* Alternatively they can be funded from disposable income.

Medium-term fees

Once the short-term plan expires, the medium-term funding is invoked to fund the education costs for a further five to ten years. Monthly amounts can be invested in a low-risk, regular premium investment ranging from a building society account to a friendly society savings plan to equity ISAs. It is important to understand the pattern of the future fees and to be aware of the timing of withdrawals.

Long-term fees

Longer term funding can incorporate a higher element of risk (as long as this is acceptable to the investor), which will offer higher potential returns. Investing in UK and overseas equities could be considered. Products may be the same as those for medium-term fees, but will have the flexibility to utilise investments that may have an increased 'equity based' content.

Finally, it is important to remember that most investments, or financial products either mature with a single payment, or provide for regular withdrawals; rarely do they provide timed termly payments. Additionally, the overall risk profile of the portfolio should lean towards the side of caution (for obvious reasons). There are any number of advisers in the country, but few who specialise in the area of planning to meet school and university fees. The SFIA Group Ltd, is the largest organisation specialising in school fees planning in the UK.

This article has been contributed by SFIA and edited by Chris Procter, Joint Managing Director.
He can be contacted at:
SFIA Ltd, 41 London Road, Twyford, Berkshire RG10 9EJ
Tel: 0845 458 3690
Fax: 0118 934 4609
Email: enquiries@sfia.co.uk
Web: www.sfia.co.uk

BEING BROAD-MINDED WIDENS HORIZONS.

QUILTER CHEVIOT
INVESTMENT MANAGEMENT

WE'RE THINKING BEYOND THE OBVIOUS TO GET THE BEST FOR YOUR INVESTMENTS. FIND OUT MORE.

CALL TIM HEALY
EXECUTIVE DIRECTOR
TEL. 020 7150 4298 OR VISIT
WWW.QUILTERCHEVIOT.COM

Managing the cost of independent schooling

Tim Healy, executive director at Quilter Cheviot Investment Management, offers some advice on managing the cost of school fees

Putting your children through independent schooling does not always come easy, financially speaking. Although a recent census by the Independent Schools Council found that between 2014 and 2015 private school fees were subject to the lowest annual increase since 1994, they still rose by an average of 3.6%. So costs remain on the up and, over the course of a child's education, they represent a substantial sum.

As with any major financial outlay, early stage planning can make a big difference. By using a combination of cost spreading, savvy saving and various tax efficiencies parents can make the, sometimes daunting, costs of private schooling far more manageable.

Once you've decided to go down the independent school route, it is important to start planning for the associated costs at the earliest opportunity. Obviously, planning for independent schooling at secondary level will allow more time to study the options and it will also mean more time for saving. Whether looking at primary or secondary schooling though, the following approaches can be considered when it comes to easing the school fees burden.

Take full advantage of tax efficiencies

There are a number of tax efficient means to help with the cost of independent school fees. Parents should know, for example, that any income from gifts given directly to their children is regarded as a child's own income. As such, a child's personal allowance of £10,000 is available to use.

An increasing number of people are sourcing support from grandparents when it comes to covering school fees and tax efficiencies can come into play here too. Advantage can be taken of a grandparent's £3,000 annual gifts exemption from inheritance tax, on a yearly basis where individuals are wanting to make a regular contribution to their grandchildren's schooling.

Tailor your investments

Having efficient investments in place can be very helpful when it comes to building a fees pot. Investing in UK gilts can be very tax efficient, for example, as any capital gain is tax exempt.

Another strategy to consider is investing in funds. The UK equity market is currently expected to yield roughly 4% for the current year and when compared against the very low interest rates offered by banks at present stock market investment clearly leads the pack in terms of value.

Of course, it is important to remember that stock markets are notorious for exaggerating fundamental economic trends and understanding how this can impact upon your financial investment over the short, medium and long term is essential. By nurturing returns though, efficient investments could enable you to withdraw money when needed while continuing to save once education has started.

Elsewhere, the tax free advantages of an ISA make it an ideal choice for parents planning and saving to pay for private schooling too. If both parents use their full ISA annual allowance, in eight years a family could have a tax free investment pot of about £300,000. This can then be used as a tax free supplement to an existing income when a family starts paying school fees, or it can simply be drawn upon to pay the school fees.

Seek solutions with schools

Beyond investment and tax efficiency strategies parents may also look to lessen the pressure of costs by spreading them over a longer period of time. Many private schools are open to individual payment schemes, so it's advisable to strike up an open dialogue with the school as soon as you identify it as a preferred choice. In some cases it will be possible for agreements to be put in place that enable parents to begin payments several years before a child joins their chosen school and finish payments after the child has left.

Whichever methods are utilised, expert advice and planning at the earliest opportunity helps to pay for the education you have chosen. At Quilter Cheviot we understand the needs of clients who are looking to develop investments that will support the cost of their childrens' education. Our aim is to help our clients fulfil their objectives over the long term and our investment process is central to achieving this goal. By combining the in-depth analysis of our dedicated research teams and the talents of our experienced investment managers, we can provide clients with a truly unique resource. It allows us to generate an investment process that is sufficiently agile to keep ahead of today's constantly changing markets, and flexible enough to incorporate the investment requirements of our clients. We choose from among the best and most suitable investments to meet your objectives, whether the priority is growth, income or capital preservation. In the case of being able to raise school fee funds, we will work hard to help you achieve that objective.

Scotland
p. 83

North-East

North-West
p. 67

Northern Ireland

Yorkshire & Humberside
p. 80

East Midlands
p. 48

West Midlands
p. 78

Wales

East of England
p. 42

Central & West
p. 36

South-East
p. 69

South-West
p. 75

Greater London p. 50
London p. 53

Prep schools in the UK

Please note that, to facilitate the use of this guide, we have introduced the geographical region 'Central & West' (see map opposite). This is not an officially designated region, and has been created solely for the purposes of this publication.

Clifton College Preparatory School

CLIFTON
COLLEGE
ESTABLISHED 1862

(Founded 1873)

The Avenue, Clifton, Bristol, BS8 3HE

Tel: +44 (0)117 3157 502

Fax: +44 (0)117 3157 504

Email: ntucker@cliftoncollege.com

Website: www.cliftoncollege.com/prep

Head of Preparatory School:

Mr John Milne

Appointed: 09/08

School type: Coeducational Day & Boarding Preparatory

Age range of pupils: 2–13

No. of pupils enrolled as at 01/01/2016: 400

Boys: 250 **Girls:** 150

No. of boarders: 80

Fees per annum as at 01/01/2016:

Day: £15,360–£16,755

Flexi Boarding: £18,360–£19,755

Full Boarding: £21,000–£26,700

Average class size: 20

Teacher/pupil ratio: 1:7

The Preparatory School was opened in 1908 and is now the region's largest boarding and day preparatory school, catering for around 400 pupils.

Clifton College Preparatory School offers first class teaching and outstanding pastoral care for girls and boys aged 2 to 13. There is no 'one size fits all' approach, each child is treated as an individual and it is our pleasure to encourage them to explore and develop their unique talents and skills. Our children are our best ambassadors. They are socially confident, intellectually agile, adventurous, well-mannered and decent young people.

We offer a tailored, all-round education with diverse and targeted co-curricular activities and excellent facilities.

Each year the Preparatory School sees more than 100 new pupils join from a wide range of schools nationwide and overseas. The main entry points are at Nursery, Year 3 and Year 7, though pupils are welcome to join into any of the Year groups.

Exceptional pastoral care

From eight years old, pastoral care is House-based, with Housemasters and Housemistresses and their teams offering a 'home from home'. Our Pre-Prep pupils' pastoral care is provided by their dedicated classroom teachers. We meet the needs of each child through their

own personal development programme. We have a culture that encourages participation and tolerance.

Inspirational teaching

We provide a rigorous and stimulating academic curriculum and we select teachers that lead in their field and share best practice. They encourage intellectual curiosity and independent learning, engendering academic self-belief and confidence in our pupils.

Diverse and targeted cocurricular activities

Our ethos encourages participation and all of our pupils engage with a diverse range of co-curricular activities and experiences. Through these activities we provide opportunities and challenges for pupils to find new strengths and talents and encourage collaboration. In all our activities we seek to perform at the highest level.

Traditional values, modern facilities

The College successfully combines heritage with modernity, enjoying the best of both. Landscaped greenery surrounds our magnificent Grade II listed buildings

which are on the outskirts of a vibrant international city. The Chapel is one of our most cherished buildings and the Redgrave is the second largest theatre in Bristol. Our superb sporting facilities include The Close and the 90-acre site known as 'Beggar's Bush' which is Bristol's biggest outdoor sports complex, providing all the latest sporting facilities.

All our pupils benefit from the Preparatory School being a boarding school, with early drop off and late pick up for our day pupils, enabling them to take part in a huge array of co-curricular activities. Our flexible and full boarding options mean that parents can choose the level of care that works best for their family, confident in the knowledge that their child will be happy, safe and secure.

Clifton College provides a supportive and welcoming atmosphere and allows pupils to benefit from the security and confidence that comes from belonging to the same school from the ages of 2 to 18. As pupils grow with the Preparatory school, their sense of independence

and responsibility prepares them for their journey into the Upper School.

Academic and sports success

We aim to unlock your son or daughter's potential to enable them to become the best version of themselves they can be. Our pupils have gone on to succeed in a variety of disciplines. Last year, our pupils gained their best ever A Level and GCSE results and 18 students were offered places at Oxbridge. Our 1st XV rugby team and girls 1st XI hockey team also achieved unbeaten seasons and former Clifton College pupils compete at international level in a range of sports. We were also in the top 100 schools in the Daily Telegraph and Sunday Times (August 2015).

Come and visit us

We understand that choosing a school is an important decision for both parents and children, so come along to one of our Open Days or book a personal visit and see why a Clifton child is a happy child.

For more information on Clifton College, or to request a prospectus or book a visit, please go to www.cliftoncollege.com

Carrdus School

(Founded 1952)
Overthorpe Hall, Banbury,

Oxfordshire OX17 2BS
Tel: 01295 263733
Fax: 01295 254644
Email: office@carrdusschool.co.uk
Website: www.carrdusschool.co.uk
Head: Mr Edward Way
Appointed: 2012
School type: Coeducational Day

Age range of boys: 3–8
Age range of girls: 3–11
No. of pupils enrolled as at 01/01/2016: 110
Boys: 11 *Girls:* 99
Fees per annum as at 01/01/2016:
Day: £1,278–£10,140
Average class size: 14
Teacher/pupil ratio: 1:7

Choosing a school for your child is one of the most important decisions that a parent makes. A good school will get the best out of every child – academically, socially, creatively and physically. All children are different. At Carrdus we encourage them to discover hidden talents and new found abilities by providing them with a wide range of opportunities, both in and out of the classroom.

There is no uniform at Carrdus. This means that each and every child is very much their own person and celebrated as an individual. The only compulsory items are a warm jacket and a pair of wellies to enjoy the enormous gardens. Boys enjoy a nurturing start to their school lives when they join us at 3 and then move onto their new schools at 7 or 8. This makes us the only girl's school (from 8-11 years) in the area. Our Year 6 girls go on to highly regarded senior schools full of confidence and enthusiasm for life – ready for the next phase.

The pupils really benefit from the small size of the school and get to know each other very well regardless of year. The staff know all the pupils as individuals and there is a huge amount of mutual respect which makes the atmosphere a very special one.

Our 11 acres of grounds provide space for the children to let off steam and learn to play without constant adult intervention, learning to share and work together. Whether it's climbing a tree, making a den, swimming in the outdoor heated pool or tending to the vegetable garden – it's important that they grasp these skills early on in life. Traditional manners are also a key ingredient of the success of Carrdus, whether it be holding the door for someone or looking people in the eye. Girls and boys leave knowing that

self-discipline, honesty, hard work and a firm handshake are key ingredients for success in the future!

Contact jcozens@carrdusschool.com to arrange a visit. We look forward to welcoming you to Carrdus.

Leaden Hall School

(Founded 1948)

70 The Close, Salisbury, Wiltshire SP1 2EP
Tel: 01722 334700
Fax: 01722 439269
Email: admin@leaden-hall.com
Website: www.leaden-hall.com
Head: Mrs Julia Eager
Appointed: January 2010
School type: Girls' Day & Boarding

Age range of girls: 3–11
No. of pupils enrolled as at 01/01/2016: 130
No. of boarders: 20
Fees per annum as at 01/01/2016:
Day: £2,670–£4,595
Full Boarding: £4,510–£6,435
Average class size: 12-15
Teacher/pupil ratio: 1:8

Set in Salisbury's stunning Cathedral Close, Leaden Hall School provides day and boarding education for girls aged 3-11 in a happy, friendly, purposeful, family atmosphere.

Much more than just a school, Leaden Hall is a family, whose members are welcomed back and who maintain strong links with each other throughout their lives.

Our unique setting – combining both historic and contemporary buildings, award-winning classrooms, studios, laboratories and performance and sports hall – provides a safe, secure and supportive environment for each pupil to grow and develop at their own pace.

The pupils at Leaden Hall are privileged to be living and learning in the ancient shadow of the Cathedral where so much is rooted in tradition. They will use these foundations to build strong lives for themselves, able to contend with all that the modern world will bring.

The girls are prepared for Wiltshire County 11+ examinations, the Common Entrance and for individual school assessments. High academic success is achieved with awards and scholarships to schools throughout the country. At the same time we have an extremely high percentage pass rate to South Wilts Grammar School every year.

The breadth of the curriculum, the numerous extra-curricular activities, a sport and music for all philosophy, all sitting alongside the academic rigour that is geared to each pupil's individual ability, ensure that Leaden Hall pupils achieve the very best education.

Boarding at Leaden Hall is very popular. We run activities in the evenings and the weekends are action-packed. As a day and boarding school, children can have 'wrap around care' from before breakfast to supper time and several day girls enjoy the option of flexiboarding.

We are always happy to welcome visitors to the school, so contact Mrs Ennew registrar@leaden-hall.com to arrange an appointment.

Find out more about the school on our website at www.leaden-hall.com

Monkton Prep School

MONKTON

(Founded 1888)
Church Road, Combe Down, Bath,
Bath & North-East Somerset BA2 7ET

Tel: +44 (0)1225 831202
Email: info@monktonprep.org.uk
Website: www.monktonprep.com
Headmaster: Mr A Marshall-Taylor
Appointed: January 2014
School type: Coeducational Day & Boarding
Age range of pupils: 2–13 (boarding from 8)
No. of pupils enrolled as at 01/01/2016: 339
Fees per annum as at 01/01/2016:

Pre-Prep (age 2-7): £2,910–£3,116 per term
Prep (Day age 7-11):
£3,660 –£3,764 per term
Prep (Boarding age 7-11):
£7,126 –£7,390 per term
Prep (Day age 11-13): £5,328 per term
Prep (Boarding age 11-13): £7,680 per term
Average class size: 15-18
Teacher/pupil ratio: 1:15-18

Setting standards for life

Monkton Prep School in the World Heritage City of Bath, is an independent, co-educational day and boarding school for pupils aged 2–13. We pride ourselves on our academic excellence, our strong pastoral care and our Christian ethos. At Monkton, we are setting standards for life; giving young people the qualities of character and values they need to become valued friends, confident team players and inspiring leaders.

A broad and varied curriculum

The syllabus in each subject is aimed at, and beyond, the requirements of National Curriculum up to the end of Year 6, and also the Common Entrance and Scholarship examinations at 13+. The Prep School has subject specialist teachers which enables both great breadth and depth of teaching. All pupils in our Year 7 and 8 year groups at Monkton have the opportunity to be leaders and mentors and take on responsibilities; this is an integral part of their education. Many opportunities are provided for children to grow as leaders, as independent thinkers and in their self-confidence, so they are well-prepared for the next step.

A wide range of activities

The activity programme is a key and exciting part of life at Monkton Prep. The choice is extremely varied and includes cub-scouts, gymnastics, swimming, choir, football and animation to name just a few. There are some brilliant events throughout the year and these together with music, drama and sporting competitions provide many opportunities for pupils to learn and grow individually and as part of a team.

Pastoral care

The happiness and well-being of each child is central to what we do. Through our inclusive approach each pupil is encouraged to try new things, develop their skills and talents and aim high in every area of school life. At Monkton we believe that every child is an individual, and we provide an education that encourages the development of every child academically, emotionally and spiritually to enable them to go out into the world and play their part in transforming the community and society around them.

'A happy place, where much is expected and much achieved'
The Good Schools Guide

Westonbirt Prep School

Westonbirt, Tetbury, Gloucestershire
GL8 8QG
Tel: 01666 881400
Email: admissions@westonbirt.org
Website: www.westonbirt.org

Headmaster: Mr Neil Shaw
School type: Coeducational Day
Age range of pupils: 3–11
Fees per annum as at 01/01/2016:
Day: £2,500–£10,950

Westonbirt Prep is an independent Preparatory and Nursery School for boys and girls aged 3-11 years. Set in 210 acres of stunning parklands, shared with Westonbirt Senior School, pupils are inspired by the beauty that surrounds them and benefit from the resources of a much larger school while maintaining the atmosphere of a small family setting.

Why Westonbirt Prep?

Smaller class sizes and the excellent ratio of staff to pupils allow children to be well supported throughout their development and for their individual abilities to be valued. Boys and girls are praised for their efforts and good behaviour and are encouraged to develop a sense of independence, mutual consideration, manners and respect for others. Our commitment to children's broader personal development combined with a structured preparation for Senior School makes us stand out.

Academic success

Prep school pupils go on to their first choice of Senior School including Westonbirt School, Grammar Schools and other top Independent schools. Academic success is strong. Emphasis is placed on sport, music, drama and art as well as wide ranging opportunities outside the classroom, including their own Forest School area.

The Good Schools' Guide

The Good Schools' Guide highlighted parents' observations that children were encouraged to find their voice at the school; "When she started my daughter was very shy, but she's flourished and has so much more confidence now."

Exceptional grounds and facilities

Westonbirt Prep successfully combines the educational quality and individual attention of an intimate, family school with the facilities and opportunities of a much larger school. The Prep school offers a £3m sports centre, indoor pool, state-of-the-art music technology suite and there is even a golf course! Pupils are given every advantage in their educational and personal development.

http://twitter.com/westonbirtprep

King's Ely Junior

(Founded 970)

Ely, Cambridgeshire CB7 4DB
Tel: 01353 660707
Email: admissions@kingsely.org
Website: www.kingsely.org
Head: Mr Richard Whymark
Appointed: 2009
School type: Co-educational Day & Boarding

Age range of pupils: 7–13
No. of pupils enrolled as at 01/01/2016: 347
Fees per annum as at 01/01/2016:
Day: £11,499–£12,546
Full Boarding: £18,333–£19,350
Average class size: 18
Teacher/pupil ratio: 1:7.5

Situated in the heart of Cambridgeshire in the cathedral city of Ely, King's Ely is a prestigious, innovative independent day and boarding school, complemented by a history that stretches back over 1,000 years. Notable academic accolades include the coveted NACE award for the excellent standard of teaching and learning, a national award for outstanding ICT facilities and various awards for international partnerships. King's Ely is also a centre of excellence for chemistry, maths and geography.

Years 3 to 8 at King's Ely Junior are full of the same excitement and energy that pervades the whole of King's Ely. A can-do atmosphere built on energy, courage and integrity, a commitment to unlocking potential and the development of conscientious, compassionate young people encourages pupils to thrive both academically and socially.

King's Ely Junior provides a broad and balanced curriculum, where pupils set their sights high and begin to take responsibility for their learning, while building strong partnerships with their teachers to ensure ongoing personal success. The school boasts modern, purpose-built teaching facilities and the remarkable backcloth of Ely Cathedral, the perfect setting for concerts and performances. Music, drama and art are embedded in the culture of the school, with opportunities for pupils of all abilities and aspirations, both within and beyond the curriculum. All major sports are offered, along with an impressive array of other activities helping every pupil to realise their sporting potential. Rowing, cricket and athletics are particularly strong, with many students representing national and regional teams.

Junior boarders and the Ely Cathedral Boy Choristers live in picturesque historic boarding houses in the cathedral grounds, well-led by caring Housemasters and Housemistresses. A strong pastoral structure where childhood is respected and cherished is a key feature of the school.

King's Ely Junior International provides an exclusive opportunity for international pupils to integrate into school life while receiving specialist language tuition.

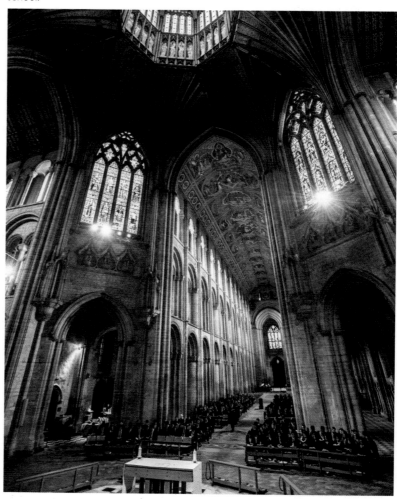

Lockers Park

(Founded 1874)

Lockers Park Lane, Hemel Hempstead,
Hertfordshire HP1 1TL
Tel: 01442 251712
Fax: 01442 234150
Email: sjohnson@lockerspark.herts.sch.uk
Website: www.lockerspark.herts.sch.uk
Headmaster: Mr C R Wilson
Appointed: September 2013
School type: Boys' Boarding, Flexible

Boarding & Day, Co-Ed Pre-Prep
Age range of boys: 4–13
Age range of girls: 4–7
No. of pupils enrolled as at 01/09/2016: 150
Fees per annum as at 01/01/2016:
Fees: £3,200–£7,450 per term
Average class size: Av 14
Teacher/pupil ratio: 1:8

Giving Boys a Great Start

Lockers Park's preparatory school is one of ambition and excellence that has been educating boys to the highest standard for over 140 years. Set in 23 acres of Hertfordshire woodland in Boxmoor, it is a day and boarding school for boys aged 4-13.

Unique to Lockers Park is an emphasis on nurturing each and every child: "The happiness of the boys is paramount." *(Tatler Schools Guide 2016).* The school fosters a love of learning through a dedicated and focussed curriculum partnered with music, sport, drama and extra-curricular activities to allow each boy to reach their potential.

A Boy's Education

"In their formative years, boys learn through being active and involved in the classroom," says Lockers Park's Headmaster Christopher Wilson. With Lockers Park's heritage in schooling boys, there is recognition that the 'sit still and listen' approach does not always ensure good results. The staff use a kinaesthetic approach with expressly small class sizes to ensure that the boys are highly engaged and achieve the best academic results.

Daily Sport

The school remains true to its 19th century roots, with a strong focus on outdoor play combined with structured sport every day. "Lockers Park makes a virtue of letting boys be boys. We believe that exploring the surrounding grounds and engaging in outdoor activities is intrinsic to good schooling, leading to increased concentration during academic lessons," continues Mr Wilson.

Prepared For The Next Step

The Year 6-8 Senior School Preparation Programme involves exam and interview practice, visits from senior school players and scholarship coaching alongside tailored advice from staff. This ensures a seamless progression onto Britain's leading public and independent senior schools.

Upcoming Open Mornings: Saturday 12th March and Saturday 14th May, 10:30am-12:30pm or call 01442 251712 to find out more.

www.lockerspark.herts.sch.uk

St Cedd's School

St Cedd's School

(Founded 1931)

178a New London Road, Chelmsford, Essex CM2 0AR
Tel: 01245 392810
Fax: 01245 392815
Email: hbrierley@stcedds.org.uk
Website: www.stcedds.org.uk
Head: Dr Pamela Edmonds
Appointed: January 2011

School type: Coeducational Day
Age range of pupils: 3–11
No. of pupils enrolled as at 01/01/2016: 400
Boys: 200 **Girls:** 200
Fees per annum as at 01/01/2016:
Day: £8,550–£9,300
Average class size: 24

St Cedd's School is a co-educational 3-11 IAPS Charitable Trust School offering pupils the opportunity to aspire and achieve in a caring environment that nurtures talent and supports individual endeavour. This is a school in which every child matters. We value and celebrate their many diverse talents and qualities and the grounded confidence the pupils develop results in great personal achievement.

Individual pupil progress

Most children exceed the Early Learning Goals by age 5 and the progress of pupils, of all abilities, throughout the school is rapid. Our internal assessment results and 11+ results far exceed national averages and annually we celebrate an unrivalled success rate to selective grammar and independent senior schools with an impressive track record of scholarship awards. This level of achievement is significant given that we are academically non-selective. Assessments on entry are designed to capture the strengths, weaknesses and areas for development of each child so that the education is tailored to their individual needs.

Centre of excellence

The Independent Schools Inspectorate (ISI) put St Cedd's School at the top level in every category of inspection in February 2013 which places the school amongst the very best 3-11 preparatory schools in the country. The accolade confirms what we witness every day; high academic achievement, excellent records of attainment in music, drama and sport, a sense of purpose and ambition that shows itself in the attitude and actions of the pupils and staff, an outstanding pastoral care system and first-rate arrangements for welfare, health and safety.

Broad and balanced curriculum

With over 70 after-school activities to choose from, extra study opportunities are balanced with a firm focus on academic work. This synergy supports the development of confident self-assured pupils ready for the challenges ahead. PE, music, art, French and science are taught by specialists with the teaching of PE, music and French starting in Nursery. Acknowledging the breadth of talents of pupils is an important aspect of life at St Cedd's School. To this end, our baccalaureate-style Year 6 curriculum, HOLDFAST, leads to awards in recognition

of 'Holistic Opportunities to Learn and Develop, Furthering Achievement, Service and Talent'.

As a member of the Choir Schools Association our Choristers sing in the Cathedral Choir.

Nurturing the future

For more than 80 years, boys and girls have been enjoying a quality of education that is among the very best you will find. Give your child the best start in our Nursery where the boys and girls thrive in a colourful and nurturing environment that widens their horizons and instils in them a love of learning. Places may also be available in other year groups.

Breakfast Club operates from 7:30am-8:00am and a wrap-around care programme is open to 6:00pm. Fees include lunch and the majority of after-school clubs.

To attend an open day, request a prospectus, or to arrange an individual tour, please contact Helen Brierley on 01245 392810 or email hbrierley@stcedds.org.uk.

Manor Lodge School

(Founded 1991)
Rectory Lane, Ridge Hill, Shenley,

Hertfordshire WD7 9BG
Tel: 01707 642424
Fax: 01707 645206
Email: enquiries@manorlodgeschool.com
Website: www.manorlodgeschool.com
Headmaster: Mr G Dunn CertEd
Appointed: June 2011
School type: Coeducational Day

Age range of pupils: 3–11
No. of pupils enrolled as at 01/01/2016: 425
Boys: 213 **Girls:** 212
Fees per annum as at 01/01/2016:
Day: £9,975–£11,235
Average class size: 19
Teacher/pupil ratio: 1:13

Manor Lodge enjoys an excellent reputation for high academic standards, innovative and exciting expressive arts and wide-ranging sporting opportunities for all. We pride ourselves in maintaining a warm, supportive atmosphere in which every individual child is allowed to blossom academically, artistically and socially at an appropriate pace as part of an inclusive family.

The school works in close partnership with parents where open dialogue is encouraged and regular meetings take place to review every aspect of the child's development. Our belief is that if a child is happy, valued and supported, they will learn and grow in all respects and thus be suitably prepared for life beyond Manor Lodge. A typical MLS child, as described by local secondary school heads, is articulate, confident, has good study habits and skills and is quick to involve themselves in all aspects of school life.

We organise over 60 clubs and activities throughout the week as well as a range of sports teams. The music department runs three separate choirs, plus a community choir, a full orchestra, a jazz band, numerous ensembles and major musical theatre productions. Manor Lodge is proud of its tradition of children performing and it is our belief that it complements and enriches the academic side of school life.

The school is proud of its record in achieving over 20 scholarships to local secondary schools in each of the past six years. On average over 95% of parents obtain their first choice of school on secondary transfer.

If you are looking for a school with a true family atmosphere where children feel loved and appreciated for who they are, where there are high academic standards and wonderful opportunities to develop artistic and sporting interests to last a lifetime, then Manor Lodge might just be the school for you.

Tring Park School for the Performing Arts

Tring Park School for the / Performing Arts

(Founded 1919)

Tring Park, Tring, Hertfordshire HP23 5LX

Tel: 01442 824255

Fax: 01442 891069

Email: info@tringpark.com

Website: www.tringpark.com

Principal:

Mr Stefan Anderson MA, ARCM, ARCT

Appointed: September 2002

School type:

Coeducational Boarding & Day

Religious Denomination:

Non-denominational

Age range of pupils: 8–19

No. of pupils enrolled as at 01/01/2016: 340

Boys: 97 **Girls:** 243 **Sixth Form:** 217

No. of boarders: 205

Fees per annum as at 01/01/2016:

Day: £13,785–£21,960

Full Boarding: £23,250–£32,880

Tring Park School for the Performing Arts is an independent, co-educational boarding and day school for over 330 pupils from ages 8-19. It offers a unique opportunity for gifted young people to specialise in ballet, dance, drama, musical theatre or commercial music, whilst gaining an excellent academic education to GCSE, BTEC and A Level.

The Prep department at Tring Park caters for pupils aged 8 – 11 years and is set within an inspiring, creative environment in a Rothschild mansion steeped in fascinating history. The Prep department offers an enriched, integrated curriculum with a unique balance between academic and vocational studies to suit the 'budding' performer plus:

- a friendly, encouraging environment enabling pupils to flourish and perform to the best of their ability building confidence to ensure progress in all areas of the curriculum giving your child an opportunity to succeed academically, whilst training in vocational activities during the school day.
- specialist teaching in dance, drama and music
- small classes set in a unique historic building
- personalised learning tailored to meet your child's needs

Pupils at Tring Park perform regularly in the school's Markova Theatre as well as in London and Europe. Performances have included Gershwin's *Crazy for You* and *Jesus Christ Superstar* at London's Shaw Theatre. The school provides young dancers to perform in the English National Ballet Christmas production of *Nutcracker* at the London Coliseum and dancers are also invited to perform with ENB on its tour of *Le Corsaire*.

Alumni include Daisy Ridley – star of *Star Wars VII*, Lily James – star of *Cinderella*, Drew McOnie – Choreographer in Residence at The Old Vic Theatre and Jessica Brown Findlay – *Downton Abbey* and *The Oresteia* in the West End.

Prep Taster Morning: 9 February 2016

Auditions: contact registrar@tringpark. com or Tel. 01442 824255

Open Days: www.tringpark.com/opendays

www.tringpark.com

Tring Park School is a registered charity no. 1040330

Leicester Grammar Junior School

(Founded 1992)
London Road, Grea Glen, Leicester,
Leicestershire LE8 9FL

Tel: 0116 259 1950
Fax: 0116 259 1951
Email: friell@leicestergrammar.org.uk
Website: www.leicestergrammar.org.uk/
junior-school-home
Head of School: Mrs C Rigby
Appointed: September 2013
School type: Coeducational Day
Age range of pupils: 3–11

No. of pupils enrolled as at 01/01/2016: 391
Fees per annum as at 01/01/2016:
Kinder – Year 2: £3,200 per term
Kinders morning (8:30 – 12:30pm):
£2,112 part time
Years 3 – 6: £3,370 per term
Average class size:
Infants 14/15, Years 3-6 18/20
Teacher/pupil ratio: Infants 1:8, Years 3-6 1:10

How we learn at LGJS is crucial to us. We are a progressive school and use the latest technology, whilst at the same time value the importance of traditional teaching of the 3Rs. This traditional and modern can be seen in our language learning, where pupils can learn Latin, French and even Mandarin. Our aim is to prepare children to have the necessary expertise for the 21st Century. We equip them with skills to question, investigate and enjoy a vast array of learning activities. We want them to explore and experience a breadth of opportunities from Forest School to Drama to Scientific Discovery. Our pupils are fortunate to work in a modern purpose

built campus which offers our own junior science laboratory, swimming pool and drama studio.

We achieve well at the traditional team sports (3rd in a National Cricket Competition) but aim to teach them sport is part of a healthy lifestyle. We are proud to be the British Champions at orienteering, and have our own bicycles for triathlon events. Music is an important part of school life with various ensembles and choirs to be part of. As expected, we offer a broad extra-curricular programme from cross-stitch to Minecraft to ballet and ukulele. The list goes on…

We encourage our pupils to take responsibility, from recycling to School Council to organising charity events. Our aim is for them to have confidence without arrogance, in order to face the challenges ahead. At the root of all of this is a happy and encouraging environment, where our pupils feel comfortable to explore, make mistakes and learn from them. Our children are happy, inspired by enthusiastic teaching and are eager to come to school. As a consequence, they achieve outstanding results.

Why not come and visit to discover more?

Worksop College Preparatory School, Ranby House

WORKSOP COLLEGE
Preparatory School, Ranby House
Co-educational, Day & Boarding, Ages 3-13

(Founded 1948)
Retford, Nottinghamshire DN22 8HX
Tel: 01777 714387 (Admissions)
Fax: 01777 702813

Email: admissionsprep@wsnl.co.uk
Website: www.wsnl.co.uk
Headmaster:
C S J Pritchard MA, BA(Hons), QTS
Appointed: September 2012
School type: Coeducational Day & Boarding
Age range of pupils: 3–13 years
No. of pupils enrolled as at 01/01/2016: 240
Fees per term as at 01/01/2016:
Day: £4,064–£4,274

Flexi-boarding 4 nights:
£1,564 (paid in addition to day fee)
Flexi-boarding 2 nights:
£814 (paid in addition to day fee)
Occasional Boarding: £38.50 (per night)
Pre-Prep Full Time: £2,625 (Pre-Prep
sessions can be divided Morning,
Afternoon or Full Day)
Creche: £10.50 (per session)
Average class size: 18-20
Teacher/pupil ratio: 1:11

More than just an education at Ranby House
We all want our children to be the best that they can be. At Worksop College Preparatory School, Ranby House, we share this ambition.

This is why we pride ourselves on providing an outstanding learning experience that supports each and every child to reach their full potential.

Set in over 60 acres of stunning countryside in the village of Ranby, Nottinghamshire, our excellent teaching standards are complemented by superb facilities for learning, sport, art, ICT, performance and music.

The site has ten sports pitches, an indoor sports centre, nine-hole golf course, tennis courts and a purpose built performing arts centre.

State-of-the-art classrooms allow children to use the latest technology, including iPads, to assist their learning in all subjects, as well as three dedicated ICT labs with an animation studio and 3D printing.

Class sizes are deliberately kept small to ensure our children get the very best from every lesson. Teachers are of the highest calibre in their subject, which is how we maintain high academic standards whilst continuing to offer non-selective admission.

Children can join our Pre-Prep department from the age of 3. Our teacher-led dedicated Nursery is a hive of activity for our youngest Ranbians.

After school children can choose from more than 30 extra-curricular activities, which are second-to-none.

There is something for everyone on offer, from rock band, glee club, orienteering and archery, to textiles, ballet lessons, horse riding and even scuba diving.

Our cosy boarding surroundings make Ranby House the ideal place for weekly, flexi or casual boarding, allowing your child to develop their independence and take full advantage of everything on offer.

For day pupils, we offer a free breakfast club and varied after school finishing times up to 6.30pm. An extensive and flexible bus service is also offered across the region.

At Ranby House we pride ourselves on giving every child the opportunity to be the best they can be.

Bromley High School GDST
A GDST School

FIDES et OPERA

(Founded 1883)

Blackbrook Lane, Bickley, Bromley, Kent BR1 2TW

Tel: 020 8781 7000/1
Fax: 020 8781 7002/3
Email: bhs@bro.gdst.net
Website: www.bromleyhigh.gdst.net
Head:
Mrs A M Drew BA(Hons), MBA (Dunelm)
Appointed: September 2014
Head of Junior School:
Mrs Claire Dickerson BA(Anglia)

School type: Independent Selective Day School for Girls
Age range of girls: 4–18
No. of pupils enrolled as at 01/01/2016: 912
Sixth Form: 125
Senior School (ages 11-18): 600
Junior School (ages 4-11): 312
Fees per annum as at 01/01/2016:
Day: £12,423–£15,405
Average class size: 20-25

Childhood is a time for curiosity, imagination and friendships. At Bromley High Junior School we provide a secure and happy environment in which we nurture these qualities. We believe in preparing the girls for the challenges beyond school and value the importance of a holistic approach.

The curriculum is designed to encourage independent thought, with opportunities for the girls to take risks to deepen their learning and embrace new experiences. We achieve high standards by providing specialist teaching and facilities in many areas including music, sport, science, computing and languages, which add an international dimension to the girls' learning as well as inspiring within them an awareness of different cultures. Physical education is an integral part of school life with many different sports on offer and opportunities to compete at all levels. The learning is enriched with a diverse programme of visits and events and a wide range of extra-curricular activities are on offer.

Creativity plays a key part in each girl's day. Girls may find themselves using Euros to buy a croissant in a French lesson or joining a Chinese Dance workshop. They may present their ideas on becoming a House Captain or design and build their own rocket after watching Tim Peak make his landmark flight to the International Space Station. Our beautiful school grounds provide opportunities for outdoor learning. Forest School enables the girls to encounter the beauty, joy, awe and wonder of the natural environment.

We understand that parents want happiness and an excellent learning environment for their daughters. Being an all through school, educating girls from childhood to adulthood brings many benefits. One school means one choice for parents as their daughters reach school age. After that the girls' educational, emotional and social progress is tracked and developed until they leave us for University, having formed long lasting relationships.

At all stages girls are encouraged to set good examples and to behave in a courteous way in order to promote self-respect. They take responsibility for their actions and show a willingness to help, support and guide others in their work within the school.

You would be very welcome to visit the Junior School at any time, and I look forward to meeting you.

Claire Dickerson, Junior Head, Bromley High School

For 4+, 7+, 11+, and 16+ Entry please visit us at our Open Events on Tuesday 17th May and Saturday 1st October 2016.

Please contact the school via our website: www.bromleyhigh.gdst.net or our admissions office on admissions@bro.gdst.net or Tel 020 8781 7000 to arrange a visit.

Croydon High School GDST

CHS
Croydon High School
ESTD. 1874

(Founded 1874)
Old Farleigh Road, Selsdon, South

Croydon, Surrey CR2 8YB
Tel: 020 8260 7500
Fax: 020 8260 7461
Email: admissions@cry.gdst.net
Website: www.croydonhigh.gdst.net
Head of Junior School:
Mrs Sophie Bradshaw
Appointed: January 2015

School type: Girls' Day
Age range of girls: 3–18
No. of pupils enrolled as at 01/01/2016: 600
Sixth Form: 110
 Fees per annum as at 01/01/2016:
Junior School: £9,030 (Nursery)
£11,808 (Years 3-6)
Senior School: £14,994 (Years 10-13)

If you are looking for the best... aim high ...Aim for Croydon High Junior School

Croydon High School in Selsdon, Surrey is an exceptional independent day school for girls aged 3 to 18. Part of the Girls' Day School Trust, the leading network of independent girls schools in the UK, Croydon High has been delivering outstanding education to local girls since 1874.

The Junior School, on the same spacious 22 acre site as the seniors, shares the excellent sports facilities, with indoor swimming pool, tennis and netball courts and a floodlit all weather artificial hockey pitch. Visitors remark on how happy, confident and well-mannered the girls are and on their sense of purpose and focus on their work.

Girls join Nursery aged 3 for mornings or full days, in recently refurbished classrooms offering a warm and caring environment where learning is both challenging and fun. Moving on to Reception, the acquisition of literacy and numeracy competence is promoted, whilst building confidence and finding out what sparks each girl's imagination.

Light, bright purpose-built classrooms and bespoke Music and Drama suites are well resourced and spacious. In the innovative 4D room, a combination of sound, light, music and touch inspires junior school pupils to produce wonderful written and creative work.

Thanks to a legacy from a former Music teacher, all girls in Year 3 have the opportunity to learn a stringed instrument with free tuition for a year and many continue with this. Many also attend the wide range of extra-curricular clubs. Pastoral care is an absolute priority with the school supporting girls as they develop socially, always encouraging them to 'have a go'. Success and effort are celebrated equally.

Inspirational teaching and a focus on the individual maximises potential and prepares girls academically and emotionally to make a seamless transition to the senior school in Year 7.

For more details or to arrange to visit the school, please contact Clare Macmillan on c.macmillan@cry.gdst.net or 020 8260 7508
www.croydonhigh.gdst.net
https://twitter.com/croydonhighjnrs

Woodford Green Preparatory School

(Founded 1932)

Glengall Road, Woodford Green, Essex
IG8 0BZ
Tel: 020 8504 5045
Email: admin@wgprep.co.uk
Website: www.wgprep.co.uk
Headmaster: Mr J P Wadge
Appointed: September 2015

School type: Co-educational Day
Age range of pupils: 3–11
No. of pupils enrolled as at 01/01/2016: 375
Fees per annum as at 01/01/2016:
Day: £2,995
Average class size: 24
Teacher/pupil ratio: 1:12

Known locally as the "Red School" because of the scarlet uniforms, Woodford Green Preparatory School was founded in 1932 to provide a non-denominational Christian education for boys and girls, a tradition that has been maintained throughout and is now enriched by a vibrant, multi-cultural environment. The school is highly regarded by parents as successful in terms of ensuring children are safe, happy and well prepared for achieving excellent results in 11+ entrance examinations. We aim to provide a learning community that lights the flame within and empowers all children to reach their educational and personal potential.

Our latest independent school inspection report highlights our outstanding work. Our school ensures that 'pupils' personal development is excellent' and that 'the quality of pupils' achievements and learning is excellent and reflects the school's aims'. It was also noted by the inspectors that our children 'are confident, self-aware and have high esteem. Pupils have a keen moral sense, awareness of others and accept responsibility willingly'.

The friendly, supportive environment, in which excellent work and behaviour fosters interest and independence, encourages all children to do their very best. We have purpose-built areas for science, sport, art, music, computing and French, complemented by specialist teachers. We have excellent teachers and modern facilities throughout the school, including a fabulous library which is regularly used by the whole school to foster a love of reading. In the Early Years, fully qualified staff ensure that children have an outstanding foundation for the rest of the school to build on. Excellent governance, leadership and management gives strong support and challenge, setting strategic priorities and building excellent teamwork, to ensure all children's needs are met. Our links with parents are very good as we strive to give parents excellent opportunities to be involved in school life and their children's progress.

We look forward to welcoming you to our very happy and successful school.

© Redcoat Photography

Bassett House School

Bassett House
School

QUISQUE PRO SUA PARTE

(Founded 1947)

60 Bassett Road, London, W10 6JP
Tel: 020 8969 0313
Email: info@bassetths.org.uk
Website: www.bassetths.org.uk
Headmistress:
Mrs Philippa Cawthorne MA (Soton) PGCE
Appointed: January 2014

School type: Co-educational Day
Age range of pupils: 3–11
No. of pupils enrolled as at 01/01/2016: 190
Fees per annum as at 01/01/2016:
Day: £7,890–£16,440
Average class size: 20
Teacher/pupil ratio: 1:7

Bassett House School, a highly successful coeducational IAPS school for children aged 3-11 situated in North Kensington, combines an extraordinarily happy atmosphere with first class academic results. It enjoys an enviable reputation, as evidenced by its ISI inspection in which in all areas assessed it was judged to be 'outstanding' or 'excellent', the highest grades they awarded. The school participates in the Minimum Funding Entitlement Scheme, which reduces the fees charged for children aged under five years old.

Bassett House is a member of House Schools Group and has as sister independent preparatory schools Orchard House School in Chiswick and Prospect House School in Putney. There will be approximately 190 children on roll in September 2013 at Bassett House School.

It is our aim that all pupils should enjoy coming to Bassett House each morning. They take full advantage of a broad-based curriculum, as well as numerous extracurricular activities. Our objective is for all pupils to be happy and fulfilled, so that they may reach their full potential across all areas of the curriculum thereby becoming confident, creative and independent learners. Teaching is supportive yet challenging and always takes into account the individual needs of the children. We also strive to develop self-respect along with a strong sense of moral values, thus enabling our pupils to become responsible and involved members of society. Underpinning all aspects of school life is an ethos that requires mutual respect and concern for all members of the school community and fosters close relationships between school and home. Good manners and courteous behaviour are encouraged at all times.

Girls continue at Bassett House until

the age of eleven, when they move to their senior schools. Boys are prepared for 7+ and 8+ assessment but increasingly continue at the school until the age of 11. Whilst the Nursery and Reception entry years are almost invariably fully subscribed (early registration is advised), the school occasionally has places for children from Year 3 upwards.

Bassett House provides a thorough grounding in the usual educational subjects and the children are prepared for the entrance examinations to leading day and boarding schools.

In recent years the entrance examination results to these schools have been excellent with the children regularly being offered places at, amongst other schools, The City of London, Colet Court, Francis Holland (Clarence Gate and Graham Terrace), Godolphin & Latymer, The Hall, The Harrodian, Highgate, Latymer, More House, Notting Hill and Ealing High, Queen's College, Queen's

Gate, South Hampstead, St Benedict's, St Paul's Girls', Sussex House, University College, Westminster Cathedral Choir School and Westminster Under School.

As at its sister schools and via the House Schools Trust, Bassett House occasionally offers scholarships for gifted children aged 7+ which contribute to or cover fees in full. The scholarships are restricted to children currently attending a maintained school who show significant promise and for whom an education in the private sector would represent a major opportunity. To learn more about the trust please visit the website www.houseschoolstrust.org.

To find out more about Bassett House, please look at the school's website www.bassetths.org.uk. Alternatively, please telephone 020 8969 0313 to order a prospectus or to join one of our regular tours. In addition, there are occasional Open Days which give an even greater opportunity to speak to our strongest supporters, namely the children!

S.R.Binney-King
1.11.00

Devonshire House Preparatory School

(Founded 1989)

2 Arkwright Road, Hampstead, London, NW3 6AE

Tel: 020 7435 1916
Email: enquiries@devonshirehouseprepschool.co.uk
Website: www.devonshirehouseschool.co.uk
Headmistress: Mrs S. Piper BA(Hons)
School type: Preparatory, Pre-preparatory & Nursery Day School

Religious Denomination: Non-denominational
Age range of boys: 2 –13
Age range of girls: 2 –11
No. of pupils enrolled as at 01/01/2016: 620
Boys: 340 **Girls:** 280
Fees per annum as at 01/01/2016:
Day: £9,060–£16,635

Academic & leisure facilities

The school is situated in fine premises in the heart of Hampstead with its own walled grounds. The aim is to achieve high academic standards whilst developing enthusiasm and initiative throughout a wide range of interests. It is considered essential to encourage pupils to develop their own individual interests and a good sense of personal responsibility.

Curriculum

Early literacy and numeracy are very important and the traditional academic subjects form the core curriculum. The younger children all have a class teacher and classroom assistant and their day consists of a mixture of formal lessons and learning through play. Whilst children of all ages continue to have a form teacher, as they grow older an increasing part of the curriculum is delivered by subject specialists. The combined sciences form an increasingly important part of the timetable as the children mature. The use of computers is introduced from an early stage, both as its own skill and as an integrated part of the pupils' education.

Expression in all forms of communication is encouraged, with classes having lessons in art, music, drama and French. Physical exercise and games also play a key part of the curriculum. Much encouragement is given to pupils to help widen their horizons and broaden their interests. The school fosters a sense of responsibility amongst the pupils, and individuality and personal attention for each pupil is considered essential to make progress in the modern world.

The principal areas of the National Curriculum are covered, though subjects may be taken at a higher level, or at a quicker pace. For the girls approaching the eleven plus senior schools' entry examinations, special emphasis is given to the requirements for these, and in the top two years for the boys, Common Entrance curriculum is taught. The pupils achieve great success in these examinations and a number also sit successfully for senior school scholarships.

The school has its own nursery, The Oak Tree Nursery, which takes children from two-and-a-half years of age.

Entry requirements

The Oak Tree Nursery: For children entering the Oak Tree Nursery, places are offered on the basis on an informal assessment made at the nursery. Children in The Oak Tree Nursery transfer directly to the Junior School.

The Junior School: For children entering the junior school from the ages of three to five, places are offered on the basis of assessment made at the school. From the age of six places are usually subject to a written test taken at school. At eight, children transfer directly into the upper school. Parents and their children are welcome to visit for interview and to see around the school.

The Upper School: Entry to the upper school is principally from the junior school. For pupils seeking to join the school from elsewhere places are normally subject to a written entrance test.

Forest School

(Founded 1834)
College Place, Snaresbrook,

London, E17 3PY
Tel: 020 8520 1744
Fax: 020 8520 3656
Email: info@forest.org.uk
Website: www.forest.org.uk
Warden: Mr Antony Faccinello
School type: Diamond structure

Age range of pupils: 4–18
No. of pupils enrolled as at 01/01/2016: 1355
Boys: 540 **Girls:** 540 **Sixth Form:** 260
Pre-Preparatory and Preparatory: 275
Fees per annum as at 01/01/2016:
Day: £11,049–£16,335
Teacher/pupil ratio: 1:9.6

Established in 1834, the school takes its name from the forest that surrounds it and is located on the edge of London's largest open space, Epping Forest.

Forest School is London's only diamond structure school and is one of the very few in the country. This means that boys and girls are taught in single-sex classes within the same grounds.

At four, boys and girls are taught together in the Pre-Preparatory School before moving into single-sex classes at seven. From 7-16, pupils are taught separately before joining a co-educational Sixth Form.

We know that boys' and girls' physiology differ as they age and these differences result in different needs for children. Life beyond the school gates, however, is not single-sex, so while boys and girls are taught separately, they play together and participate in clubs, excursions, productions and events together.

It really is the best of both worlds. Boys and girls can grow up without the pressures that come from direct competition with the opposite sex in the classroom, and teachers have the flexibility to tailor their teaching methods according to both the age and sex of the class.

If you feel Forest Preparatory School may be a match for your son or daughter then do please get in touch with us.

Herne Hill School

CELEBRATING 40 YEARS

(Founded 1976)

The Old Vicarage, 127 Herne Hill, London, SE24 9LY
Tel: 020 7274 6336
Email: enquiries@hernehillschool.co.uk
Website: www.hernehillschool.co.uk
Headteacher: Mrs Ngaire Telford

Director: Mr Dominik Magyar
School type: Coeducational Day
Age range of pupils: 2+ to 7
No. of pupils enrolled as at 01/01/2016: 275
Fees per annum as at 01/01/2016:
Day: £1,790–£4,435

Herne Hill School has much to offer – caring and enthusiastic staff, happy and confident children, and excellent results at 7+ years.

In the UK, it is the largest independent pre-school and pre-prep focusing exclusively on 2+ to 7 year olds. In South London, it is well known as an oasis of happy learning and as the largest feeder into the reputable Dulwich schools. Children join the Kindergarten in the year they become three years old, Pre-Reception in the year they become four or then Reception. Chance vacancies are occasionally available in Years 1 and 2.

The school lies tucked away behind St Paul's Church on Herne Hill. Its grounds and facilities provide a 'homely', safe and nurturing feel while at the same time being open, green and deceptively large – the perfect environment for young children to blossom and enjoy discovering how to learn. Since January 2016, a new hall and Kindergarten has become fully operational and enabled a number of additional benefits:

- the provision of healthy hot lunches freshly cooked on site daily;

- a large, state-of-the-art Kindergarten with free-flow access to a covered outdoor play area;
- a modern, multi-purpose hall for sports, drama, dance, assemblies, lunches, etc.; and
- upgraded playground facilities with a new, enlarged all-weather surface and a trim trail in the nature area.

By focusing on Early Years and Key Stage 1, Herne Hill School has developed a strong expertise in making the critical transition from "nursery" to "school" seamless. Children joining the Kindergarten and Pre-

Reception can avoid the disruption of a 4+ change and have continuity for up to five years in what are arguably their most important formative years. Children joining in Reception also benefit from the smooth progression from a play-based learning approach to more structured lessons.

"Love Care Excellence" encapsulates the school philosophy that love, nurture and a caring environment foster the children's self-confidence, sense of achievement and happiness, thereby stimulating their curiosity and desire to learn. The school's atmosphere lives this philosophy. It is a caring, friendly and fun place, and at the same time there is an air of achievement, respect and discipline.

The proprietary curriculum is finely balanced to take account of each child's individual needs as well as the requirements of the 7+ entry tests – and to make learning fun! It is designed to develop the skills of independent learning and to sustain the children's innate joy of learning. Music, drama, gym, dancing and French are emphasised and taught by specialists. Wrap-around care is available from 8am to 6pm through a broad offering of attractive clubs aimed at satisfying the children's various interests and enabling earlier drop-off and later

pick-up for parents.

The latest ISI inspection report delivered a strong endorsement of the school's ethos, staff, curriculum, modus operandi and infrastructure by giving the highest possible rating of 'excellent' or 'outstanding' to every aspect of the school. The inspectors deemed overall achievement to be excellent and that pupils are very well educated and achieve very high standards in both their

learning and personal development. The full report can be found on www.isi.net.

The school holds two open mornings a year, typically in March and September. Prospective parents may also see the school 'in action' by joining one of the regular tours held during school hours. The school's website contains relevant information about life at the school, its curriculum and the destination of its leavers.

Hawkesdown House School Kensington

Hawkesdown House School
Endeavour • Courage • Truth

27 Edge Street, Kensington, London, W8 7PN

Tel: 020 7727 9090
Email: admin@hawkesdown.co.uk
Website: www.hawkesdown.co.uk
Head: Mrs C Bourne MA(Cantab)
Appointed: January 2010
School type:
Boys' Independent Pre-Prep Day

Religious Denomination: Non-denominational
Age range of boys: 3–8
No. of pupils enrolled as at 01/01/2016: 141
Fees per annum as at 01/01/2016:
Day: £14,550–£16,725
Average class size: 18-21
Teacher/pupil ratio: 1:9

Hawkesdown House is an independent school for boys from the age of 4 to 8 with a Nursery Class for boys of 3 years old. It is housed in a fine building in Edge Street, off Kensington Church Street, and most of the boys live within walking distance. Founded in 2001, the School's reputation has spread by word of mouth and it is an important part of the community.

The Headmistress, Mrs Claire Bourne, a Cambridge Classics graduate, is a firm believer in single sex education for this age group. "Boys learn in such a different way from girls and we understand that completely here and cater to their needs."

She leads a young and enthusiastic staff who all have high expectations of the boys. "Our main curriculum focus is on literacy and numeracy but our syllabus is wonderfully broad. We want the boys to leave Hawkesdown House with a joy of learning so we ensure that their education is enriched in every way. Music, chess, judo, fencing and Mandarin are just some of the subjects on offer." After school clubs, School Council and a House system offer the boys many opportunities to contribute to school life. The Friday assembly for parents, where the boys' achievements are celebrated, is always packed.

"Hawkesdown House is a big family" says Mrs Bourne, "we are immensely proud of our boys and everyone here is valued for their contribution and effort."

The School is dedicated to providing an outstanding early education for the boys, who are prepared for examinations at 8 years old to London's most selective Prep Schools including Westminster Under, Colet Court and Sussex House.

Parents who would like further information or to visit the school and meet the Head, should contact the School Office for a prospectus or an appointment.

Lyndhurst House Prep School

LYNDHURST HOUSE
PREPARATORY SCHOOL

(Founded 1952)

24 Lyndhurst Gardens, Hampstead,
London, NW3 5NW
Tel: 020 7435 4936
Email: pmg@lyndhursthouse.co.uk
Website: www.lyndhursthouse.co.uk
Headmaster: Andrew Reid MA(Oxon)
Appointed: September 2008

School type: Boys' Day
Age range of boys: 4–13
No. of pupils enrolled as at 01/01/2016: 165
Fees per annum as at 01/01/2016:
Day: £5,515–£6,160
Average class size: 18
Teacher/pupil ratio: 1:8

Lyndhurst House Pre-Prep & Prep School for boys was founded by Vernon Davies in 1952, in a tall, handsome Willett-style building in leafy Lyndhurst Gardens, Hampstead.

For over 60 years Lyndhurst has played a full part in the range of local independent educational provision, sending on its 13-year-olds to the many renowned senior schools in London, and some to boarding further afield with an excellent record of academic success and achievement, matched by a strong participation in sports, music and art.

Pupils develop a good knowledge of their own and other cultures and traditions. Visits to theatres, museums and art galleries feature prominently throughout the year. A significant strength of the school is the way pupils from a wide range of cultural backgrounds work and play together harmoniously.

One of the smaller prep schools in the area, Lyndhurst provides a structured but individually responsive education from reception at four-plus up to Common Entrance and scholarship at 13, delivered by an experienced, well-qualified, and stable staff team, and the abiding characteristics of its pupils seem to be a lively enthusiasm and sense of engagement and belonging. Lyndhurst House is a non-denominational school.

For all enquiries, please contact
Mrs P M Green
Lyndhurst House Preparatory
24 Lyndhurst Gardens
Hampstead
London NW3 5NW
Tel: 020 7435 4936
Email: pmg@lyndhursthouse.co.uk
Website: www.lyndhursthouse.co.uk
We look forward to meeting you.

Newton Prep

(Founded 1991)

149 Battersea Park Road, London, SW8 4BX

Tel: 020 7720 4091

Fax: 020 7498 9052

Email: admin@newtonprep.co.uk

Website: www.newtonprepschool.co.uk

Headmistress: Mrs Alison Fleming BA, MA Ed, PGCE

Appointed: September 2013

School type: Coeducational Pre-

Preparatory & Preparatory Day

Age range of pupils: 3–13

No. of pupils enrolled as at 01/01/2016: 640

Boys: 352 **Girls:** 288

Fees per annum as at 01/01/2016:

Day: £8,310–£17,625

Average class size: 20

Bright children, exceptional opportunities. Newton Prep is a modern exciting school which has spacious, state of the art facilities including a fully-equipped 300-seat auditorium, three science labs, ICT suites and a new music school which includes a 120-seat recital hall, a music technology studio, a recording studio and multiple practice rooms, not to mention the school's 'rolling acre', the constantly used, on-site all-weather pitch. Three sports halls and a dance suite complete the indoor sports facilities. Both the children and visiting authors rave about the huge, bright and popular library.

Newton Prep teachers encourage all pupils into flashes of brilliance by supporting them to access a stretching, broad and creative curriculum. Newton pupils are bright, confident, kind, happy and keen to articulate their ideas and many questions.

A wide range of extracurricular activities are available, including judo, fencing, ballet, art, Mandarin, music-tech and speech and drama. Please visit www.newtonprepschool.co.uk for more information.

Entry requirements

Places are allocated to Nursery ensuring that there is gender balance and that there is an even spread of autumn, spring and summer birthdays. Children joining Reception are assessed individually. Entry into Years 1-8 is by academic assessment and interview. Scholarships and means-tested bursaries are available from Year 3.

Examinations offered

Entrance examinations to Senior Schools, Common Entrance and scholarships at 11 and 13, supported by a Deputy Head with responsibility for Senior School Transfer.

North Bridge House Preparatory School

 North Bridge House Preparatory School

(Founded 1939)
1 Gloucester Avenue, London, NW1 7AB

Tel: 020 7267 6266
Email:
admissions@northbridgehouse.com
Website:
www.northbridgehouse.com/prep
Head: Brodie Bibby

School type: Co-educational Day
Age range of pupils: 7–13
No. of pupils enrolled as at 01/01/2016: 486
Fees per annum as at 01/01/2016:
Day: £15,585
Average class size: Circa 20

Located in an impressive former convent on the edge of Regent's Park, North Bridge House Preparatory School provides a high quality, 'all-round' education for girls and boys.

In December 2015 we were, once again, recognised for our on-going commitment to our pupils and awarded *"outstanding in all areas"* by the inspectorate, receiving the following comments… *"The school is a close-knit learning community in which pupils are very well behaved, happy and high achieving. From an early age, pupils develop a strong sense of self-esteem"*

We know, support and inspire every pupil to achieve their full potential and provide a solid foundation for a successful academic career and adult life.

Thanks to our nurturing approach and thorough academic preparation, a consistently high number of children are accepted by their first choice Senior School, with many winning much sought-after academic, music, sport, drama and art scholarships. To ensure each individual flourishes and achieves their aspirations, we work closely with the pupil and parents to choose the right school for them. Both boys and girls have the option to move onto our Senior School in Hampstead in year 7, or stay with us until age 13 and choose to join our Senior and Sixth form in Canonbury.

At North Bridge House Prep, we teach a rich and varied curriculum, tailor-made to challenge, stimulate and reward every pupil. We also endeavour to go that bit further than the norm and equip our pupils with more than just the basic understanding of a subject. What's more, the inspection described our *"quality of teaching as outstanding"* with *"Teachers bring a lively enthusiasm to their teaching, which encourages and enthuses pupils in their learning."*

Sport is essential to our pupils' physical and emotional wellbeing and development – with PE and games sessions held in Regent's Park or the school gym, rock-climbing at a local sports club and winter cricket in our Senior School's state-of-the-art sports hall.

In addition, our extra-curricular offering is rich, diverse and character-building with activities ranging from music, art, drama and sport (also enjoyed as part of the curriculum) – to chess, cookery, design technology, Spanish, ballet and street dance.

Our inspection also lauded the leadership of the school as *"outstanding"* and remarked how pupils' behaviour *"is founded on the high levels of mutual trust and respect between pupils and staff"*. We were also praised for the excellent quality of safeguarding and the provision for the welfare, health and safety of pupils.

North Bridge House is very proud to be recognised as one of London's most prestigious Prep Schools and welcome you and your family to visit us during one of our open days or for a private tour. Find out more at northbridgehouse.com/open.

Orchard House School

Orchard House
School

(Founded 1993)

16 Newton Grove, Bedford Park, London, W4 1LB
Tel: 020 8742 8544 Registrar: 020 8987 9886
Email: registrar@orchardhs.org.uk
Website: www.orchardhs.org.uk
Headmistress: Mrs M V Edwards BEd (Bedford), CertEd (Man)
Appointed: September 2015

School type: Co-educational Day
Age range of pupils: 3–11
No. of pupils enrolled as at 01/01/2016: 290
Fees per annum as at 01/01/2016:
Day: £7,890–£16,440
Average class size: 20
Teacher/pupil ratio: 1:7

Orchard House School, a highly successful coeducational IAPS school for children aged 3-11 situated in Chiswick, combines an extraordinarily happy atmosphere with first class academic results. It enjoys an enviable reputation, as evidenced by its ISI inspection in which in all areas assessed it was judged to be 'outstanding' or 'excellent', the highest grades that are awarded. The school participates in the Minimum Funding Entitlement Scheme, which reduces the fees charged for children aged under 5 years old.

Orchard House is a member of House Schools Group and has as sister independent preparatory schools Bassett House School in North Kensington and Prospect House School in Putney. There will be approximately 290 children on roll in September 2013 at Orchard House School.

It is our aim that all pupils should enjoy coming to Orchard House each morning. They take full advantage of a broad-based curriculum, as well as numerous extracurricular activities. Our objective is for all pupils to be happy and fulfilled, so that they may reach their full potential across all areas of the curriculum thereby becoming confident, creative and independent learners. Teaching is supportive yet challenging and always takes into account the individual needs of the children. We also strive to develop self-respect along with a strong sense of moral values, thus enabling our pupils to become responsible and involved members of society. Underpinning all aspects of school life is an ethos that requires mutual respect and concern for all members of the school community and fosters close relationships between school and home. Good manners and courteous behaviour are encouraged at all times.

Girls continue at Orchard House until the age of 11, when they move to their senior schools. Boys are prepared for 7+ and 8+ assessment but increasingly continue at the school until the age of 11. Whilst the Nursery and Reception entry years are almost invariably fully subscribed (early registration is advised), the school occasionally has places for children from Year 3 upwards.

Orchard House provides a thorough grounding in the usual educational subjects and the children are prepared for the entrance examinations to leading day and boarding schools.

In recent years the entrance examination results to these schools have been excellent with the children regularly being offered places at, amongst other schools, Colet Court, Caldicott, Godolphin & Latymer, King's House, The Harrodian, The Lady Eleanor Holles School, Latymer Preparatory and Upper, Ludgrove, Notting Hill and Ealing High, St Paul's Girls', Sussex House, University College, Westminster Cathedral Choir School and Westminster Under School.

As at its sister schools and via the House Schools Trust, Orchard House occasionally offers scholarships for gifted children aged 7+ which contribute to or cover fees in full. The scholarships are restricted to children currently attending a maintained school who show significant promise and for whom an education in the private sector would represent a major opportunity. To learn more about the trust please visit the website www.houseschoolstrust.org.

To find out more about Orchard House, please look at the school's website www.orchardhs.org.uk. Alternatively, please telephone 020 8742 8544 to order a prospectus or to join one of our regular tours. In addition, there are occasional Open Days which give an even greater opportunity to speak to our strongest supporters, namely the children!

Prospect House School

Prospect House
School

QUISQUE PRO SUA PARTE

(Founded 1991)

75 Putney Hill, London, SW15 3NT
Tel: 020 8780 0456 Registrar: 020 8246 4897
Email: registrar@prospecths.org.uk
Website: www.prospecths.org.uk
Headmistress: Mrs Dianne Barratt MEd
(Newcastle-upon-Tyne)
Appointed: 2004

School type: Co-educational Day
Age range of pupils: 3–11
No. of pupils enrolled as at 01/01/2016: 300
Fees per annum as at 01/01/2016:
Day: £7,890–£16,440
Average class size: 20
Teacher/pupil ratio: 1:7

Prospect House School, a highly successful co-educational IAPS school for children aged 3-11 situated in Putney, combines an extraordinarily happy atmosphere with first class academic results. It enjoys an enviable reputation, as evidenced by its ISI school inspection this year in which in all areas assessed it was judged to be 'excellent', the highest grade that is awarded. The school participates in the Minimum Funding Entitlement Scheme, which reduces the fees charged for children aged under 5 years old.

Prospect House is a member of House Schools Group and has as sister independent preparatory schools Bassett House School in North Kensington and Orchard House School in Chiswick. There will be approximately 290 children on roll in September 2013 at Prospect House School.

It is our aim that all pupils should enjoy coming to Prospect House each morning. They take full advantage of a broad-based curriculum, as well as numerous extracurricular activities. Our objective is for all pupils to be happy and fulfilled, so that they may reach their full potential across all areas of the curriculum thereby becoming confident, creative and independent learners. Teaching is supportive yet challenging and always takes into account the individual needs of the children. We also strive to develop self-respect along with a strong sense of moral values, thus enabling our pupils to become responsible and involved members of society. Underpinning all aspects of school life is an ethos that requires mutual respect and concern for all members of the school community and fosters close relationships between school and home. Good manners and courteous behaviour are encouraged at all times.

Boys and girls continue at Prospect House until the age of 11, when they move to their senior schools. Whilst the Nursery and Reception entry years are almost invariably fully subscribed (early registration is advised), the school occasionally has places for children from Year 3 upwards.

Prospect House provides a thorough grounding in the usual educational subjects and the children are prepared for the entrance examinations to leading day and boarding schools.

In recent years the entrance examination results to these schools have been excellent with the children regularly being offered places at, amongst other schools, Benenden, City of London Freemen's, Colet Court, Downe House, Emanuel, Francis Holland (both Regent's Park and Sloane Square), Godolphin & Latymer, Hampton, The Harrodian, The Lady Eleanor Holles, Ibstock Place, King's College, Kew House, Latymer Upper, Notre Dame, Putney High, Radnor House, Reed's, St Paul's Girls', Surbiton High, Tiffin, Westminster Under School, Wimbledon High and Wycombe Abbey.

As at its sister schools and via the House Schools Trust, Prospect House occasionally offers scholarships for gifted children aged 7+ which contribute to or cover fees in full. The scholarships are restricted to children currently attending a maintained school who show significant promise and for whom an education in the private sector would represent a major opportunity. To learn more about the trust please visit the website www.houseschoolstrust.org.

To find out more about Prospect House, please look at the school's website www.prospecths.org.uk. Alternatively, please telephone 020 8780 0456 to order a prospectus or to join one of our regular tours. In addition, there are occasional Open Days which give an even greater opportunity to speak to our strongest supporters, namely the children!

Queen's Gate School

Queen's Gate

(Founded 1891)

133 Queen's Gate, London, SW7 5LE

Tel: 020 7589 3587
Fax: 020 7584 7691
Email: registrar@queensgate.org.uk
Website: www.queensgate.org.uk
Principal:
Mrs R M Kamaryc BA, MSc, PGCE
Appointed: January 2006
School type: Girls' Day

Age range of girls: 4–18
No. of pupils enrolled as at 01/01/2016: 523
Sixth Form: 90
Fees per annum as at 01/01/2016:
Junior School: £15,750
Senior School: £18,300
Average class size: 23
Teacher/pupil ratio: 1:10

Queen's Gate School is an independent day school for girls between the ages of 4 and 18 years. Established in 1891, the school is an Educational Trust situated in five large Victorian Houses within easy walking distance of Kensington Gardens, Hyde Park, and many of the main London museums.

We offer girls a friendly, supportive environment, where individuality is nurtured, academic standards are high and where a broad based curriculum ensures a well-rounded education.

Sport is highly valued at Queen's Gate with two compulsory sessions for all girls each week. We have many sports available at other times during the school day including netball, athletics, basketball, hockey, fencing, swimming, rowing, horse riding, cross-country running, biathlon and dance.

Admission is by test and interview in the Junior School. Girls for 4+ entry are invited for an assessment in early January of the year of entry. Parents will be invited to meet the Junior School Headmistress during the preceding half term. Entrance to the Senior School is by the North London Independent Girls' Schools' Consortium entrance examination at 11+, and the school's own entrance examinations to other years in the Senior School. Applicants for the Sixth Form are expected to have passed six GCSEs at A grade with A grades in those subjects they wish to pursue to A level.

In addition to the Open Events that take place in the Senior and Junior Schools throughout the year, parents are always welcome to make a private visit to see the schools at work. Appointments can be made by contacting the Registrar, Janette Micklewright, on 0207 594 4982 or by email registrar@queensgate.org.uk.

Read more about Queen's Gate on our website, www.queensgate.org.uk.

St Paul's Cathedral School

ST PAUL'S CATHEDRAL SCHOOL

(Founded 12th Century or earlier)

2 New Change, London, EC4M 9AD

Tel: 020 7248 5156

Fax: 020 7329 6568

Email: admissions@spcs.london.sch.uk

Website: www.spcslondon.com

Headmaster: Mr Neil Chippington MA, MEd, FRCO

Appointed: September 2009

School type: Coeducational Pre-Prep, Day Prep & Boarding Choir School

Religious Denomination: Church of England, admits pupils of all faiths

Age range of pupils: 4–13

No. of pupils enrolled as at 01/01/2016: 252

Boys: 143 **Girls:** 99

No. of boarders: 36

Fees per annum as at 01/01/2016:

Day: £12,939–£13,932

Full Boarding: £8,057

Average class size: 15-20

Teacher/pupil ratio: 1:10

Curriculum

A broad curriculum, including the International Primary Curriculum, prepares all pupils for 11+, 13+, scholarship and Common Entrance examinations. There is a strong musical tradition and choristers' Cathedral choral training is outstanding. A wide variety of games and other activities is offered.

Entry requirements

Entry at 4+ and 7+ years: Pre-prep and day pupils interview and short test; Choristers voice trials and tests held throughout the year for boys between 6 -8 years.

St Paul's Cathedral School is a registered charity (No. 312718), which exists to provide education for the choristers of St Paul's Cathedral and for children living in the local area.

The Hampshire School, Chelsea

The Hampshire School
C H E L S E A

(Founded 1928)

15 Manresa Road, Chelsea, London, SW3 6NB

Tel: 020 7352 7077
Fax: 020 7351 3960
Email: o.baskett@thehampshireschoolchelsea.co.uk
Website: www.thehampshireschoolchelsea.co.uk
Principal: Mr Dónal Brennan
Appointed: January 2014
School type: Co-educational Day

Age range of pupils: 3–13
No. of pupils enrolled as at 01/01/2016: 307
Boys: 187 **Girls:** 120
Fees per annum as at 01/01/2016:
Day: £14,925–£16,440
Average class size: Early Years: 13, Main School: 20
Teacher/pupil ratio: 1:6.4

Founded in 1928 and located in Chelsea, The Hampshire School provides the top class education one would expect from a traditional English Preparatory School. It is an inter-denominational day school providing outstanding learning in small classes, led by our highly qualified and dedicated teaching staff. The school offers a stimulating curriculum, ensuring that learning is interactive, fun and that every child is confident and valued.

The Early Years School is situated a mile away from the main school and is housed in a newly renovated classical London townhouse, providing children with the 'home away from home' secure and nurturing environment they need at this young age. The Early Years Foundation Stage curriculum is followed and the school puts emphasis on the children becoming happy, confident and polite learners who are engaged and enthusiastic in their education. Visits to the Forest School at Holland Park Ecology Centre and exciting, original bespoke programmes occur throughout the year.

The main school's outstanding facilities include a galleried library, gymnasium, science laboratory, art and design studio, fully equipped stage and large outdoor playground.

Children excel academically at The Hampshire School, Chelsea, successfully navigating the 11+ and 13+ to gain entry to their first choice school. Both schools have invitation only academic clubs to either extend or support children if required. Music is a strong point with over three quarters of children learning an instrument ranging from piano, guitar, cello to drums. There is a head of both boys' and girls' sports, encouraging excellence in both. Many matches are played against other schools enhancing the community feel of the school.

We also offer a choice of 70 extra-curricular activities including judo, gymnastics, fencing, archery, touch typing, dancing, art, languages, music, a radio station, ukulele and cross stitch.

For more information about The Hampshire School, Chelsea, Email: **o.baskett@thehampshireschoolchelsea.co.uk**
www.thehampshireschoolchelsea.co.uk

Kirkham Grammar Junior School

Ribby Road, Kirkham, Preston, Lancashire
PR4 2BH
Tel: 01772 684264
Fax: 01772 672747
Email: info@kirkhamgrammar.co.uk
Website: www.kirkhamgrammar.co.uk

Head of Junior School:
Ms Annette Roberts
School type: Coeducational Day
Age range of pupils: 3–11
No. of pupils enrolled as at 01/01/2016: 250
Teacher/pupil ratio: 1:12

Kirkham Grammar Junior School is a thriving co-educational day school for children aged 3-11 years, providing outstanding teaching, pastoral care and extra-curricular activities, which are designed to give girls and boys the best possible start in life. We offer a safe and secure environment in which every child is nurtured to achieve their full potential within a well-developed system of pastoral care, and we enjoy the support of parents, grandparents and other family members in creating a close-knit school community.

Kirkham Grammar Junior School, founded in 1991, is situated opposite the Senior School (founded 1549) on Ribby Road, West of Kirkham. As well as enjoying its own state of the art facilities within the Junior School site, the Junior School also has access to Senior School facilities, including an Astroturf pitch and Multi-purpose Hall.

There are nearly 250 boys and girls in school – in more or less equal numbers – aged between three and eleven.

Some children exhibit obvious ability in academic, sporting or creative endeavours from an early age; others do not, and may lack confidence as a result. We strive to discover the aptitudes, build the self-esteem and develop the potential of every one of these children. High levels of individual attention are central to achieving this aim, with the School's excellent staff the key resource.

We see extra-curricular opportunities, easily accessed and essential to every child's full development. Girls' and boys' sport flourishes at all ages, a full musical scheme is in place and every child has the opportunity to appear in a theatrical production at least once a year.
Twitter: https://twitter.com/KGJS
Facebook: https://www.facebook.com/KirkhamGrammarJuniorSchool

Stonyhurst St Mary's Hall

STONYHURST
ST MARY'S HALL

(Founded 1945)

Stonyhurst, Lancashire BB7 9PU

Tel: 01254 827073

Fax: 01254 827135

Email: admissions@stonyhurst.ac.uk

Website: www.stonyhurst.ac.uk

Headmaster:

Mr Ian Murphy BA (Hons), PGCE Durham

Appointed: September 2014

School type:

Coeducational Boarding & Day

Age range of pupils: 3–13

No. of pupils enrolled as at 01/01/2016: 262

Fees per annum as at 01/01/2016:

Day: £8,013–£14,907

Weekly Boarding: £19,449

Full Boarding: £22,950

Average class size: Max 20

Teacher/pupil ratio: 1:8

Stonyhurst St Mary's Hall is the Preparatory School of Stonyhurst College, providing the first steps in a seamless education from age 3 to 18. We are a Roman Catholic school in the Jesuit tradition offering an excellent education for boarders and day pupils alike. Stonyhurst St Mary's Hall is housed in its own buildings on the same site as the senior school with which it shares several facilities.

Stonyhurst St Mary's Hall is a place of enthusiastic learning, achievement and energy, with a genuine sense of family. Our pupils are proud of their school's distinguished heritage: Stonyhurst was founded in 1593 and is the oldest surviving Jesuit school in the world. We bring out and celebrate the best in every individual and we follow a broad, innovative curriculum that leaves children ready to consider their future path in life. Our pupils are aware of their responsibility to maximise their unique talents and thrive as they engage in the school's many opportunities in sport, music and drama; they are also grounded in values that give them a robust moral code for the challenges of modern life and they share the necessary awareness and compassion to put themselves forward for the needs of others.

The curriculum followed from 7-11 ensures that pupils are fully engaged with their school work, achieving high academic standards with small classes and individual attention. From the age of 11, delivery of the academic programme is overseen by the Heads of Department from Stonyhurst College and is taught by highly qualified specialist teachers, ensuring continuity as they move across to the College at the age of 13.

Stonyhurst St Mary's Hall has excellent facilities, which include a new science lab, extensive music department (all pupils in Year 4 learn a musical instrument and many have tuition before this), an art studio, a swimming pool, sports hall and a theatre, in which all children have their drama lessons. We also have a Learning Support department and a full-time English as an Additional Language teacher.

Boarders

Our boarders are cared for by houseparents, who are supported by an enthusiastic and caring team. While boarders are given maximum support and supervision, they are encouraged to do things for themselves, keep track of their timetable and manage their time effectively.

At Stonyhurst St Mary Hall, boarders can be as young as eight. Operating very much on a family basis, the boarding house is a very happy and well-ordered environment with separate boys' and girls' accommodation. The children enjoy exciting weekend trips, many clubs and activities and love to play in the school's extensive grounds and beautiful surroundings. On Sundays they join the boarders of the College for Mass in Stonyhurst's St Peter's Church.

Stonyhurst St Mary's Hall is in a beautiful rural location about an hour from Manchester, two hours from London by train and 40 minutes from Preston.

Hodder House

For children aged 3 to 7

Welcoming children from the age of three, Hodder House is our purpose built, award-winning pre-prep unit at St Mary's Hall.

Set in beautiful surroundings and equipped with exceptional facilities from the latest iPads to a unique woodland classroom, it is the ideal environment for indoor/outdoor play and learning.

Children work in small classes under the care and guidance of highly skilled and experienced early years teachers. In addition to literacy, numeracy, science and ICT, children learn modern languages, enjoy the arts, PE and swimming and can take part in our extensive after school activities programme until 18:00 (including a nutritious and delicious tea).

Cranmore School

(Founded 1968)
Epsom Road, West Horsley, Surrey KT24 6AT

Tel: 01483 280340
Fax: 01483 280341
Email: admissions@cranmoreprep.co.uk
Website: www.cranmoreprep.co.uk
Headmaster:
Mr Michael Connolly BSc, BA, MA, MEd
Appointed: September 2006
School type: Coeducational Day

Religious Denomination:
Catholic; other faiths welcome
Age range of pupils: 2–13
No. of pupils enrolled as at 01/01/2016: 475
Fees per annum as at 01/01/2016:
Nursery: £3,500
Junior: £3,795
Senior: £4,550

Cranmore School, one of Surrey's leading prep schools, offers an unrivalled, broad-ranging academic focus that challenges young enquiring minds. It has announced that it will become fully co-educational, welcoming girls and boys from aged 2 to 13.

Headmaster, Michael Connolly, commented "We are implementing this change from a position of strength. Increasingly parents want their sons and daughters to be educated together and we feel sure that Cranmore is well placed to deliver an outstanding education for both boys and girls." The school has been commended for its academic reputation, excellent facilities and high quality music and sport.

Cranmore was awarded the top grade in every category for its most recent inspection: "The pupils' achievements are excellent." and "The pupils' personal development is supported by excellent pastoral care." There is a very broad curriculum. Pupils study both modern and classical languages: French, Spanish, Mandarin, Latin and Greek. As you would expect for a leading school, Maths, English and Science are very strong with the latter being taught as Physics, Chemistry and Biology from Year 6 onwards. The sporting opportunities are phenomenal as the school has its own extensive playing fields, golf course, swimming pool, gymnasium with climbing wall and a sports hall which incorporates a fitness centre and several

squash courts. Children can pursue all the major sports but also do rowing, skiing or even golf.

Specialist subject teaching begins when pupils enter the senior department (8+). The older children also relish the benefits of the House System, part of the pastoral network reflecting Cranmore's Catholic ethos that cares for and encourages each individual.

Younger pupils, including those in the Nursery (Bright Stars at Cranmore), receive an excellent start which includes access to a fantastic Forest School with bespoke log cabin. In addition to the Nursery, the main entry points are for Reception (4+) and Year 3 (7+).

Hurstpierpoint College Prep School

Hurstpierpoint, West Sussex BN6 9JS
Tel: 01273 834975

Fax: 01273 836900
Email: hurstprep@hppc.co.uk
Website: www.hppc.co.uk
Head: Mr I D Pattison BSc
Appointed: September 2013
School type: Coeducational Day
Age range of pupils: 4–13

No. of pupils enrolled as at 01/01/2016: 360
Fees per annum as at 01/01/2016:
Reception: £7,140
Years 1-2: £7,680
Year 3: £12,075
Years 4-6: £13,875
Years 7-8: £14,280

Hurst Prep: Laying the foundations for children to thrive.

Hurst Prep School enjoys a stunning, safe and superbly equipped 140 acre country campus located amid beautiful countryside on the border of Sussex's South Downs National Park. Set within the Hurst College campus alongside the Senior School, Hurst Prep provides the first step on the education journey.

Enjoying their childhood

Hurst Prep is a very safe, caring and inspirational community where every pupil grows in confidence, knowing that they are respected, valued, praised and cherished. Within this positive and supportive environment, our children prosper and, over time, develop the essential values, skills, attributes and, most importantly, knowledge that will enable them to face the future with assurance.

Becoming lifelong learners

We feed the natural curiosity that lies within every child. Our boys and girls quickly discover that learning and self improvement can be enjoyable and rewarding activities in their own rights. Our focus on the quality and depth of the academic foundations laid down during these years means that, as each child grows in understanding, they also gain the knowledge and develop the intellectual maturity they need to become curious and capable lifelong learners.

Developing into well-rounded individuals

Throughout the pupils' time at Hurst Prep, we work in close partnership with parents to ensure that each and every one of our children thrives academically. Through the community of everyday school life, as well as the rich opportunities available in the creative and performing arts, activities and sport, Hurst children gain the broad-based skills, confidence and emotional maturity to prepare them for the coming stages of their school and adult lives.

Ludgrove

(Founded 1892)
Wokingham, Berkshire RG40 3AB

Tel: 0118 978 9881
Fax: 0118 979 2973
Email: registrar@ludgroveschool.co.uk
Website: www.ludgrove.net
Head of School: Mr Simon Barber
Appointed: Sept 2008
School type: Boys' Boarding

Religious Denomination: Church of England
Age range of boys: 8–13
No. of pupils enrolled as at 01/01/2016: 190
Fees per annum as at 01/01/2016:
Fees: £8,450 per term
Average class size: 12
Teacher/pupil ratio: 1:8

Ludgrove is a thriving full boarding school for 190 boys age 8 to 13, which sits in 130 acres of spectacular grounds. It is a magical place to spend five years of childhood, where outstanding pastoral care lies at the heart of everything and with fortnightly exeats we have a wonderful balance between school and home life.

We are a strong community where respect and kindness towards others and traditional values are paramount. Our boys relish their independence and enjoy nothing more than an hour or so of free time in which they can make the most of the extensive grounds and facilities; building camps, playing golf, digging in gardens, throwing a pot on the wheel or just kicking a ball with friends.

As a school, we are unashamedly ambitious for every boy and are proud of our strong academic record. We have a non-selective intake in year 4 and in recent years over 75% of boys have gone onto Eton, Harrow and Radley, in addition to other distinguished public schools.

The boys have a wealth of opportunities: a stimulating curriculum, exceptional facilities including a new 350 seat theatre and a vibrant extra-curricular programme with exposure to music, drama, sport and art. We aim to develop the boys' confidence in a caring supportive environment, where they are valued as individuals and learn to live as a community. Friendships are made for life and the unique Ludgrove spirit allows boys to thrive in an atmosphere of happiness, good manners and kindness.

Ludgrove is conveniently placed just 50 minutes from central London, with easy access to Heathrow and Gatwick.

Bursaries are available.

Milbourne Lodge School

Arbrook Lane, Esher, Surrey KT10 9EG
Tel: 01372 462737
Fax: 01372 471164
Email: registrar@milbournelodge.co.uk
Website: www.milbournelodge.co.uk
Head: Mrs Judy Waite

School type: Coeducational Day
Age range of pupils: 4–13
No. of pupils enrolled as at 01/01/2016: 236
Boys: 191 **Girls:** 45
Fees per annum as at 01/01/2016:
Day: £10,845–£13,500

Milbourne Lodge is a selective Pre-Prep and Prep School for boys and girls aged 4 to 13. Founded in 1912, the school has a long-standing tradition of preparing children for Common Entrance and Scholarship exams to the most prestigious and well known public schools. In the past five years alone over 50 academic, art, music and sports scholarships have been won by our pupils.

We strive to set the academic bar high, to value sport and extra-curricular activities, to instil a sense of responsibility and good manners and to develop children that are resilient and confident. Our academic curriculum, taught by a highly experienced and dedicated team of staff, is supported by excellent music, art and sports programmes, with games played every day. A strong emphasis is also placed on pastoral care and the school provides a warm and supportive environment in which each child feels valued and can flourish.

Milbourne Lodge is a very energetic school which provides endless opportunities and variety. Every child is encouraged to build on their own particular talents and to discover new ones. Here at Milbourne we work hard and play hard!

"Our overriding objective is to prepare your child for his or her next school. We will prepare each child to be ready to relish the experience of their new school, to be confident in their own skin and to be eager to take the next steps", Judy Waite, Head.

Following an extensive building programme, four new classrooms and a specialist science laboratory have recently been opened and from September 2016 there will be two form entry throughout the school. Located in Esher, Surrey, the school is situated in over eight acres of beautiful grounds within easy access of the A3 and M25. A daily bus runs from SW London.

Notre Dame School

Cobham, Surrey KT11 1HA
Tel: 01932 869990
Website: www.notredame.co.uk
Head of Seniors: Mrs Anna King MEd, MA (Cantab), PGCE

Head of Prep: Ms Merinda D'Aprano BEd, MA, CTC, FRSA
School type: Girls' Day 2-18, Boys' Day 2-7
Religious Denomination: Roman Catholic
Age range of pupils: 2–18
No. of pupils enrolled as at 01/01/2016: 600

Notre Dame School with its exceptional on-site facilities provides a dynamic environment giving every pupil the opportunity to develop and excel. The talented and dedicated teaching staff ensures the girls achieve outstanding results in all areas of the academic curriculum. Set in 17 acres of Surrey parkland Notre Dame girls enjoy high levels of success in all areas of Sport while the professional, 380-seat professional theatre gives pupils a really unique opportunity to tread the boards from a very young age; in drama, singing, ballet and dance or playing their individual instrument of choice.

Notre Dame's facilities include an outstanding Nursery which welcomes boys and girls from the age of two and follows the Early Years Foundation Stage Guidance. As well as their own classrooms and outdoor play areas they can access the whole school facilities such as the indoor swimming pool, the treehouse, large indoor sports arena, and enjoy specialist teaching for music, ballet, Spanish and swimming. Our curriculum is further enhanced with our forest school activities which take place within the 25 acres of secure parkland.

Sessions are flexible to suit the family's needs. Hot lunches and teas are available. Early Birds opens at 8:15am and Night Owls after school club runs until 5:30pm.

New facilities are currently under construction for completion in 2016. A new all-weather hockey pitch and six netball courts with a new pavilion are planned, from where parents can enjoy watching their daughters compete in the many matches and tournaments they participate in. In the prep school, Notre Dame will also be offering places to boys up to age 7 from September 2016.

Sutton High School GDST

SUTTON HIGH SCHOOL

(Founded 1884)

55 Cheam Road, Sutton, Surrey SM1 2AX
Tel: 020 8642 0594
Fax: 020 8642 2014
Email: admissions@sut.gdst.net
Website: www.suttonhigh.gdst.net
Headmistress: Mrs Katharine Crouch
Appointed: Septermber 2012

Head of Junior School: Miss Anne Musgrove
School type: Girls' Day
Age range of girls: 3–18
No. of pupils enrolled as at 01/01/2015: 600
Sixth Form: 60
 Fees per annum as at 01/01/2016:
Day: £9,153–£15,450

Sutton High School is an academically selective independent school for girls aged 3 to 18 which provides a broad and challenging curriculum to its pupils.

Strikingly positive relationships between our girls and their teachers, both within the classroom and beyond, make a significant contribution to the quality of the girls' academic and personal development. Our girls feel safe and cared for in a warm and secure environment which gives them the space to develop a strong sense of who they are and their place in the community. Frequent leadership opportunities at all levels of the school enable our girls to become articulate, confident and resilient adults.

The Nursery and Junior School is a vibrant and positive community, which visitors frequently comment upon. A strong emphasis on pastoral care and our nurturing environment enables the girls to learn and grow into confident, active and enthusiastic learners from the very start. Our broad curriculum offers the girls a wide range of learning experiences but, alongside this, priority is always given to the development of English and mathematical skills. All girls, including those in the Nursery, have the advantage of French, PE and music lessons taught by specialists. Other foreign languages are introduced from Year 3.

Extended opportunities are provided when girls take part in form assemblies, performances and whole school concerts and plays. This allows them to develop their talents to the full. Our Junior School prepares girls extremely well for the next stage in their learning; ensuring that every girl meets with both challenge and support and thus reaches her full potential.

Transition into the Senior School and later on into the Sixth Form is seen as a natural progression for our Junior School girls. At GCSE we offer a broad range of subjects, including more demanding but rewarding IGCSE courses in mathematics, English and the sciences and girls value the variety of A Level courses offered to them.

We look forward to welcoming you to Sutton High School and showing you what a vibrant and happy community we are.

Exeter Cathedral School

(Founded 1159)

UT VOCE, ITA VITA

The Chantry, Palace Gate,
Exeter, Devon EX1 1HX
Tel: 01392 255298
Email: admissions@exetercs.org
Website: www.exetercs.org
Headmaster: James Featherstone
Appointed: 2015
School type: Co-educational Day & Boarding

Age range of pupils: 3–13
No. of pupils enrolled as at 01/01/2016: 275
Boys: 138 **Girls:** 137
No. of boarders: 17
Fees per annum as at 01/01/2016:
Day: £6,519–£10,872
Full Boarding: £16,683–£17,658
Average class size: 17

There are currently 275 boys and girls between the ages of 2 and 13 at Exeter Cathedral School, 36 of them being Cathedral Choristers. Our size allows us to nurture and know each of our pupils as individuals, but also to have the energy, vibrancy and expertise to offer a truly all-round Prep School education.

Children as young as 2 years old attend our bright and energetic Pre-Prep department, with a brand new purpose-built Nursery, housed within the Cathedral Close, opened in summer 2015.

Pupils have an enormous number of challenging opportunities available to them as they progress through the school, from sport and outdoor pursuits to design technology, drama and art. Children's academic achievements are testament to their teachers' enthusiasm and expertise. Pupils leave at age 13 (at the end of Year 8) and, despite a non-selective admission system, the School has an excellent and proven record of academic, music, art, drama and all-rounder scholarship success to a wide range of leading senior schools.

Exeter Cathedral School is proud to educate the boy and girl Choristers of Exeter Cathedral, who continue the centuries-old tradition of singing the daily services and leading the pattern of worship. Whilst the vast majority of pupils are not here for their singing ability, music is nonetheless an important part of our School – children grow up with it all around them and are encouraged to participate.

A small number of pupils board in our cosy and friendly boarding house. Some come from a distance and have to board; some live nearby but enjoy being a part of the flexible and friendly boarding environment. Occasional boarding is a popular option for some families. Breakfast club from 7.30 am, and a wide range of after school activities until 7 pm, provide a service to busy parents and enthusiastic children.

Do come and see for yourself what Exeter Cathedral School has to offer: you will certainly be made to feel very welcome. Your daughter/son is also warmly invited to spend a 'taster day' with us at a time of your choosing.

Kingsley School

KINGSLEY SCHOOL
BIDEFORD

(Founded 2009)
Northdown Road, Bideford, Devon EX39 3LY
Tel: 01237 426200

Fax: 01237 425981
Email:
admissions@kingsleyschoolbideford.co.uk
Website: www.kingsleyschoolbideford.co.uk
Headmaster: Mr Simon Woolcott BSc ARCS
Appointed: October 2013
Head of the Junior School:
Mrs Jane Bruce BA Dip. SpLD
School type: Coeducational Day & Boarding

Age range of pupils: 0–18
No. of pupils enrolled as at 01/01/2016: 395
No. of boarders: 100
Fees per annum as at 01/01/2016:
Day: £1,870–£3,180
Weekly Boarding: £5,410
Full Boarding: £6,870
Average class size: 14
Teacher/pupil ratio: 1:9

Welcome to Kingsley School

Kingsley School is set in the beautiful North Devon town of Bideford on the banks of the River Torridge. It is surrounded by stunning countryside, just two kilometers from popular surfing beaches.

We are an inclusive day and boarding school where every child is important and is treated with dignity and respect. As a relatively small school of around 400 boys and girls from Nursery to Sixth Form, Kingsley's atmosphere is like that of a large family where everybody knows each other well. The school's philosophy encourages personal qualities such as courage, generosity, honesty, imagination, tolerance and kindness. In addition we develop the students' wider interests and skills in sport, music, art, and drama. Overall, a Kingsley education develops the individual character and talents of each and every student both inside and outside the classroom.

Kingsley Juniors

Kingsley Juniors educates boys and girls from Nursery through to Year 6. Kingsley Juniors sits within the main site and offers its own dedicated facilities. We are most proud of our friendly and happy atmosphere, where individuality is nurtured, imagination is ignited and our children thrive.

Kingsley enrichment

Kingsley School is much more than a narrow academic institution. We believe that the best learning is enjoyable and that school life must offer a wide range of opportunities socially, artistically and in sport.

We offer all the traditional English sports which we play on our own sports fields and in addition we compete on an international level with judo, and nationally in handball and gymnastics. Amongst other sports we also offer dance, surfing, badminton and trampolining. We also make extensive use of our surrounding countryside with many opportunities for walking and camping.

The school has outstanding academic strengths in mathematics, the sciences and geography, while music and drama benefit from using our own purpose-designed 400 seat theatre. The school also has a distinguished UK-wide reputation for academic success in our Dyslexia Centre where students achieve their full potential – which is often way beyond previous expectations – and are totally integrated into every aspect of school life, inside and outside the classroom.

Headmaster Simon Woolcott said "Inspirational teachers have unlocked the talents and the desire to learn which has uncovered the potential of our students. We are all delighted when our pupils find their passion and are inspired. Alongside our tremendous academic results I am most proud that our departing students are polite and well grounded as well as engaging and confident. In life this is just as important as their results."

Wells Cathedral School

(Founded AD 909)
The Liberty, Wells, Somerset BA5 2ST
Tel: 01749 834200
Fax: 01749 834201

Email:
admissions@wells-cathedral-school.com
Website:
www.wells-cathedral-school.com
Head: Mrs Elizabeth Cairncross
Appointed: September 2000
Head of Junior School: Mrs Julie Barrow
School type: Coeducational Day & Boarding

Age range of pupils: 3–18
No. of pupils enrolled as at 01/11/2015: 730
Boys: 385 **Girls:** 345
Fees per annum as at 01/11/2015:
Day: £6,999–£17,223
Full Boarding: £23,196–£28,824
Average class size: 14

Founded in AD 909 and one of the oldest schools in Europe, Wells Cathedral School offers a unique opportunity for students to enjoy a hi-tech, state of the art education with a beautiful, musical and historic backdrop.

Our school motto, 'esto quod es', encourages all students to be what they are, allowing a broad variety of pupils to thrive and develop their unique talents here at Wells. This philosophy, our flexible approach to education and our emphasis on pastoral care enables us to produce well-rounded and enquiring young adults ready to face the challenges of the modern world.

In addition to our established record in academic excellence, Wells provides a range of opportunities to meet our students' talents and interests. We offer a specialist mathematics scheme, 40+ co-curricular activities, an exciting outdoor education programme which incorporates both CCF and the Duke of Edinburgh Award, an extensive creative arts programme, as well as enthusiastic and competitive sports provision, which emphasises five major sports, and offers opportunities in many more. Wells acknowledges excellence with a range of scholarships for academic, creative, choral, musical and sporting excellence.

Wells is the only specialist music school running alongside a regular school, with students following a full academic curriculum. All Wells pupils benefit from the atmosphere that our internationally-renowned music specialism creates, whether they are at Wells for music, sport, academics or a general education.

Located in the medieval heart of the stunning Somerset market town of Wells, our students enjoy the combined benefits of the surrounding countryside with easy access to the nearby cities of Bath and Bristol, with its international airport.

"Tracing its roots back to 909, Wells is one of the world's oldest schools, and wears its age beautifully; there surely can't be a lovelier place of learning anywhere."
– Good Schools Guide, 2015

King Henry VIII Preparatory School

(Founded 2008)

Kenilworth Road, Coventry, West Midlands CV3 6PT
Tel: 024 7627 1307
Fax: 024 7627 1308
Email: swallows@khps.co.uk
Website: www.khps.co.uk
Headteacher: Mrs Gillian Bowser
Appointed: 2015

School type: Coeducational Day
Age range of pupils: 3–11
No. of pupils enrolled as at 01/01/2016:
Boys: 224 **Girls:** 281
Fees per annum as at 01/01/2016:
Day: £8,052–£8,580
Average class size: 16-20
Teacher/pupil ratio: 1:10

King Henry VIII Preparatory School is a co-educational school serving the needs of children aged from 3 to 11. We work closely with parents ensuring the many and varied gifts of all children are given the opportunity to shine. The positive relationships between talented staff and pupils, alongside the obvious benefits of small class sizes and excellent facilities, help to ensure that each child is known as an individual and can flourish academically, socially and emotionally.

The school motto, Confide Recte Agens – Have the confidence to do what is right, is the driver for the moral compass we aim to develop in our pupils. We promise that the best interests of the child will always be at the heart of our decision making and as such our motto is equally applicable to our staff.

Rooted in a long standing history of excellence, we are able to hold fast to the many positive traditions of the British preparatory education system whilst selecting the most effective contemporary, engaging and innovative teaching methods to ensure our children are fully equipped for the next stage of their educational journey and beyond. The benefits of this approach can be seen throughout the school in the happy faces, friendly voices and enquiring minds of our pupils.

The school is based on 2 campuses Swallows and Hales. Swallows caters for children in Nursery (from the age of 3) up to the end of Year 3. Hales campus was purpose built in 1996. Children in Years 4, 5 and 6 learn happily each day in a mix of general classrooms and specialist facilities.

On his return from the First World War Rev Kenelm Swallow M.C. wanted the school to be 'a place to inspire pupils, a place they would love when they were there and after they had left, and a place they would look upon as their second home.' In this he succeeded.

Moor Park

MOOR PARK

(Founded 1963)
Ludlow, Shropshire SY8 4DZ

Tel: 01584 872342
Fax: 01584 877311
Email: head@moorpark.org.uk
Website: www.moorpark.org.uk
Headmaster: Mr Charles G O'B Minogue
Appointed: September 2015
School type: Co-educational Day, Full & Flexi Boarding

Age range of pupils: 3–13 years
No. of pupils enrolled as at 01/01/2016: 226
Boys: 120 **Girls:** 106
Fees per annum as at 01/01/2016:
Day: £6,930–£15,465
Full Boarding: £18,990–£22,785
Average class size: 12
Teacher/pupil ratio: 1:8

"Moor Park is a rural school, embracing the rural life."

Moor Park is an independent co-educational day and boarding school providing wrap around care from 3 months to 13 years. Just another Prep School I hear you say? Well in many aspects yes, you may be right. But in many, many more you may be surprised.

Many schools claim to offer an all-round education but Moor Park take this to extremes. They use every square inch of the 84 acres as one big classroom. In free time, the children use the woods to build dens, climb trees and allow their elastic to stretch just a little. And in doing this, Moor Park allow children to be children, being supervised, while allowing them every opportunity to build confidence and independence. Moor Park is a rural school, embracing the rural life.

The school aims to prepare the children for the next stage of life and entry into senior schools. In 2015 alone, Moor Park students gained 18 scholarships to 12 different senior schools, with every child gaining a place, from all-rounder scholarships to academic, art, music and sport. These results are gained despite running a non-selective entrance policy and emphatically not being a hothouse where pressure is put on young people to prepare for the exam above all else. Every child is focused on individually with strengths being encouraged from an early age. Moor Park children are nurtured and developed at a pace which suits them; happy children and great results speak for themselves.

Boarding is offered to everyone from Year 3 upwards but the school operates a flexible approach to boarding and families are free to choose the option which best suits their circumstances, or indeed choose not to board at all. The boarders have a lot of fun with Wacky Wednesdays and, of course, the Boarding Award finalist 'Big Weekends', the most recent version being Nerf Warfare. It was difficult to see who had more fun, the children or the staff and the Headmaster was a natural target!

For more information, to arrange a visit or to request a prospectus, please visit www.moorpark.org.uk or call 01584 876061.

Fulneck Junior School

(Founded 1753)
Fulneck, Pudsey, Leeds, West Yorkshire
LS28 8DS

Tel: 0113 257 0235
Fax: 0113 255 7316
Email: enquiries@fulneckschool.co.uk
Website: www.fulneckschool.co.uk
Head of Junior School: Mr Chris Bouckley
Principal: Mrs Deborah Newman **School type:** Co-educational Day & Boarding
Age range of pupils: 3–11 (boarding from age 9)

No. of pupils enrolled as at 01/01/2015: 128
Fees per annum as at 01/01/2016:
Foundation Stage: £2,250 per term
Key Stage 1 – 2: £2,445 –£3,030 per term
Boarding: £6,055 per term
Flexi-Boarding: £30 per night
Average class size: 15
Teacher/pupil ratio: 1:8

A vibrant, happy, aspirational community where we focus on one child. Yours.

Finding the right school is one of the most important decisions that you will make for your child, and the strong foundations laid by a high quality and nurturing education will give them the best start in life. Fulneck Junior School provides a caring community where children benefit from a unique, all round education in an inspirational historic setting. Each and every child is encouraged to reach their full potential.

With highly trained and experienced teachers and an enviable staff to pupil ratio, the Extended Early Years and Junior Curriculum provides breadth, excellence and excitement both in the classroom and outside in our beautiful outdoor learning space. Specialist teachers in PE, Spanish, Music and Dance enhance the learning experience whilst our tracking and monitoring system for learning ensures progress.

Personalised learning is supported by individual assessment and teaching strategies which differentiate and engage children at their own level. Our acclaimed Learning Support Unit provides specialist one-to-one tuition for dyslexic pupils as well as support in all areas of the curriculum.

Our core values, 'In essentials Unity, in non-essentials Liberty, in all things Charity' underpin every aspect of school life. Your children are the life of our School and everything we do revolves around them and their development.

But life at Fulneck offers so much more than what goes on inside the classroom, and the exciting and varied activities outside of lessons are just as important. An extensive extra-curricular programme allows children to try out sporting activities including gymnastics and cross-country as well as music, dance, cooking and much more.

Our 'home from home' boarding houses welcome children from age 9, and busy parents can also take advantage of our flexi-boarding.

Why not come and visit to discover how your child will flourish at Fulneck Junior School? We look forward to welcoming you and your family very soon!

Pocklington Prep School

POCKLINGTON PREP SCHOOL

Ages 4 to 11

(Pocklington School founded 1514)
West Green, Pocklington, York, North Yorkshire YO42 2NH

Tel: 01759 321228

Email: enquiry@pocklingtonprepschool.com

Website: www.pocklingtonschool.com

Headmaster: Mr I D Wright BSc(Hons), PGCE, NPQH

Appointed: January 2009

School type: Co-educational Day & Boarding

Age range of pupils: 4–11

No. of pupils enrolled as at 01/01/2016: 218

Boys: 124 **Girls:** 94

No. of boarders: 10

Fees per annum as at 01/01/2016:

Day: £7,080–£11,106

Weekly Boarding: £18,975

Full Boarding: £20,439

Average class size: 16-20

Teacher/pupil ratio: 1:11

Pocklington Prep School – a strong and caring community

Children flourish in the supportive environment of Pocklington Prep School, where an excellent all-round education inspires a lifelong enthusiasm for learning.

Our strong and caring community, for day and boarding pupils aged 4-11, includes a vibrant co-curricular life and sense of involvement in the rounded education we are renowned for. It is underpinned by a deep-rooted belief in and commitment to pastoral care, which allows staff to support children as they grow.

Innovative teaching

Specialist and innovative teachers focus on each individual and stretch and challenge them to ensure they are happy, confident learners who achieve their full potential. Pupils' natural talents and curiosity are encouraged while developing the core skills of reading, writing and numeracy. Our ambition aim is to embed the skill of independent thought so that pupils can draw on a solid foundation of knowledge to form and apply new ideas.

Continually evolving

Pocklington Prep School lies 12 miles east of York, on the edge of Pocklington, and shares a 65-acre campus with Pocklington School, which caters for 11 to 18-year-olds. The school was founded in 1514 and has continually evolved since then to combine the best teaching methods with the latest technologies.

Extensive facilities

The schools' superb classroom facilities are complemented by a 300-seat theatre, an indoor sports hall and a swimming pool, plus 21 acres of grass sports pitches and two full-sized synthetic pitches. Numerous co-curricular activities take place every day and each child is encouraged to develop their own interests.

The school has good public transport links and its own minibus pick-up service. Full, flexible and casual boarding options are available. Junior boarders live in modern single-sex houses and enjoy a dedicated programme of weekend and after-school activities, in addition to the normal school calendar.

Inspired for Life

Our aim is that when our pupils move on to their senior schools, they will be confident independent thinkers who are proud of their achievements and 'Inspired for Life'.

https://twitter.com/PockSchool

The Froebelian School

(Founded 1913)

Clarence Road, Horsforth, Leeds,
West Yorkshire LS18 4LB
Tel: 0113 2583047
Email: admissions@froebelian.co.uk
Website: www.froebelian.com
Head Teacher:
Mrs Catherine Dodds B.Ed (Hons), PGCE

Appointed: 2015
School type: Co-educational Day
Age range of pupils: 3–11
No. of pupils enrolled as at 01/11/2015: 185
Fees per annum as at 01/11/2015:
Day: £4,590–£6,850
Teacher/pupil ratio: 1:10

The Froebelian School is one of the leading independent preparatory schools in Leeds for boys and girls aged 3 to 11 years. Our motto of 'Giving a flying start to the citizens of tomorrow' sums up our determination to provide the best possible start to lifelong education.

Our pupils reach the highest possible standards in academic work, sport, music, technology, art and drama. We offer an excellent staff: pupil ratio (1:10), modern facilities and the support of highly dedicated, professional teachers.

We aim to provide children with a happy learning environment, one where they are challenged and supported to achieve personal excellence. Each year approximately 24 children aged 3+ are admitted to the Lower Kindergarten (Nursery) class. Other places for an older child are sometimes available and enquires are always welcome.

Situated in Horsforth, a pleasant suburb of Leeds near to the ring road, the school is easily accessible from most areas of Leeds, Bradford and Harrogate. Our site is very secure with a wooded area offering delightful views over the Aire valley.

In 2015, the Froebelian School opened a new day nursery close to the school in a purposely-renovated building. First Steps at Froebelian shares the Froebelian goals of nurturing children and allowing them to fulfill their potential. It is open to all children aged 3 months to 5 years old and children may have preferential entry at age 3 to the main school.

The Froebelian School is the only school in Leeds to appear consistently in The Sunday Times Parent Power 'Top 100' Independent Schools and we are ranked at number 22 in 2015. Please explore our website and arrange to visit us soon, you will receive a warm welcome. You will also be able to see at first hand why Froebelian really is the best choice of the private preparatory schools in Leeds.

Gordonstoun

(Founded 1934)
Elgin, Moray IV30 5RF

Tel: 01343 837829
Fax: 01343 837808
Email: admissions@gordonstoun.org.uk
Website: www.gordonstoun.org.uk
Principal: Mr Simon Reid BA
Appointed: April 2011
School type: Coeducational Boarding & Day
Age range of pupils: 7–18

No. of pupils enrolled as at 01/01/2016: 104
No. of boarders: 41
Fees per annum as at 01/01/2016:
Day: £13,176
Weekly Boarding: £21,429
Full Boarding: £21,429
Average class size: 15
Teacher/pupil ratio: 1:7

"Gordonstoun Junior School brings out the best in my daughter. Her self-assurance has improved and she is willing to tackle any challenge with enthusiasm." **Mother of Year 7 girl**

"The School really does focus on finding out what your child is both good at and capable of and getting it out of them!" **Father of Year 7 boy**

At Gordonstoun Junior School children can be children, living in a happy and caring environment, fulfilling their academic potential and inspired to pursue new passions. The famous Gordonstoun broader curriculum develops every child through a wide range of experiences beyond the classroom to learn more about themselves, about taking responsibility and about living and contributing to a community.

Academically we follow the English National curriculum and focus on developing the key skills needed as they progress through the school. Class sizes are small, no more than 15, so individual attention can be given to support and stretch every child.

There are few children of this age who can treasure experiences such as sailing on an 80 foot yacht, spending a week camping at the most northerly part of the Scottish Highlands, playing sport at a highly competitive level and at the same time making lifelong friendships.

"I love the school grounds because they are so big and you are free to go where you want. You can play in the woods or on the field, you can have a game of football on the pitches or you can just gossip with your friends in the sun." **Ben, Year 7**

"The School's motto is Plus est en Vous which means there is more in you and I think everyone believes and follows it." **Robbie, Year 6**

Merchiston Castle School

MERCHISTON
JUNIORS | Boys first

(Founded 1833)

294 Colinton Road, Edinburgh, EH13 0PU

Tel: 0131 312 2201

Fax: 0131 441 6060

Email: admissions@merchiston.co.uk

Website: www.merchiston.co.uk

Headmaster: Mr A R Hunter BA

Appointed: September 1998

Deputy Head: Mr Peter Hall MA

School type: Boys' Boarding & Day

Age range of boys: 7–18

No. of pupils enrolled as at 01/01/2016: 460

No. of boarders: 330

Fees per annum as at 01/01/2016:

Day: £12,525–£20,190

Full Boarding: £17,545–£27,465

Teacher/pupil ratio: 1:9

Think about a world in which boys can be boys but where in time, they will grow to become ambitious, aspirational, and sensitive, yet gentle-men! Think about a wonderfully caring and nurturing family environment, where they will learn to like learning more. Then, think about igniting their interests in such diverse things as … cooking … cricket … and chemistry!

Merchiston is a school of contrasts: located just five minutes from a village; in a parkland setting, but with easy access into the wonderful, cosmopolitan capital city that is Edinburgh. Nearly everything boys could imagine by way of co-curricular activity is available here on campus, whilst only a short drive from the nearest beach, ski-slope, sailing school or golf course.

We are a Scottish school, offering the English curriculum, with a global, outward-looking dimension.

Merchiston Juniors

Merchiston Juniors caters for boys from age 7. Teaching for the youngest boys takes place in a purpose-built teaching centre. Small class sizes and dedicated teachers ensure individual attention. There is a smooth transition from Junior to Senior education as pupils are introduced to Senior School teachers and teaching methods from age 10. The timetable offers a full programme of trips, outings and activities, particularly at weekends. The safe and secluded Pringle boarding house is a great place to introduce boys to the concept of boarding, with taster weekends and flexible boarding options available.

Boarding life

We provide a stimulating, challenging, yet supportive and encouraging environment where your son can grow up surrounded

by his friends within our unique house structure. All the junior boarders live in Pringle House, which is within the school grounds but separate from the main school and is their base for homework, relaxation and sleeping. The boys are cared for by their female Housemaster, the Housekeepers and House Mother, whose role extends to a wide range of pastoral and domestic issues. In addition, there is a dedicated team of House Tutors, and a team of residential Prefects who assist with the running of the House and the supervision of the many activities on offer. The Prefects are excellent role models for the younger boys and play a vital role in all aspects of House life.

Academic Record

Merchiston delivers an extraordinary, value added academic experience. The school has an impressive record of helping boys excel far beyond their expected results at GCSE and A Level. Merchiston's Academic Leadership Team is building close links with admissions departments in leading American universities to ensure the success of applications to the USA. The 2015 A Level results were again outstanding, with many pupils successfully combating stiffer marking standards and tougher exams. The results show a 100% pass rate and 40% of boys achieving A* and A grades. Additionally, 70% of boys gained A*/A grades at GCSE: a school record!

Merchiston is committed to leading students towards 'personal excellence'. Currently, our extra-mural initiatives include entry for the Mathematics and Physics Challenges and Olympiads, English Speaking Board examinations, foreign language trips, Arkwright Scholarships (Design and Technology), and many others.

Sport for all

Merchiston's sporting programme plays an extremely important role in school life, and the team of staff works hard to achieve excellence within a 'sport for all' philosophy, offering training and competition in over 20 sports.

In rugby, Merchiston won the top league of the Scottish Schools Rugby Conference for the year 2015-16. The conference consists of five rounds of matches, and each round is made up of games between teams at all age groups from U13 to U18. All teams are awarded points to contribute to a whole school points total.

Merchiston's two specialist academies in golf and tennis combine a bespoke academic education with world-class training for aspiring tennis players and golfers. The Tennis Academy has been the Scottish Schools Tennis Champions for the last six out of eight years, and is ranked number two in the UK in the LTA Team Tennis Schools rankings. Our squad was chosen to represent Scotland in the ISF World Schools Championships in Doha, and finished sixth in the world.

Merchiston's Golf Academy is based at the Kings Acre Golf Club, a short drive from Merchiston. Due to the Golf Academy's recent success, it represented Scotland at this year's ISGA Home Internationals in Wales, coming second to England. Merchiston is also the number one ranked ISGA Junior School.

Plans for the future

Merchiston is turning its attention to upgrading its sporting facilities for "it's time for sport": plans have been drawn up to construct a new sports complex consisting of two multi-use sports halls, a large fitness suite, dedicated classrooms and meeting spaces, and a six-lane 25 metre swimming pool. Alongside this will be an all-weather multi-purpose (2G) artificial grass playing surface, and, uniquely in Scotland, an all-weather rugby (3G) pitch.

Kilgraston School
NURSERY · PREP · SENIOR · SIXTH FORM

(Founded 1930)

Bridge of Earn, Perth, Perth & Kinross
PH2 9BQ

Tel: 01738 812257

Fax: 01738 813410

Email: headoffice@kilgraston.com

Website: www.kilgraston.com

Headmistress: Mrs. Dorothy MacGinty

Appointed: April 2014

School type: Girls' Day & Boarding

Religious Denomination: Catholic

Age range of boys: 3–5

Age range of girls: 3–18

No. of pupils enrolled as at 01/01/2016: 285

Boys: 5 **Girls:** 280 **Sixth Form:** 60

Prep: Senior: No. of boarders: 116

Fees per annum as at 01/01/2016:

Day: £8,985–£16,305

Full Boarding: £21,285–£27,855

Average class size: Av 15

Teacher/pupil ratio: 1:9

Kilgraston Preparatory School and Nursery is the junior school for Kilgraston, a leading boarding and day school for girls in Scotland. Located in its own building, the Preparatory School is surrounded by 54 acres of stunning parkland in Bridge of Earn, three miles from the centre of Perth, 45 minutes from Edinburgh and an hour's drive from Glasgow.

The Nursery is an integral part of Kilgraston Prep School providing a flexible and caring pre-school education where boys and girls between the ages of 3 and 5 years enjoy a secure, happy, creative day. As Kilgraston is an all-through school, the nursery children have the opportunity to benefit from specialist teachers in physical education, swimming, tennis, music and science.

Admission to Kilgraston Preparatory School is by interview. Girls are able to progress into Kilgraston Senior School, or prepare for scholarship exams for Kilgraston and Common Entrance exams for other schools. The academic standard is high with all pupils completing the Preparatory School and achieving a place in their senior school of choice.

Pupils are taught by class teachers until the age of 9, with specialist teachers for PE, French, music and drama. Form teachers hold pastoral responsibility for the pupils and classes are small with provision for additional support needs. From age 10, the curriculum becomes more specialised with increasing input from specialised subject staff and use of the facilities in the Senior School. Pastoral care is the responsibility of a tutor.

The core academic curriculum is enhanced by a wide range of co-curricular subjects. While academic excellence is a priority, art, drama and music flourish and are an important feature of life at Kilgraston. Classrooms are well equipped and modern IT facilities are spread throughout the school. Opportunities are provided throughout the year for pupils to perform in groups or as soloists and they compete successfully in local festivals and events. The girls have the opportunity to take LAMDA, Associated Board and Trinity examinations. There is an annual production involving all pupils.

Sports and recreation thrive within the superb Sports Hall, which includes a climbing wall and gym. Pupils benefit from a 25m indoor swimming pool, 9 floodlit all-weather courts, playing fields and athletics track. Kilgraston is the only school in Scotland with an equestrian facility on campus and also hosts the Scottish Schools Equestrian Championships each year at Gleneagles.

The school's main sports are: hockey, netball, tennis, rounders, swimming and athletics, and fixtures are regularly played against other preparatory schools. The school has a an excellent skiing record.

Kilgraston Preparatory School has a pastoral house system. Inter-House competitions and challenges in games, music and debating provide an opportunity for friendly competition and fun. The family atmosphere in the newly refurbished boarding area, Butterstone, is enhanced by the wide range of weekend activities that make use of the superb local facilities in and around Perthshire.

Directory

Please note the following: The user will find Essex and Hertfordshire in Greater London and East of England; Kent and Surrey in Greater London and South-East. When seeking schools in any of these counties, therefore, the user is advised to check both regional sections.

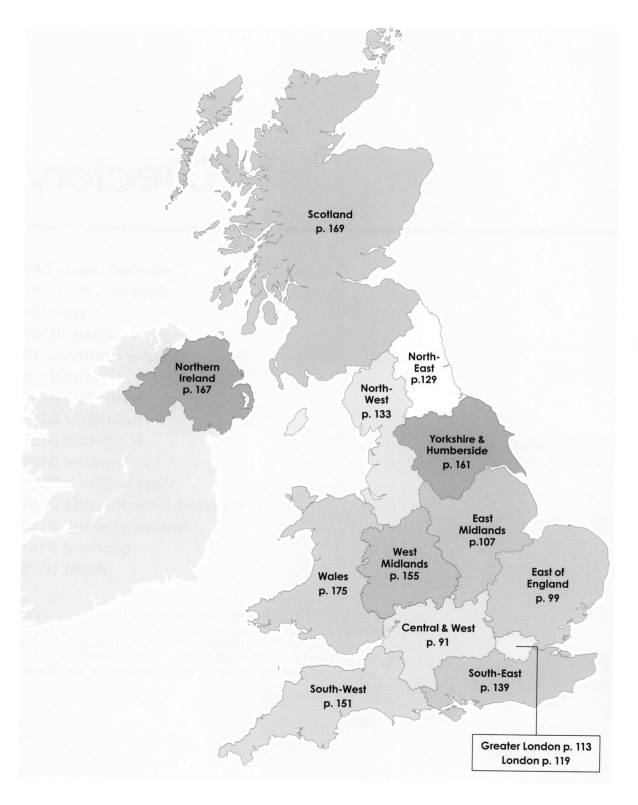

Scotland
p. 169

Northern
Ireland
p. 167

North-
East
p.129

North-
West
p. 133

Yorkshire &
Humberside
p. 161

East
Midlands
p.107

West
Midlands
p. 155

Wales
p. 175

East of
England
p. 99

Central & West
p. 91

South-East
p. 139

South-West
p. 151

Greater London p. 113
London p. 119

Channel Islands

KEY TO SYMBOLS

- ⚤ Boys' school
- ⚤ Girls' school
- 🌐 International school
- 16ᵗ Tutorial or sixth form college
- Ⓐ A levels
- 🏫 Boarding accommodation
- £ Bursaries
- IB International Baccalaureate
- 🖋 Learning support
- 16+ Entrance at 16+
- 🎓 Vocational qualifications
- (IAPS) Independent Association of Prep Schools
- (HMC) The Headmasters' & Headmistresses' Conference
- (ISA) Independent Schools Association
- (GSA) Girls' School Association
- (BSA) Boarding Schools' Association
- Ⓢ Society of Heads

Unless otherwise indicated, all schools are coeducational day schools. Single-sex and boarding schools will be indicated by the relevant icon.

Guernsey

Elizabeth College
The Grange, St Peter Port,
Guernsey GY1 2PY
Tel: +44 (0)1481 726544
Principal: G J Hartley MA, MSc
Age range: B3–18 G3–11
No. of pupils: 712 VIth115
Fees: Day £6,633–£7,250
(A) (£) (✎)

The Ladies' College
Les Gravees, St Peter Port,
Guernsey GY1 1RW
Tel: 01481 721602
Principal: Mrs J Riches
Age range: G4–18
No. of pupils: 555 VIth100
Fees: Day £5,385–£5,964
(⚡) (A)

Jersey

Beaulieu Convent School
Wellington Road, St
Helier, Jersey JE2 4RJ
Tel: 01534 731280
Headmaster: Mr C Beirne
Age range: G4–18
No. of pupils: 762 VIth127
Fees: Day £4,584
(⚡) (A) (£) (✎)

De La Salle College
Wellington Road, St
Saviour, Jersey JE2 7TH
Tel: 01534 754100
Head of College: Mr Jason Turner
Age range: 4–18
No. of pupils: 762
Fees: Day £5,103
(A)

FCJ Primary School
Deloraine Road, St Saviour,
Jersey JE2 7XB
Tel: 01534 723063
Headmistress: Ms Maureen Doyle
Age range: 4–11
No. of pupils: 290
Fees: Day £2,820
(✎)

Helvetia House School
14 Elizabeth Place, St
Helier, Jersey JE2 3PN
Tel: 01534 724928
Headmistress: Mrs Ann
Atkinson BA, DipEd
Age range: G4–11
No. of pupils: 82
Fees: Day £4,200
(⚡)

St George's Preparatory School
La Hague Manor, Rue de la
Hague, St Peter, Jersey JE3 7DB
Tel: 01534 481593
Headmaster: Mr Colin Moore
Age range: 2–11
No. of pupils: 210
Fees: Day £4,890–£13,440
(£) (✎)

St Michael's Preparatory School
La Rue de la Houguette, St
Saviour, Jersey JE2 7UG
Tel: 01534 856904
Head of School: Mr Mike Rees
Age range: 3–13
No. of pupils: 357
Fees: Day £8,250–£12,717
(£) (✎)

Victoria College Preparatory School
Pleasant Street, St Helier,
Jersey JE2 4RR
Tel: 01534 723468
Headmaster: Russell
Price BSc, MPhil
Age range: B7–11
No. of pupils: 300
Fees: Day £1,476
(⚡) (✎)

Central & West

KEY TO SYMBOLS

- 🛉 *Boys' school*
- 🛉 *Girls' school*
- 🌐 *International school*
- 16 *Tutorial or sixth form college*
- Ⓐ *A levels*
- 🏛 *Boarding accommodation*
- £ *Bursaries*
- IB *International Baccalaureate*
- ✐ *Learning support*
- 16 *Entrance at 16+*
- ⚒ *Vocational qualifications*
- (IAPS) *Independent Association of Prep Schools*
- (HMC) *The Headmasters' & Headmistresses' Conference*
- (ISA) *Independent Schools Association*
- (GSA) *Girls' School Association*
- (BSA) *Boarding Schools' Association*
- Ⓢ *Society of Heads*

Unless otherwise indicated, all schools are coeducational day schools. Single-sex and boarding schools will be indicated by the relevant icon.

Bath & North-East Somerset

Downside School
Stratton-on the-Fosse,
Radstock, Bath, Bath & North-
East Somerset BA3 4RJ
Tel: 01761 235103
Head Master: Dr J Whitehead
Age range: 11–18
No. of pupils: 458 VIth140
Fees: Day £12,900–£14,352
FB £20,940–£26,361

**King Edward's
Junior School**
North Road, Bath, Bath &
North-East Somerset BA2 6JA
Tel: 01225 463218
Head: Mr Greg Taylor
Age range: 7–11
No. of pupils: 196
Fees: Day £9,795

**King Edward's Pre-
Prep School**
Weston Lane, Bath, Bath &
North-East Somerset BA1 4AQ
Tel: 01225 421681
Head: Ms. Jayne Gilbert
Age range: 3–7
No. of pupils: 110
Fees: Day £8,850

**Kingswood
Preparatory School**
College Road, Lansdown,
Bath, Bath & North-East
Somerset BA1 5SD
Tel: 01225 734460
Headmaster: Mr Marcus E Cornah
Age range: 3–11
No. of pupils: 335
Fees: Day £7,125–£8,250 WB
£14,118 FB £16,806–£17,808

MONKTON PREP SCHOOL
For further details see p. 40
Church Road, Combe
Down, Bath, Bath & North-
East Somerset BA2 7ET
Tel: +44 (0)1225 831202
Email:
info@monktonprep.org.uk
Website:
www.monktonprep.com
Headmaster:
Mr A Marshall-Taylor
Age range: 2–13
(boarding from 8)
No. of pupils: 339

The Paragon School
Lyncombe House, Lyncombe
Vale, Bath, Bath & North-
East Somerset BA2 4LT
Tel: 01225 310837
Headmaster: Mr Titus Mills BA
Age range: 3–11
No. of pupils: 252
Fees: Day £5,835–£6,504

**The Royal High
School, Bath GDST**
Lansdown Road, Bath, Bath &
North-East Somerset BA1 5SZ
Tel: +44 (0)1225 313877
Head: Mrs Jo Duncan BA, MA
Age range: G3–18
No. of pupils: 640
Fees: Day £4,212 WB
£8,105 FB £8,105

Bristol

Badminton Junior School
Westbury-on-Trym, Bristol BS9 3BA
Tel: 0117 905 5200
**Head of the Junior
School:** Mrs E Davies
Age range: G3–11
No. of pupils: 130
Fees: Day £8,040–£10,830
FB £20,190–£21,240

Bristol Grammar School
University Road, Bristol BS8 1SR
Tel: 0117 973 6006
Headmaster: R I Mackinnon
Age range: 4–18
No. of pupils: 1137 VIth288
Fees: Day £5,700–£10,590

Bristol Steiner School
Redland Hill House,
Redland, Bristol BS6 6UX
Tel: 0117 933 9990
Age range: 3–16
No. of pupils: 213
Fees: Day £1,728–£4,800

Carmel Christian School
817A Bath Road, Brislington,
Bristol BS4 5NL
Tel: 0117 977 5533
Headteacher: Mr David Owens
Age range: 5–16
No. of pupils: 28
Fees: Day £480–£720

Cleve House School
254 Wells Road, Knowle,
Bristol BS4 2PN
Tel: 0117 9777218
Headmaster: Mr. Craig Wardle
Age range: 2–11
No. of pupils: 90
Fees: Day £5,985

**CLIFTON COLLEGE
PREPARATORY SCHOOL**
For further details see p. 36
The Avenue, Clifton,
Bristol BS8 3HE
Tel: +44 (0)117 3157 502
Email: ntucker@
cliftoncollege.com
Website:
www.cliftoncollege.com/prep
**Head of Preparatory
School:** Mr John Milne
Age range: 2–13
No. of pupils: 400
Fees: Day £6,000–£12,000
WB £16,305–£16,920 FB
£17,070–£17,700

Clifton High School
College Road, Clifton,
Bristol BS8 3JD
Tel: 0117 973 0201
Head: Dr Alison M Neill
BSc, PhD, PGCE
Age range: 4–18
No. of pupils: 527
Fees: Day £7,605–£10,905 FB £19,605

Colston's School
Stapleton, Bristol BS16 1BJ
Tel: 0117 965 5207
Headmaster: Peter Fraser
Age range: 3–18
No. of pupils: 581 VIth138
Fees: Day £5,160–£7,110 FB £15,045

Fairfield School
Fairfield Way, Backwell,
Bristol BS48 3PD
Tel: 01275 462743
Headmistress: Mrs Lesley Barton
Age range: 3–11
No. of pupils: 101
Fees: Day £2,025–£7,995

**Gracefield
Preparatory School**
266 Overndale Road,
Fishponds, Bristol BS16 2RG
Tel: 0117 956 7977
Headmistress: Mrs E Morgan
Age range: 4–11
No. of pupils: 90
Fees: Day £2,725

Queen Elizabeth's Hospital
Berkeley Place, Clifton,
Bristol BS8 1JX
Tel: 0117 930 3040
Head: Mr Stephen Holliday
MA (Cantab)
Age range: B7–18
No. of pupils: 670
Fees: Day £8,793–£13,455

**Redland High
School for Girls**
Redland Court, Redland,
Bristol BS6 7EF
Tel: 0117 924 5796
Headmistress: Mrs Caroline
Bateson BA(Hons)
Age range: G3–18
No. of pupils: 450 VIth90
Fees: Day £5,760–£9,600

Silverhill School
Swan Lane, Winterbourne,
Bristol BS36 1RL
Tel: 01454 772156
Principal: Mr Julian Capper
Age range: 2–11
No. of pupils: 185
Fees: Day £4,800–£6,255

The Downs School
Wraxall, Bristol BS48 1PF
Tel: 01275 852008
Head: M A Gunn MA(Ed), BA, PGCE
Age range: 4–13
No. of pupils: 262

**The Red Maids'
Junior School**
Grange Court Road, Westbury-
on-Trym, Bristol BS9 4DP
Tel: 0117 962 9451
Headteacher: Mrs Lisa
Brown BSc (Hons)
Age range: G7–11
No. of pupils: 120
Fees: Day £2,780

Tockington Manor School
Washingpool Hill Road,
Tockington, Bristol BS32 4NY
Tel: 01454 613229
Headmaster: Mr Stephen Symonds
Age range: 2–14
No. of pupils: 250
Fees: Day £7,650–£12,510 FB £17,070

Torwood House School
8, 27-29 Durdham Park,
Redland, Bristol BS6 6XE
Tel: 0117 9735620
Headmistress: Mrs D Seagrove
Age range: 0–11
No. of pupils: 70
Fees: Day £1,964–£2,049

Buckinghamshire

Akeley Wood School
Akeley Wood, Buckingham,
Buckinghamshire MK18 5AE
Tel: 01280 814110
Headmaster: Dr Jerry
Grundy BA, PhD
Age range: 12 months–18 years
No. of pupils: 833 VIth119
Fees: Day £7,185–£10,575
Ⓐ Ⓔ ✐

Ashfold School
Dorton House, Dorton, Aylesbury,
Buckinghamshire HP18 9NG
Tel: 01844 238237
Headmaster: Mr M O M Chitty BSc
Age range: 3–13
No. of pupils: 280 VIth28
Fees: Day £7,320–£12,900
WB £15,084
♞ Ⓔ ✐

Broughton Manor Preparatory School
Newport Road, Broughton, Milton
Keynes, Buckinghamshire MK10 9AA
Tel: 01908 665234
Headmaster: Mr Ross Urquhart
Age range: 2 months–11 years
No. of pupils: 250
Fees: Day £9,600
Ⓔ

Chesham Preparatory School
Two Dells Lane, Chesham,
Buckinghamshire HP5 3QF
Tel: 01494 782619
Headmaster: Mr Michael
Davies BA, PGCE
Age range: 3–13
No. of pupils: 392
Fees: Day £8,700–£12,300
✐

Childfirst Day Nursery Aylesbury
Green End, off Rickford's Hill,
Aylesbury, Buckinghamshire
HP20 2SA
Tel: 01296 392516
Registrar: Mrs Carole Angood
Age range: 2 months–7 years
No. of pupils: 80
Fees: Day £6,276

Childfirst Pre School Aylesbury
35 Rickfords Hill, Aylesbury,
Buckinghamshire HP20 2RT
Tel: 01296 433224

Crown House School
19 London Road, High Wycombe,
Buckinghamshire HP11 1BJ
Tel: 01494 529927
Headmaster: Ben Kenyon
Age range: 4–11
No. of pupils: 120
Fees: Day £5,985–£6,570
✐

Davenies School
Station Road, Beaconsfield,
Buckinghamshire HP9 1AA
Tel: 01494 685400
Headmaster: C Rycroft
Age range: B4–13
No. of pupils: 325
Fees: Day £12,180–£15,540
♞ Ⓔ ✐

Fernwood School
Church Road, Aspley Heath, Milton
Keynes, Buckinghamshire MK17 8TJ
Tel: 01908 583541
Head: Mrs M E Denyer
Age range: 1–9
No. of pupils: 75

Filgrave School
Filgrave Village, Newport
Pagnell, Milton Keynes,
Buckinghamshire MK16 9ET
Tel: 01234 711534
Headteacher: Mrs H Schofield
BA(Hons), MA, PGCE
Age range: 2–7
No. of pupils: 27
Fees: Day £5,160
Ⓔ ✐

Gateway School
1 High Street, Great Missenden,
Buckinghamshire HP16 9AA
Tel: 01494 862407
Headteacher: Mrs Sue
LaFarge BA(Hons), PGCE
Age range: 2–11
No. of pupils: 355
Fees: Day £10,002
✐

Godstowe Preparatory School
Shrubbery Road, High Wycombe,
Buckinghamshire HP13 6PR
Tel: 01494 529273
Headmaster: Mr David Gainer
Age range: B3–7 G3–13
No. of pupils: 409
Fees: Day £8,505–£13,245
WB £19,455 FB £19,455
♞ Ⓔ ✐

Griffin House School
Little Kimble, Aylesbury,
Buckinghamshire HP17 0XP
Tel: 01844 346154
Headmaster: Mr Tim Walford
Age range: 3–11
No. of pupils: 100
Fees: Day £7,395–£7,695
Ⓔ ✐

High March School
23 Ledborough Lane, Beaconsfield,
Buckinghamshire HP9 2PZ
Tel: 01494 675186
Headmistress: Mrs S J Clifford
Age range: G3–11
No. of pupils: 292
Fees: Day £903–£12,510
♞ Ⓔ ✐

Milton Keynes Preparatory School
Tattenhoe Lane, Milton Keynes,
Buckinghamshire MK3 7EG
Tel: 01908 642111
Headmistress: Mrs Hilary Pauley BEd
Age range: 0–11
No. of pupils: 500
Fees: Day £10,374
Ⓔ

Pipers Corner School
Pipers Lane, Great
Kingshill, High Wycombe,
Buckinghamshire HP15 6LP
Tel: 01494 718 255
Headmistress: Mrs H J Ness-
Gifford BA(Hons), PGCE
Age range: G4–18
No. of pupils: VIth72
Fees: Day £7,230–£14,010
WB £18,750–£222,845 FB
£18,990–£23,085
♞ Ⓐ ♞ Ⓔ ✐

St Teresa's Catholic School & Nursery
Aylesbury Road, Princes
Risborough, Buckinghamshire
HP27 0JW
Tel: 01844 345005
Head: Mr Simon Detre
Age range: 3–11
No. of pupils: 132
Fees: Day £5,775–£7,308
✐

Swanbourne House School
Swanbourne, Milton Keynes,
Buckinghamshire MK17 0HZ
Tel: 01296 720264
Headmaster: Mr Simon
Hitchings MA (Oxon)
Age range: 3–13
No. of pupils: 361
Fees: Day £4,155–£15,780 FB £21,250
♞ Ⓔ ✐

The Beacon School
Chesham Bois, Amersham,
Buckinghamshire HP6 5PF
Tel: 01494 433654
Headmaster: P Brewster
BSc(Hons), PGCE
Age range: B3–13
No. of pupils: 470
Fees: Day £4,695–£13,200
♞ Ⓔ ✐

The Grove Independent School
Redland Drive, Loughton, Milton
Keynes, Buckinghamshire MK5 8HD
Tel: 01908 690590
Principal: Mrs Deborah Berkin
Age range: 3 months–13 years
No. of pupils: 210

The Webber Independent School
Soskin Drive, Stantonbury
Fields, Milton Keynes,
Buckinghamshire MK14 6DP
Tel: 01908 574740
Principal: Hilary Marsden
Age range: 3–18
No. of pupils: 300 VIth15
Fees: Day £3,894–£10,371
Ⓐ Ⓔ ✐

Thornton College
Thornton, Milton Keynes,
Buckinghamshire MK17 0HJ
Tel: 01280 812610
Headmistress: Miss Agnes T Williams
Age range: B2–4+ G2–16
No. of pupils: 370
Fees: Day £6,300–£10,095 WB
£10,500–£13,305 FB £13,305–£16,545
♞ ♞ ♞ Ⓔ ✐

Walton Pre-Preparatory School & Nursery
The Old Rectory, Walton
Drive, Milton Keynes,
Buckinghamshire MK7 6BB
Tel: 01908 678403
Headmistress: Mrs M
Ramsbotham CertEd
Age range: 2 months–7 years
No. of pupils: 120
Fees: Day £8,316

Gloucestershire

Airthrie School
29 Christchurch Road, Cheltenham,
Gloucestershire GL50 2NY
Tel: 01242 512837
Principal: Mrs A E Sullivan DipEd,
DipIM, CertCounselling
Age range: 3–11
No. of pupils: 168
Fees: Day £5,280–£7,494

Beaudesert Park School
Minchinhampton, Stroud,
Gloucestershire GL6 9AF
Tel: 01453 832072
Headmaster: Mr J P R
Womersley BA, PGCE
Age range: 3–13
No. of pupils: 430
Fees: Day £2,710–£5,310 WB £6,900

Berkhampstead School
Pittville Circus Road, Cheltenham,
Gloucestershire GL52 2QA
Tel: 01242 523263
Head: R P Cross BSc(Hons)
Age range: 3–11
No. of pupils: 215
Fees: Day £2,793–£7,470

Bredon School
Pull Court, Bushley, Tewkesbury,
Gloucestershire GL20 6AH
Tel: 01684 293156
Headmaster: Mr John
Hewitt MBA, BA
Age range: 4–18
No. of pupils: 224 VIth40
Fees: Day £6,045–£16,410 WB
£17,715–£25,260 FB £18,180–£25,740

Cheltenham College Preparatory School
Thirlestaine Road, Cheltenham,
Gloucestershire GL53 7AB
Tel: 01242 522697
Headmaster: Mr
Jonathan Whybrow
Age range: 3–13
No. of pupils: 420
Fees: Day £2,421–£15,442
FB £5,424–£7,074

Dean Close Pre-Preparatory & Preparatory School
Lansdown Road, Cheltenham,
Gloucestershire GL51 6QS
Tel: 01242 512217
Head of School: Paddy Moss
Age range: 2+–13
No. of pupils: 292
Fees: Day £10,485–£15,852
FB £18,405–£23,310

Dormer House School
High Street, Moreton-in-Marsh,
Gloucestershire GL56 0AD
Tel: 01608 650758
Headmistress: Mrs Alison Thomas
Age range: 2–11
Fees: Day £7,425

Hatherop Castle School
Hatherop, Cirencester,
Gloucestershire GL7 3NB
Tel: 01285 750206
Headmaster: P Easterbrook BEd
Age range: 2–13
No. of pupils: 190
Fees: Day £6,285–£10,455
FB £15,270–£16,110

Hopelands Preparatory School
38 Regent Street, Stonehouse,
Gloucestershire GL10 2AD
Tel: 01453 822164
Headmistress: Mrs S Bradburn
Age range: 3–11
No. of pupils: 59
Fees: Day £4,479–£5,322

Kitebrook House
Little Compton, Moreton-in-Marsh,
Gloucestershire GL56 0RP
Tel: 01608 674350
Headmistress: Mrs Susan McLean
Age range: 3–13
No. of pupils: 134
Fees: Day £8,790–£11,200
WB £14,940

Rendcomb College
Rendcomb, Cirencester,
Gloucestershire GL7 7HA
Tel: 01285 831213
Headmaster: Mr R Jones
BA(Hons), MEd
Age range: 3–18
No. of pupils: 371 VIth54
Fees: Day £5,205–£7,150 WB
£7,480–£9,885 FB £7,480–£9,885

St. Edward's Preparatory School
London Road, Charlton
Kings, Cheltenham,
Gloucestershire GL52 6NR
Tel: 01242 538900
Headmaster: Mr Stephen
McKernan BA(Hons) MEd NPQH
Age range: 2–11 years
No. of pupils: 366
Fees: Day £6,750–£10,800

The Acorn School
Church Street, Nailsworth,
Gloucestershire GL6 0BP
Tel: 01453 836508
Headmaster: Mr Graeme
E B Whiting
Age range: 3–19
No. of pupils: VIth30
Fees: Day £3,800–£6,000

The King's School
Gloucester, Gloucestershire
GL1 2BG
Tel: 01452 337337
Headmaster: Alistair K
J Macnaughton
Age range: 3–18
No. of pupils: VIth80
Fees: Day £5,985–£15,960

The Richard Pate School
Southern Road, Cheltenham,
Gloucestershire GL53 9RP
Tel: 01242 522086
Headmaster: Mr Robert
MacDonald
Age range: 3–11 years
No. of pupils: 300
Fees: Day £3,000–£9,360

WESTONBIRT PREP SCHOOL
For further details see p. 41
Westonbirt, Tetbury,
Gloucestershire GL8 8QG
Tel: 01666 881400
Email:
admissions@westonbirt.org
Website: www.westonbirt.org
Headmaster: Mr Neil Shaw
Age range: 3–11
Fees: Day £2,500–£10,950

Wycliffe Preparatory & Senior School
Bath Road, Stonehouse,
Gloucestershire GL10 2JQ
Tel: 01453 822432
Senior School Head: Mrs M
E Burnet Ward MA(Hons)
Age range: 2–18
No. of pupils: VIth178
Fees: Day £5,295–£15,870
FB £13,620–£25,800

Wynstones School
Whaddon Green, Gloucester,
Gloucestershire GL4 0UF
Tel: 01452 429220
Chair of the College of Teachers:
Marianna Law-Lindberg
Age range: 3–18
No. of pupils: VIth9
Fees: Day £4,956–£7,236 FB £4,835

North Somerset

Ashbrooke House School
9 Ellenborough Park North,
Weston-Super-Mare, North
Somerset BS23 1XH
Tel: 01934 629515
Headteacher: Karen Wallington
Age range: 3–11
Fees: Day £4,494–£5,277

Sidcot School
Oakridge Lane, Winscombe,
North Somerset BS25 1PD
Tel: 01934 843102
Head: Iain Kilpatrick
Age range: 3–18
No. of pupils: 515 VIth170
Fees: Day £6,150–£14,250
FB £22,050–£27,750

Oxfordshire

Abingdon Preparatory School
Josca's House, Frilford, Abingdon, Oxfordshire OX13 5NX
Tel: 01865 391570
Headmaster: Mr C Hyde-Dunn
Age range: B4–13
Fees: Day £10,080–£13,860

CARRDUS SCHOOL
For further details see p. 38
Overthorpe Hall, Banbury, Oxfordshire OX17 2BS
Tel: 01295 263733
Email: office@carrdusschool.co.uk
Website: www.carrdusschool.co.uk
Head: Mr Edward Way
Age range: B3–8 G3–11
No. of pupils: 110
Fees: Day £1,278–£10,140

Chandlings
Bagley Wood, Kennington, Oxford, Oxfordshire OX1 5ND
Tel: 01865 730771
Head: Mrs S Ashworth Jones
Age range: 2–11
Fees: Day £9,540–£12,540

Childfirst Day Nursery Banbury
The Old Museum, 8 Horsefair, Banbury, Oxfordshire OX16 0AA
Tel: 01295 273743

Childfirst Day Nursery Bicester
32 Launton Road, Bicester, Oxfordshire OX26 6PY
Tel: 01869 323730
Headmistress: Miss J Fowler BA(Hons), QTS
Age range: 2 months–7 years
Fees: Day £7,500

Christ Church Cathedral School
3 Brewer Street, Oxford, Oxfordshire OX1 1QW
Tel: 01865 242561
Headmaster: Martin Bruce MA, BA, FCollP
Age range: B3–13 G3–4
No. of pupils: 159
Fees: Day £5,409–£12,123 FB £7,560

Cokethorpe School
Witney, Oxfordshire OX29 7PU
Tel: 01993 703921
Headmaster: Mr D Ettinger BA, MA, PGCE
Age range: 4–18
No. of pupils: 666 VIth133
Fees: Day £11,025–£15,974

Cothill House
Abingdon, Oxfordshire OX13 6JL
Tel: 01865 390800
Headmaster: Mr D M Bailey
Age range: B8–13
No. of pupils: 250
Fees: FB £24,300

Cranford House School
Moulsford, Wallingford, Oxfordshire OX10 9HT
Tel: 01491 651218
Headmistress: Mrs Claire Hamilton MA(Cantab)
Age range: B3–7 G3–16
No. of pupils: 377
Fees: Day £4,350–£12,975

Dragon School
Bardwell Road, Oxford, Oxfordshire OX2 6SS
Tel: 01865 315400
Head: Mr John R Baugh BEd
Age range: 4–13
No. of pupils: 844
Fees: Day £10,500–£18,690 FB £26,940

Emmanuel Christian School
Sandford Road, Littlemore, Oxford, Oxfordshire OX4 4PU
Tel: 01865 395236
Principal: Mr P Bate
Age range: 3–11
No. of pupils: 73
Fees: Day £5,040

Ferndale Preparatory School
5-7 Bromsgrove, Faringdon, Oxfordshire SN7 7JF
Tel: 01367 240618
Head of School: Mrs Fiona Shires
Age range: 2–11
No. of pupils: 100
Fees: Day £7,725–£8,175

Headington Preparatory School
26 London Road, Oxford, Oxfordshire OX3 7PB
Tel: +44 (0)1865 759400
Head: Mrs Jane Crouch BA (Hons) Keele, MA London
Age range: G3–11
No. of pupils: 250

Magdalen College School
Cowley Place, Oxford, Oxfordshire OX4 1DZ
Tel: 01865 242191
Master: Dr Tim Hands
Age range: B7–18
No. of pupils: 669 VIth161
Fees: Day £8,018–£9,880

Moulsford Preparatory School
Moulsford, Wallingford, Oxfordshire OX10 9HR
Tel: 01491 651438
Headmaster: Mr B Beardmore-Gray
Age range: B4–13
Fees: Day £9,840–£14,700 WB £18,450

New College School
2 Savile Road, Oxford, Oxfordshire OX1 3UA
Tel: 01865 285 560
Headmaster: Mr N R Gullifer MA
Age range: B4–13
No. of pupils: 160
Fees: Day £7,413–£11,985

Our Lady's Abingdon School
Radley Road, Abingdon, Oxfordshire OX14 3PS
Tel: 01235 524658
Principal: Mr Stephen Oliver
Age range: 3–18
No. of pupils: VIth74
Fees: Day £7,314–£12,399

Oxford High School GDST
Belbroughton Road, Oxford, Oxfordshire OX2 6XA
Tel: 01865 559888
Head: Mrs Judith Carlisle BA(Hons)
Age range: B6–7 G4–18
No. of pupils: VIth160
Fees: Day £2,812–£3,867

Oxford Montessori School
Forest Farm, Elsfield, Oxford, Oxfordshire OX3 9UW
Tel: 01865 358210
Principal: Judith Walker Mont Dip, NNEB
Age range: 5–10
No. of pupils: 169

Rupert House School
90 Bell Street, Henley-on-Thames, Oxfordshire RG9 2BN
Tel: 01491 574263
Headmistress: Mrs N J Gan MA(Ed), FRSA
Age range: B4–7 G4–11
No. of pupils: 214
Fees: Day £3,810–£9,150

Rye St Antony
Pullens Lane, Oxford, Oxfordshire OX3 0BY
Tel: 01865 762802
Headmistress: Miss A M Jones BA, PGCE
Age range: B3–11 G3–18
No. of pupils: 400 VIth70
Fees: Day £9,360–£14,175 WB £18,930–£22,275 FB £20,040–£23,400

Sibford School
Sibford Ferris, Banbury, Oxfordshire OX15 5QL
Tel: 01295 781200
Head: Mr Michael Goodwin BA
No. of pupils: VIth840
Fees: Day £7,758–£12,453 WB £15,555–£22,530 FB £23,718–£24,195

St Helen and St Katharine
Faringdon Road, Abingdon, Oxfordshire OX14 1BE
Tel: 01235 520173
Headmistress: Miss R Edbrooke
Age range: G9–18
No. of pupils: VIth170
Fees: Day £12,420

St Hugh's School
Carswell Manor, Faringdon, Oxfordshire SN7 8PT
Tel: 01367 870700
Headmaster: A J P Nott BA(Hons), PGCE
Age range: 3–13
Fees: Day £8,505–£14,430 WB £16,200–£17,280

St John's Priory School
St John's Road, Banbury, Oxfordshire OX16 5HX
Tel: 01295 259607
Headmaster: Paul Cawley-Wakefield
Age range: 3–11
Fees: Day £3,400–£8,130

St Mary's School
13 St Andrew's Road, Henley-on-Thames, Oxfordshire RG9 1HS
Tel: 01491 573118
Headmaster: Mr Rob Harmer (BA)Hons
Age range: 2–11
No. of pupils: 143
Fees: Day £3,320

Summer Fields
Mayfield Road, Oxford, Oxfordshire OX2 7EN
Tel: 01865 454433
Headmaster: Mr David Faber MA(Oxon)
Age range: B7–13
No. of pupils: 256
Fees: Day £17,700 FB £22,857

The European School
Culham, Abingdon, Oxfordshire OX14 3DZ
Tel: 01235 522621
Head: Mrs Leene Soekov
Age range: 9–18
No. of pupils: 540 VIth95
Fees: Day £3,363–£4,586

The King's School, Witney
New Yatt Road, Witney,
Oxfordshire OX29 6TA
Tel: 01993 778463
Principal: Mr Steve Beegoo
Age range: 3–16
No. of pupils: 185
Fees: Day £4,140

The Manor Preparatory School
Faringdon Road, Abingdon,
Oxfordshire OX13 6LN
Tel: 01235 858458
Headmaster: Mr Piers
Heyworth MA, PGCE
Age range: B2–7 years G2–11 years
No. of pupils: 375
Fees: Day £10,800–£13,155

Windrush Valley School
The Green, London Lane,
Ascott-under-Wychwood,
Oxfordshire OX7 6AN
Tel: 01993 831793
Headmaster: Mr Alan Wood MEd,
TCert, DipSpEd, ACP, FCollP
Age range: 3–11
No. of pupils: 125
Fees: Day £5,970

West Berkshire

Brockhurst & Marlston House Schools
Hermitage, Newbury,
Berkshire RG18 9UL
Tel: 01635 200293
Joint Heads: Mr David Fleming
& Mrs Caroline Riley
Age range: G3–13
No. of pupils: 275
Fees: Day £7,410–£12,450
WB £16,530 FB £16,530

Cheam School
Headley, Newbury, West
Berkshire RG19 8LD
Tel: +44 (0)1635 268242
Headmaster: Mr Mark
Johnson BEd (Hons)
Age range: 3–13
No. of pupils: 401
Fees: Day £10,260–
£17,940 FB £24,270

Horris Hill
Newtown, Newbury, West
Berkshire RG20 9DJ
Tel: 01635 40594
Headmaster: Mr G F Tollit B.A.(Hons)
Age range: B8–13
No. of pupils: 120
Fees: Day £17,250 FB £23,250

Marlston House Preparatory School
Hermitage, Newbury, West
Berkshire RG18 9UL
Tel: 01635 200293
Headmistress: Mrs Caroline
Riley MA, BEd
Age range: G3–13
No. of pupils: 110
Fees: Day £7,410–£12,450
WB £16,530

St Gabriel's
Sandleford Priory, Newbury,
West Berkshire RG20 9BD
Tel: 01635 555680
Principal: Alun S Jones
LTCL, LWCMD
Age range: B3–7 G3–18
No. of pupils: 462 VIth59
Fees: Day £9,945–£14,205

St Michael's School
Harts Lane, Burghclere, Newbury,
West Berkshire RG20 9JW
Tel: 01635 278137
Headmaster: Rev. Fr.
Patrick Summers
Age range: 5–18
No. of pupils: VIth5

The Cedars School
Church Road, Aldermaston,
West Berkshire RG7 4LR
Tel: 0118 971 4251
Headteacher: Mrs Jane O'Halloran
Age range: 4–11
No. of pupils: 50
Fees: Day £8,250

Thorngrove School
The Mount, Highclere, Newbury,
West Berkshire RG20 9PS
Tel: 01635 253172
Headmaster: Mr Adam King
Age range: 2–13
Fees: Day £11,070–£13,860

Wiltshire

Avondale School
High Street, Bulford, Salisbury,
Wiltshire SP4 9DR
Tel: 01980 632387
Headmaster: Mr Stuart Watson
Age range: 3–11
Fees: Day £5,625–£5,685

Chafyn Grove School
Bourne Avenue, Salisbury,
Wiltshire SP1 1LR
Tel: 01722 333423
Headmaster: Mr E J Newton
BA(Hons) PGCE (Cantab),
IAPS Chairman 2013/14
Age range: 3–13
No. of pupils: 307
Fees: Day £7,560–£14,985
FB £16,995–£20,643

Emmaus School
School Lane, Staverton,
Trowbridge, Wiltshire BA14 6NZ
Tel: 01225 782684
Head: Mrs M Wiltshire
Age range: 5–16
No. of pupils: 54
Fees: Day £2,900

Godolphin Preparatory School
Laverstock Road, Salisbury,
Wiltshire SP1 2RB
Tel: 01722 430 652
Headmistress: Mrs P White
BEd(Winchester)
Age range: G3–11
No. of pupils: 85
Fees: Day £5,535–£10,692

Grittleton House School
Grittleton, Chippenham,
Wiltshire SN14 6AP
Tel: 01249 782434
Headmaster: Mr N J Dawes
Age range: 2–16
No. of pupils: 283
Fees: Day £6,375–£9,570

Heywood Prep
The Priory, Corsham,
Wiltshire SN13 0AP
Tel: 01249 713379
Headmaster: Mr Guy
Barrett BSc(Hons)
Age range: 2–11
No. of pupils: 140
Fees: Day £6,450–£7,410

LEADEN HALL SCHOOL
For further details see p. 39
70 The Close, Salisbury,
Wiltshire SP1 2EP
Tel: 01722 334700
Email: admin@leaden-hall.com
Website: www.leaden-hall.com
Head: Mrs Julia Eager
Age range: G3–11
No. of pupils: 130
Fees: Day £2,670–£4,595
FB £4,510–£6,435

Leehurst Swan
Campbell Road, Salisbury,
Wiltshire SP1 3BQ
Tel: 01722 333094
Headmaster: Mr R N Leake
Age range: 2–16
Fees: Day £7,365–£12,600

Maranatha Christian School
Queenlaines Farm, Sevenhampton,
Swindon, Wiltshire SN6 7SQ
Tel: 01793 762075
Headteacher: Mr Paul Medlock
Age range: 3–18
No. of pupils: 68
Fees: Day £1,935–£7,470

Meadowpark Nursery & Pre-Preparatory
Calcutt Street, Cricklade,
Wiltshire SN6 6BA
Tel: 01793 752600
Headteacher: Mrs R Kular
Age range: 0–11
Fees: Day £4,900

Pinewood School
Bourton, Swindon, Wiltshire SN6 8HZ
Tel: 01793 782205
Headmaster: Mr P J Hoyland
Age range: 3–13
No. of pupils: 313
Fees: Day £6,485–£13,410 WB
£13,800–£14,670 FB £14,310–£15,210

Prior Park Preparatory School
Calcutt Street, Cricklade,
Wiltshire SN6 6BB
Tel: 01793 750275
Headteacher: Mr M A Pearce
Age range: 3–13
No. of pupils: 240
Fees: Day £10,212–£12,804
FB £15,009–£17,898

Salisbury Cathedral School
The Old Palace, 1 The Close,
Salisbury, Wiltshire SP1 2EQ
Tel: 01722 555300
Head Master: Mr Clive
Marriott BEd MA
Age range: 3–13
No. of pupils: 200
Fees: Day £2,385–£4,535 FB £18,270
🏛️ £ ✏️

Sandroyd School
Rushmore, Tollard Royal,
Salisbury, Wiltshire SP5 5QD
Tel: 01725 516264
Headmaster: Martin J
Harris BSc(Hons), PGCE
Age range: 5–13
No. of pupils: 225
Fees: Day £7,470–£17,505
FB £16,650–£20,940
🏛️ £ ✏️

South Hills School
Home Farm Road, Wilton,
Salisbury, Wiltshire SP2 8PJ
Tel: 01722 744971
Principal: Mrs A Proctor
Age range: 3 months–7 Years

St Francis School
Marlborough Road, Pewsey,
Wiltshire SN9 5NT
Tel: 01672 563228
Headmaster: Mr David Sibson
Age range: 2–13 years
Fees: Day £684–£12,216
£ ✏️

St Margaret's Preparatory School
Curzon Street, Calne,
Wiltshire SN11 0DF
Tel: 01249 857220
Headmistress: Mrs Karen Cordon
Age range: 3–11
No. of pupils: 220
Fees: Day £9,060–£11,910
£ ✏️

Stonar School
Cottles Park, Atworth,
Melksham, Wiltshire SN12 8NT
Tel: 01225 701740
Head: Mr Toby Nutt
Age range: B2–11 G2–18
No. of pupils: 330 VIth46
Fees: Day £7,665–£14,895 WB
£16,350–£19,050 FB £18,060–£26,880
🏃 🏇 Ⓐ 🏛️ £ ✏️

Warminster School
Church Street, Warminster,
Wiltshire BA12 8PJ
Tel: +44 (0)1985 210160
Headmaster: Mr Mark
Mortimer MBA BA
Age range: 3–18
No. of pupils: 550
Fees: Day £4,815 FB £9,995
🏇 Ⓐ 🏛️ £ IB ✏️

East

*See also Greater London (D113)
for schools in Essex and Hertfordshire

KEY TO SYMBOLS

- ⚤ *Boys' school*
- ⚤ *Girls' school*
- 🌐 *International school*
- 16· *Tutorial or sixth form college*
- Ⓐ *A levels*
- 🏛 *Boarding accommodation*
- £ *Bursaries*
- ⒾⒷ *International Baccalaureate*
- ✎ *Learning support*
- 16· *Entrance at 16+*
- ❀ *Vocational qualifications*
- (IAPS) *Independent Association of Prep Schools*
- (HMC) *The Headmasters' & Headmistresses' Conference*
- (ISA) *Independent Schools Association*
- (GSA) *Girls' School Association*
- (BSA) *Boarding Schools' Association*
- Ⓢ *Society of Heads*

*Unless otherwise indicated, all schools are
coeducational day schools. Single-sex and boarding
schools will be indicated by the relevant icon.*

Bedfordshire

Bedford Girls' School
Cardington Road, Bedford,
Bedfordshire MK42 0BX
Tel: 01234 361900
Headmistress: Miss Jo
MacKenzie BSc, MSc
Age range: G7–18
No. of pupils: 1000
Fees: Day £7,602–£10,683
(symbols) A £ IB

Bedford Modern School
Manton Lane, Bedford,
Bedfordshire MK41 7NT
Tel: 01234 332500
Headmaster: Mr M Hall
BA(Hons) MA
Age range: 7–18
No. of pupils: 1195
Fees: Day £8,000–£11,499
(A) £ (symbol)

Bedford Preparatory School
De Parys Avenue, Bedford,
Bedfordshire MK40 2TU
Tel: 01234 362271/362274
Headmaster: Mr C Godwin BSc, MA
Age range: B7–13
No. of pupils: 438
Fees: Day £9,312–£12,204 WB
£14,694–£17,586 FB £15,414–£18,306
(symbols)

Luton Pentecostal Church Christian Academy
15 Church Street, Luton,
Bedfordshire LU1 3JE
Tel: 01582 412276
Head: Rev C Oakey
Age range: 3–13
Fees: Day £2,400
£

Orchard School & Nursery
High Gobion Road, Barton-le-Clay,
Bedford, Bedfordshire MK45 4LT
Tel: 01582 882054
Headteacher: Mrs A Burton
Age range: 0–6
No. of pupils: 127

Pilgrims Pre-Preparatory School
Brickhill Drive, Bedford,
Bedfordshire MK41 7QZ
Tel: 01234 369555
Head: Mrs J Webster
BEd(Hons), EYPS
Age range: 3 months–8 years
No. of pupils: 385
Fees: Day £2,795–£7,590

Polam School
43–45 Lansdowne Road, Bedford,
Bedfordshire MK40 2BU
Tel: 01234 261864
Head: Mrs Phillipa Villa
Age range: 2–9
No. of pupils: 120
Fees: Day £7,500

Rabia Girls School
12–16 Portland Road, Luton,
Bedfordshire LU4 8AX
Tel: 01582 493239
Headteacher: Mrs F Shaikh
Age range: G4–16
No. of pupils: 265

Rushmoor School
58–60 Shakespeare Road,
Bedford, Bedfordshire MK40 2DL
Tel: 01234 352031
Headteacher: Ian Daniel BA, NPQH
Age range: B3–16 G3–11
Fees: Day £4,890–£8,985
£ (symbol)

St Andrew's School
78 Kimbolton Road, Bedford,
Bedfordshire MK40 2PA
Tel: 01234 267272
Headmistress: Mrs J E
Marsland BPhil(Ed)
Age range: B3–9 G3–16
No. of pupils: 385
Fees: Day £5,205–£8,505
(symbols)

St George's School
28 Priory Road, Dunstable,
Bedfordshire LU5 4HR
Tel: 01582 661471
Headmistress: Mrs Plater
Age range: 3–11
No. of pupils: 120
Fees: Day £4,020–£4,560
(symbol)

Cambridgeshire

Cambridge International School
Cherry Hinton Hall, Cherry
Hinton Road, Cambridge,
Cambridgeshire CB1 8DW
Tel: +44 (0)1223 416938
Principal: Dr. Harriet Sturdy
Age range: 2–18 years
No. of pupils: 350
(symbols) £

Cambridge Steiner School
Hinton Road, Fulbourn, Cambridge,
Cambridgeshire CB21 5DZ
Tel: 01223 882727
Age range: 2–11
No. of pupils: 100
Fees: Day £6,300
£

Kimbolton School
Kimbolton, Huntingdon,
Cambridgeshire PE28 0EA
Tel: 01480 860505
Headmaster: Jonathan Belbin BA
Age range: 4–18
No. of pupils: Vith170
Fees: Day £8,625–£13,425 FB £22,215
(symbols) A £ (symbol)

King's Acremont, King's Ely Nursery & Pre-Prep
30 Egremont Street, Ely,
Cambridgeshire CB6 1AE
Tel: 01353 660702
Head: Lynda Brereton
Age range: 3–7
Fees: Day £7,563–£8,136
(symbol)

King's College School
West Road, Cambridge,
Cambridgeshire CB3 9DN
Tel: 01223 365814
Headmaster: Mr Nicholas
Robinson BA, PGCE, FRSA
Age range: 4–13
No. of pupils: 418
Fees: Day £10,755–£13,680
WB £21,300
(symbols) £ (symbol)

KING'S ELY JUNIOR
For further details see p. 42
Ely, Cambridgeshire CB7 4DB
Tel: 01353 660707
Email: admissions@kingsely.org
Website: www.kingsely.org
Head: Mr Richard Whymark
Age range: 7–13
No. of pupils: 347
Fees: Day £11,499–£12,546
FB £18,333–£19,350
(symbols) £ (symbol)

Kirkstone House School
Main Street, Baston, Peterborough,
Cambridgeshire PE6 9PA
Tel: 01778 560350
Head: Mrs C Jones BSocSc
Age range: 5–16
No. of pupils: 234
Fees: Day £5,688–£8,493
£ (symbol)

Magdalene House Preparatory School
North Brink, Wisbech,
Cambridgeshire PE13 1JX
Tel: 01945 586 780
Head: Mr Chris Moxon BA, PGCE
Age range: 4–11
No. of pupils: 180
Fees: Day £8,200
£

Phoenix School Cambridge
Willow Tree, Twenty Pence
Road, Wilburton, Ely,
Cambridgeshire CB6 3PX
Tel: 01353 967581
Headteacher: Mrs Gill Cooke
Age range: 3–11
No. of pupils: 11

Sancton Wood School
2 St Paul's Road, Cambridge,
Cambridgeshire CB1 2EZ
Tel: 01223 471703
Head Teacher: Mr Richard Settle
Age range: 3–16
No. of pupils: 193
Fees: Day £3,546–£11,337
£ (symbol)

St Faith's
Trumpington Road, Cambridge,
Cambridgeshire CB2 8AG
Tel: 01223 352073
Headmaster: Mr N L Helliwell
Age range: 4–13
No. of pupils: 539
Fees: Day £9,735–£12,270
£ (symbol)

St John's College School
73 Grange Road, Cambridge,
Cambridgeshire CB3 9AB
Tel: 01223 353532
Headmaster: Mr K L
Jones MA(Cantab)
Age range: 4–13
No. of pupils: 458
Fees: Day £11,223–£14,100
FB £22,269
(symbols) £ (symbol)

St Mary's School
Bateman Street, Cambridge,
Cambridgeshire CB2 1LY
Tel: 01223 353253
Headmistress: Miss Charlotte Avery
Age range: G4–18
No. of pupils: 650 Vith105
Fees: Day £12,465 WB
£23,100 FB £26,862
(symbols) A £ (symbol)

Stephen Perse Foundation Junior School
St Eligius Street, Cambridge,
Cambridgeshire CB2 1HX
Tel: 01223 346 140
Head: Miss K Milne
Age range: 7–11
No. of pupils: 135
Fees: Day £11,610
£

Stephen Perse Pre-prep, Madingley
Cambridge Road,
Madingley, Cambridge,
Cambridgeshire CB23 8AH
Tel: 01954 210309
Head of Pre-prep: Mrs
Sarah Holyoake
Age range: 3–7
No. of pupils: 60
Fees: Day £10,200

The Perse Pelican Nursery and Pre-Preparatory School
Northwold House, 92
Glebe Road, Cambridge,
Cambridgeshire CB1 7TD
Tel: 01223 403940
Headmistress: Mrs S C
Waddington MA
Age range: 3–7
No. of pupils: 154
Fees: Day £11,640

The Perse Preparatory School
Trumpington Road, Cambridge,
Cambridgeshire CB2 8EX
Tel: 01223 403920
Head: James Piper
Age range: 7–11
Fees: Day £13,119

The Peterborough School
Thorpe Road, Peterborough,
Cambridgeshire PE3 6AP
Tel: 01733 343357
Headmaster: Mr A D
Meadows BSc(Hons)
Age range: 6 weeks–18 years
No. of pupils: 430
Fees: Day £9,893–£14,121

Whitehall School
117 High Street, Somersham,
Cambridgeshire PE28 3EH
Tel: 01487 840966
Principal: Rebecca Hutley
Age range: 3–11
No. of pupils: 109
Fees: Day £1,510–£1,953

Essex

Alleyn Court Preparatory School
Wakering Road, Southend-on-Sea, Essex SS3 0PW
Tel: 01702 582553
Headmaster: Mr Gareth
Davies BA(Hons), PGCE
Age range: 2–11
Fees: Day £2,607–£10,881

Braeside School for Girls
130 High Road, Buckhurst
Hill, Essex IG9 5SD
Tel: 020 8504 1133
Head Teacher: Mrs G
Haddon BA(Hons), PGCE
Age range: G3–16
No. of pupils: 199
Fees: Day £5,175–£10,875

Brentwood Preparatory School
Middleton Hall Lane,
Brentwood, Essex CM15 8EQ
Tel: 01277 243333
Headmaster: Mr Jason Whiskerd
Age range: 3–11
Fees: Day £5,889–£11,640

Brentwood Pre-Preparatory School
Shenfield Road, Brentwood,
Essex CM15 8BD
Tel: 01277 243239
Headmistress: Mrs S E
Wilson BEd, CertEd
Age range: 3–7
Fees: Day £5,130

Chigwell School
High Road, Chigwell, Essex IG7 6QF
Tel: 020 8501 5700
Headmaster: Mr M E Punt MA, MSc
Age range: 4–18
No. of pupils: 915 VIth185
Fees: Day £10,200–£16,020
FB £26,730–£26,730

Colchester High School
Wellesley Road, Colchester,
Essex CO3 3HD
Tel: 01206 573389
Principal: David Young
BA(Hons), PGCE
Age range: 2–16
No. of pupils: 486
Fees: Day £3,300–£10,000

Coopersale Hall School
Flux's Lane, off Stewards Green
Road, Epping, Essex CM16 7PE
Tel: 01992 577133
Headmistress: Miss Kaye Lovejoy
Age range: 2–11
No. of pupils: 275
Fees: Day £3,645–£7,275

Crowstone Preparatory School
121-123 Crowstone Road,
Westcliff-on-Sea, Southend-on-Sea, Essex SS0 8LH
Tel: 01702 346758
Headmaster: J P Thayer
Age range: 3–11
No. of pupils: 133
Fees: Day £2,655

Dame Bradbury's School
Ashdon Road, Saffron
Walden, Essex CB10 2AL
Tel: 01799 522348
Headmistress: Ms Tracy Handford
Age range: 3–11
No. of pupils: 254
Fees: Day £2,000–£10,950

Elm Green Preparatory School
Parsonage Lane, Little Baddow,
Chelmsford, Essex CM3 4SU
Tel: 01245 225230
Principal: Ms Ann Milner
Age range: 4–11
No. of pupils: 220
Fees: Day £7,449

Felsted Preparatory School
Felsted, Great Dunmow,
Essex CM6 3JL
Tel: 01371 822610
Headmistress: Mrs Jenny Burrett
BA(Dunelm), MEd(Cantab), PGCE
Age range: 4–13
No. of pupils: 460
Fees: Day £6,390–£13,965 FB £17,850

FKS Schools
Edwards House, Braintree Road,
Felsted, Essex CM6 3DS
Tel: 01371 820638
Headmistress: Mrs A Woods
Age range: 4–11
No. of pupils: 161
Fees: Day £6,219–£6,864

Friends' School
Mount Pleasant Road, Saffron
Walden, Essex CB11 3EB
Tel: 01799 525351
Head: Ms Anna Chaudhri MA
Age range: 3–18
No. of pupils: 390 VIth50
Fees: Day £2,375–£5,305 WB
£6,615–£7,690 FB £7,190–£8,590

Gosfield School
Cut Hedge Park, Halstead Road,
Gosfield, Halstead, Essex CO9 1PF
Tel: 01787 474040
Principal: Dr Sarah Welch
Age range: 4–18
No. of pupils: VIth21
Fees: Day £4,740–£13,695 WB
£15,465–£17,310 FB £17,985–£23,130

Great Warley School
Warley Street, Great Warley,
Brentwood, Essex CM13 3LA
Tel: 01277 233288
Head: Mrs B Harding
Age range: 3–11
Fees: Day £2,250–£3,500

Guru Gobind Singh Khalsa College
Roding Lane, Chigwell,
Essex IG7 6BQ
Tel: 020 8559 9160
Principal: Mr Amarjit Singh
Toor BSc(Hons), BT
Age range: 3–17
Fees: Day £3,900

Heathcote School
Eves Corner, Danbury,
Chelmsford, Essex CM3 4QB
Tel: 01245 223131
Head Teacher: Miss H Petersen
Age range: 2–11
Fees: Day £4,830–£7,245

Herington House School
1 Mount Avenue, Hutton,
Brentwood, Essex CM13 2NS
Tel: 01277 211595
Principal: Mr R Dudley-Cooke
Age range: 3–11
No. of pupils: 129
Fees: Day £4,365–£8,670

Holmwood House Preparatory School
Chitts Hill, Lexden, Colchester,
Essex CO3 9ST
Tel: 01206 574305
Headmaster: Alexander Mitchell
Age range: 4–13
No. of pupils: 302
Fees: Day £7,920–£14,079
WB £18,258

Hutton Manor School
428 Rayleigh Road, Hutton,
Brentwood, Essex CM13 1SD
Tel: 01277 245585
Head: Mr P Pryke
Age range: 3–11
Fees: Day £2,975–£3,995

Littlegarth School
Horkesley Park, Nayland,
Colchester, Essex CO6 4JR
Tel: 01206 262332
Headmaster: Mr Peter H Jones
Age range: 2–11 years
No. of pupils: 318
Fees: Day £2,700–£3,140
(£)(✎)

Loyola Preparatory School
103 Palmerston Road,
Buckhurst Hill, Essex IG9 5NH
Tel: 020 8504 7372
Headmaster: Mr P G M
Nicholson CertEd, BEd(Hons)
Age range: B3–11
No. of pupils: 195
Fees: Day £8,820
(†)(£)(✎)

Maldon Court Preparatory School
Silver Street, Maldon,
Essex CM9 4QE
Tel: 01621 853529
Headteacher: Mrs L Guest
Age range: 3–11
Fees: Day £7,305

New Hall School
The Avenue, Boreham,
Chelmsford, Essex CM3 3HS
Tel: 01245 467588
Principal: Mrs Katherine Jeffrey
MA, BA, PGCE, MA(Ed Mg), NPQH
Age range: 3–18
No. of pupils: 1132 VIth166
Fees: Day £7,392–£15,225
FB £16,110–£22,860
(♿)(A)(♨)(£)(✎)

Oaklands School
8 Albion Hill, Loughton,
Essex IG10 4RA
Tel: 020 8508 3517
Headmistress: Mrs Cheryl Macnair
Age range: B2–7 G2–11
No. of pupils: 243
Fees: Day £3,795–£7,650

Oxford House School
2-4 Lexden Road, Colchester,
Essex CO3 3NE
Tel: 01206 576686
Headteacher: Mrs E Hill
Age range: 2–11
No. of pupils: 152
Fees: Day £4,305–£8,565

Saint Pierre School
16 Leigh Road, Leigh-on-Sea,
Southend-on-Sea, Essex SS9 1LE
Tel: 01702 474164
Headmaster: Mr Chris Perkins
Age range: 2–11+
Fees: Day £2,062–£6,186
(£)

St Anne's Preparatory School
New London Road, Chelmsford,
Essex CM2 0AW
Tel: 01245 353488
Head: Mrs S Robson
Age range: 3–11
No. of pupils: 160
Fees: Day £6,300–£6,600

ST CEDD'S SCHOOL
For further details see p. 44
178a New London Road,
Chelmsford, Essex CM2 0AR
Tel: 01245 392810
Email: hbrierley@stcedds.org.uk
Website: www.stcedds.org.uk
Head: Dr Pamela Edmonds
Age range: 3–11
No. of pupils: 400
Fees: Day £8,550–£9,300
(✎)

St John's School
Stock Road, Billericay,
Essex CM12 0AR
Tel: 01277 623070
Head Teacher: Mrs F
Armour BEd(Hons)
Age range: 3–16
No. of pupils: 392
Fees: Day £4,470–£10,650
(✎)

St Margaret's Preparatory School
Gosfield Hall Park, Gosfield,
Halstead, Essex CO9 1SE
Tel: 01787 472134
Principal: Mrs E Powling
Age range: 2–11
No. of pupils: 250
Fees: Day £45.50–£2,975
(£)(✎)

St Mary's School
Lexden Road, Colchester,
Essex CO3 3RB
Tel: 01206 572544   Admissions:
01206 216420
Principal: Mrs H K Vipond
MEd, BSc(Hons), NPQH
Age range: B3–4 G3–16
No. of pupils: 430
Fees: Day £7,464–£11,340
(♿)(£)(✎)

St Michael's Church Of England Preparatory School
198 Hadleigh Road, Leigh-on-Sea,
Southend-on-Sea, Essex SS9 2LP
Tel: 01702 478719
Head: Steve Tompkins
BSc(Hons), PGCE, MA, NPQH
Age range: 3–11
No. of pupils: 271
Fees: Day £3,510–£6,990
(£)(✎)

St Nicholas School
Hillingdon House, Hobbs Cross
Road, Harlow, Essex CM17 0NJ
Tel: 01279 429910
Headmaster: Mr K M
Knight BEd, MA, NPQH
Age range: 4–16
No. of pupils: 400
Fees: Day £7,470–£9,660
(£)

St Philomena's Catholic School
Hadleigh Road, Frinton-on-
Sea, Essex CO13 9HQ
Tel: 01255 674492
Headmistress: Mrs B
McKeown DipEd
Age range: 3–11
Fees: Day £5,190–£6,360
(£)(✎)

The Daiglen School
68 Palmerston Road, Buckhurst
Hill, Essex IG9 5LG
Tel: 020 8504 7108
Headteacher: Mrs M Bradfield
Age range: 3–11
No. of pupils: 130
Fees: Day £6,360
(£)(✎)

Thorpe Hall School
Wakering Road, Southend-
on-Sea, Essex SS1 3RD
Tel: 01702 582340
Headmaster: Mr Andrew Hampton
Age range: 2–16 years
No. of pupils: 359
Fees: Day £7,695–£10,620
(£)(✎)

Trinity School
Brizes Park, Ongar Road, Kelvedon
Hatch, Brentwood, Essex CM15 0DG
Tel: 01277 374123
Headmaster: Reverend
M S B Reid BD
Age range: 4–18
(A)

Ursuline Preparatory School
Old Great Ropers, Great
Ropers Lane, Warley,
Brentwood, Essex CM13 3HR
Tel: 01277 227152
Headmistress: Mrs
Pauline Wilson MSc
Age range: 3–11
Fees: Day £2,610–£4,950
(✎)

Widford Lodge School
Widford Road, Chelmsford,
Essex CM2 9AN
Tel: 01245 352581
Headmaster: Mr Simon Trowell
Age range: 2–11
Fees: Day £5,400–£7,050
(✎)

Hertfordshire

Abbot's Hill School
Bunkers Lane, Hemel Hempstead,
Hertfordshire HP3 8RP
Tel: 01442 240333
Headmistress: Mrs E Thomas
BA (Hons), PGCE, NPQH
Age range: B3–5 G3–16
Fees: Day £9,159–£16,332
(♨)(£)(✎)

Aldenham School
Elstree, Hertfordshire WD6 3AJ
Tel: 01923 858122
Headmaster: James C Fowler MA
Age range: 3–18
No. of pupils: 700 VIth158
Fees: Day £13,626–£19,500
FB £18,768–£28,410
(♿)(A)(♨)(£)(✎)

Aldwickbury School
Wheathampstead Road,
Harpenden, Hertfordshire AL5 1AD
Tel: 01582 713022
Headmaster: Mr V W Hales
Age range: B4–13
No. of pupils: 330
Fees: Day £2,002–£3,012
WB £3,800–£3,884
(†)(♨)(£)(✎)

Beechwood Park School
Markyate, St Albans,
Hertfordshire AL3 8AW
Tel: 01582 840333
Headmaster: Mr E Balfour
Age range: 3–13
Fees: Day £9,765–£14,640
WB £18,120
(♨)(£)(✎)

Berkhamsted School
Overton House, 131 High Street,
Berkhamsted, Hertfordshire HP4 2DJ
Tel: 01442 358001
Principal: Mr Richard
Backhouse MA(Cantab)
Age range: 3–18 years
No. of pupils: 1680 VIth361
Fees: Day £10,065–£19,095
WB £25,565 FB £30,415

Bhaktivedanta Manor School
Hilfield Lane, Aldenham, Watford,
Hertfordshire WD25 8EZ
Tel: 01923 851000 Ext:241
Headteacher: Mrs. Wendy Harrison
Age range: 4–12
No. of pupils: 40
Fees: Day £1,680

Bishop's Stortford College Prep School
Maze Green Road, Bishop's
Stortford, Hertfordshire CM23 2PH
Tel: 01279 838607
Head of Prep School:
Mr Bill Toleman
Age range: 4–13
Fees: Day £8,088–£13,998 WB
£18,114–£19,671 FB 18,312–£19,866

Charlotte House Preparatory School
88 The Drive, Rickmansworth,
Hertfordshire WD3 4DU
Tel: 01923 772101
Head: Miss P Woodcock
Age range: G3–11
No. of pupils: 140
Fees: Day £6,900–£11,100

Duncombe School
4 Warren Park Road, Bengeo,
Hertford, Hertfordshire SG14 3JA
Tel: 01992 414100
Headmaster: Mr Jeremy
Phelan M.A. (Ed)
Age range: 2–11
No. of pupils: 325
Fees: Day £9,075–£12,585

Edge Grove School
Aldenham Village,
Hertfordshire WD25 8NL
Tel: 01923 855724
Headmaster: Mr Ben Evans
Age range: 3–13
Fees: Day £11,100–£114,835 WB
£15,870–£19,305 FB £15,870–£19,305

Egerton Rothesay School
Durrants Lane, Berkhamsted,
Hertfordshire HP4 3UJ
Tel: 01442 865275
Headteacher: Mr Colin Parker
BSc(Hons), Dip.Ed (Oxon),
PGCE, C.Math MIMA
Age range: 6–19
No. of pupils: 143
Fees: Day £14,310–£20,370

Haberdashers' Aske's School
Butterfly Lane, Elstree,
Borehamwood,
Hertfordshire WD6 3AF
Tel: 020 8266 1700
Headmaster: Mr P B Hamilton MA
Age range: B5–18
No. of pupils: 1402 VIth310
Fees: Day £10,641–£14,103

Haberdashers' Aske's School for Girls
Aldenham Road,
Elstree, Borehamwood,
Hertfordshire WD6 3BT
Tel: 020 8266 2300
Headmistress: Miss Biddie
A O'Connor MA (Oxon)
Age range: G4–18
No. of pupils: 1185
Fees: Day £13,269–£15,516

Haresfoot School
Chesham Road, Berkhamsted,
Hertfordshire HP4 2SZ
Tel: 01442 872742
Principal: Mrs Carole
Hawkins BA, PGCE
Age range: 0–11
Fees: Day £1,845–£7,770

Heath Mount School
Woodhall Park, Watton-at-Stone,
Hertford, Hertfordshire SG14 3NG
Tel: 01920 830230
Headmaster: Mr R Middleton
MSc, BEd(Hons)
Age range: 3–13
Fees: Day £2,715–£9,315
WB £12,630–£12,960

High Elms Manor School
High Elms Manor, High Elms Lane,
Watford, Hertfordshire WD25 0JX
Tel: 01923681103
Headmistress: Mrs Sheila O'Neill
MontDipDist, TCert, BA, AMI Dip
Age range: 0–12
No. of pupils: 90
Fees: Day £11,136

Howe Green House School
Great Hallingbury, Bishop's
Stortford, Hertfordshire CM22 7UF
Tel: 01279 657706
Head of School: Mrs Deborah Mills
Age range: 2–11
Fees: Day £5,946–£9,444

Kingshott
St Ippolyts, Hitchin,
Hertfordshire SG4 7JX
Tel: 01462 432009
Headmaster: Mr Iain Gilmour
Age range: 3–13
No. of pupils: 372
Fees: Day £4,770–£10,350

Little Acorns Montessori School
Lincolnsfield Centre,
Bushey Hall Drive, Bushey,
Hertfordshire WD23 2ER
Tel: 01923 230705
Head of School: Lola
Davies BPA, AMIDip
Age range: 2–6
No. of pupils: 28
Fees: Day £2,120

Lochinver House School
Heath Road, Little Heath, Potters
Bar, Hertfordshire EN6 1LW
Tel: 01707 653064
Headmaster: Ben Walker
BA(Hons), PGCE, CELTA
Age range: B4–13
No. of pupils: 349
Fees: Day £9,000–£11,826

LOCKERS PARK
For further details see p. 43
Lockers Park Lane,
Hemel Hempstead,
Hertfordshire HP1 1TL
Tel: 01442 251712
Email: sjohnson@
lockerspark.herts.sch.uk
Website:
www.lockerspark.herts.sch.uk
Headmaster: Mr C R Wilson
Age range: B4–13 G4–7
No. of pupils: 150

Longwood School
Bushey Hall Drive, Bushey,
Hertfordshire WD23 2QG
Tel: 01923 253715
Head Teacher: Mrs Muriel Garman
Age range: 3–11
Fees: Day £4,590–£5,790

MANOR LODGE SCHOOL
For further details see p. 46
Rectory Lane, Ridge Hill,
Shenley, Hertfordshire WD7 9BG
Tel: 01707 642424
Email: enquiries@
manorlodgeschool.com
Website:
www.manorlodgeschool.com
Headmaster: Mr G Dunn CertEd
Age range: 3–11
No. of pupils: 425
Fees: Day £9,975–£11,235

Merchant Taylors' Prep
Moor Farm, Sandy Lodge
Road, Rickmansworth,
Hertfordshire WD3 1LW
Tel: 01923 825648
Headmaster: Dr T D Lee BEd(Hons)
Age range: B4–13
No. of pupils: 300
Fees: Day £2,613–£9,414

Radlett Preparatory School
Kendal Hall, Watling Street,
Radlett, Hertfordshire WD7 7LY
Tel: 01923 856812
Principal: Mr G White BEd (Hons)
Age range: 4–11
Fees: Day £7,140–£7,250

Rudolf Steiner School
Langley Hill, Kings Langley,
Hertfordshire WD4 9HG
Tel: 01923 262505
Age range: 3–19
No. of pupils: 405
Fees: Day £2,985–£7,800

Sherrardswood School
Lockleys, Welwyn,
Hertfordshire AL6 0BJ
Tel: 01438 714282
Headmistress: Mrs L Corry
Age range: 2–18
No. of pupils: 357
Fees: Day £6,720–£12,750

St Albans High School for Girls
Townsend Avenue, St Albans,
Hertfordshire AL1 3SJ
Tel: 01727 853800
Headmistress: Mrs Jenny
Brown MA (Oxon)
Age range: G4–18
No. of pupils: 940 VIth170

St Christopher School
Barrington Road, Letchworth,
Hertfordshire SG6 3JZ
Tel: 01462 650 850
Head: Richard Palmer
Age range: 3–18
No. of pupils: 511 VIth78
Fees: Day £3,375–£14,505
FB £15,600–£25,470

St Columba's College Prep School
King Harry Lane, St Albans,
Hertfordshire AL3 4AW
Tel: 01727 862616
Head of Prep: Mrs Ruth Loveman
Age range: B4–11
No. of pupils: 275
Fees: Day £8,550–£9,714

St Edmund's College & Prep School
Old Hall Green, Nr Ware,
Hertfordshire SG11 1DS
Tel: 01920 824247
Head: Paulo Durán BA MA
Age range: 3–18
No. of pupils: 799 VIth135
Fees: Day £9,465–£14,955 WB
£19,830–£22,575 FB £21,855–£24,990

St Edmund's Prep
Old Hall Green, Ware,
Hertfordshire SG11 1DS
Tel: 01920 824239
Head: Mr Steven Cartwright
BSc (Surrey)
Age range: 3–11
No. of pupils: 185
Fees: Day £8,484–£12,252

St Francis' College
Broadway, Letchworth Garden
City, Hertfordshire SG6 3PJ
Tel: 01462 670511
Headmistress: Mrs D MacGinty
BEd, NPQH, DipMontEd
Age range: G3–18
No. of pupils: 460 VIth75
Fees: Day £8,370–£11,385 WB
£15,555–£18,630 FB £19,140–£22,155

St Hilda's School
28 Douglas Road, Harpenden,
Hertfordshire AL5 2ES
Tel: 01582 712307
Headmaster: Mr Dan Sayers
Age range: G3–11 years
No. of pupils: 165
Fees: Day £5,715–£9,975

St Hilda's School
High Street, Bushey,
Hertfordshire WD23 3DA
Tel: 020 8950 1751
Headmistress: Mrs Tracy
Handford MA
Age range: B2–4 G2–11
No. of pupils: 142
Fees: Day £4,635–£8,685

St John's Preparatory School
The Ridgeway, Potters Bar,
Hertfordshire EN6 5QT
Tel: 01707 657294
Headmistress: Mrs C
Tardios BA(Hons)
Age range: 4–11
No. of pupils: 184
Fees: Day £8,190–£8,730

St Joseph's In The Park
St Mary's Lane, Hertingfordbury,
Hertford, Hertfordshire SG14 2LX
Tel: 01992 581378
Headmaster: Mr Neil Jones
Age range: 3–11
No. of pupils: 161
Fees: Day £5,298–£14,247

St Margaret's School, Bushey
Merry Hill Road, Bushey,
Hertfordshire WD23 1DT
Tel: 020 8416 4400
Head: Mrs Rose Hardy
MA(Oxon), MEd, FRSA
Age range: G4–18 years
No. of pupils: 450 VIth100
Fees: Day £14,730 WB
£20,220–£23,670 FB £27,600

Stanborough School
Stanborough Park, Garston,
Watford, Hertfordshire WD25 9JT
Tel: 01923 673268
Head: Mr Roger Murphy
Age range: 3–19
No. of pupils: 300 VIth20
Fees: Day £3,660–£5,500
WB £12,834–£15,846

Stormont
The Causeway, Potters Bar,
Hertfordshire EN6 5HA
Tel: 01707 654037
Head of School: Mrs Sharon Martin
Age range: G4–11
Fees: Day £10,215–£10,680

The Christian School (Takeley)
Dunmow Road, Brewers End,
Takeley, Bishop's Stortford,
Hertfordshire CM22 6QH
Tel: 01279 871182
Headmaster: M E Humphries
Age range: 5–16
Fees: Day £3,720

The King's School
Elmfield, Ambrose Lane,
Harpenden, Hertfordshire AL5 4DU
Tel: 01582 767566
Principal: Mr Clive John
Case BA, HDE
Age range: 5–16
Fees: Day £4,380

The Purcell School, London
Aldenham Road, Bushey,
Hertfordshire WD23 2TS
Tel: 01923 331100
Headmaster: Mr Peter Crook
MA, BMus, ARAM, ARCO
Age range: 8–18
No. of pupils: 167 VIth70
Fees: WB £22,452 FB £28,716

TRING PARK SCHOOL FOR THE PERFORMING ARTS
For further details see p. 47
Tring Park, Tring,
Hertfordshire HP23 5LX
Tel: 01442 824255
Email: info@tringpark.com
Website: www.tringpark.com
Principal: Mr Stefan Anderson
MA, ARCM, ARCT
Age range: 8–19
No. of pupils: 340 VIth217
Fees: Day £13,785–£21,960
FB £23,250–£32,880

Westbrook Hay Prep School
London Road, Hemel Hempstead,
Hertfordshire HP1 2RF
Tel: 01442 256143
Headmaster: Keith D
Young BEd(Hons)
Age range: 3–13
No. of pupils: 300
Fees: Day £9,225–£13,275

York House School
Redheath, Sarratt Road,
Croxley Green, Rickmansworth,
Hertfordshire WD3 4LW
Tel: 01923 772395
Headmaster: Jon Gray BA(Ed)
Age range: 3–13
No. of pupils: 240
Fees: Day £10,845

Norfolk

All Saints School
School Road, Lessingham,
Norwich, Norfolk NR12 0DJ
Tel: 01692 582083
Headmistress: J N Gardiner
Age range: 3–16
Fees: Day £2,736–£4,455

Beeston Hall School
Beeston Regis, West Runton,
Cromer, Norfolk NR27 9NQ
Tel: 01263 837324
Headmaster: Mr R C
Gainher BSc(Hons)
Age range: 7–13
Fees: Day £15,333 FB £20,709

Downham Preparatory School & Montessori Nursery
The Old Rectory, Stow Bardolph,
Kings Lynn, Norfolk PE34 3HT
Tel: 01366 388066
Headmistress: Mrs E Laffeaty-
Sharpe MontDip
Age range: 2–11
No. of pupils: 170
Fees: Day £4,959–£6,702

Glebe House School
2 Cromer Road, Hunstanton,
Norfolk PE36 6HW
Tel: 01485 532809
Headmaster: Mr Crofts
Age range: 0–13
No. of pupils: 110
Fees: Day £7,200–£10,800
WB £9,180–£12,780

Gresham's Prep School
Cromer Road, Holt,
Norfolk NR25 6EY
Tel: 01263 714600
Headmaster: Mr J H W
Quick BA, PGCE
Age range: 7–13
No. of pupils: 225
Fees: Day £16,845 FB £23,265

Gresham's Pre-Prep School
Market Place, Holt,
Norfolk NR25 6BB
Tel: 01263 714575
Headmistress: Janette Davidson
Age range: 3–8
No. of pupils: 107
Fees: Day £9,045–£10,290

Hethersett Old Hall School
Hethersett, Norwich,
Norfolk NR9 3DW
Tel: 01603 810390
Headmaster: Mr S Crump
Age range: B3–11 G3–18
No. of pupils: 197 VIth29
Fees: Day £5,850–£12,450 WB
£13,395–£17,850 FB £15,585–£23,175

Norwich High School for Girls GDST
95 Newmarket Road,
Norwich, Norfolk NR2 2HU
Tel: 01603 453265
Headmaster: Mr J J
Morrow BA(Oxon), MA
Age range: G3–18
No. of pupils: VIth120
Fees: Day £6,906–£11,031

Norwich School
70 The Close, Norwich,
Norfolk NR1 4DD
Tel: 01603 728430
Head Master: Steffan D A Griffiths
Age range: 7–18
No. of pupils: 1035
Fees: Day £11,535–£12,660

Norwich Steiner School
Hospital Lane, Norwich,
Norfolk NR1 2HW
Tel: 01603 611175
Headteacher: Mr Andrew Vestrini
Age range: 3–18
No. of pupils: 91
Fees: Day £2,419–£6,515

Notre Dame Preparatory School
147 Dereham Road, Norwich,
Norfolk NR2 3TA
Tel: 01603 625593
Headmaster: Mr K O'Herlihy
Age range: 2–11
No. of pupils: 140
Fees: Day £810–£5,445

Riddlesworth Hall Preparatory School
Garboldisham, Diss,
Norfolk IP22 2TA
Tel: 01953 681 246
Headmaster: Paul Cochrane
Age range: 2–13
No. of pupils: 137
Fees: Day £10,470 WB
£16,500 FB £17,535

Sacred Heart School
17 Mangate Street, Swaffham,
Norfolk PE37 7QW
Tel: 01760 721330/724577
Headmistress: Sr Francis Ridler
FDC, BEd(Hons), EYPS
Age range: 3–16 years
No. of pupils: 156
Fees: Day £7,935–£11,775 WB
£16,845–£18,045 FB £21,825–£21,825

St Nicholas House School
Yarmouth Road, North
Walsham, Norfolk NR28 9AT
Tel: 01692 403143
Headteacher: Mr Martin Castle
Age range: 3–11
No. of pupils: 65
Fees: Day £4,260

Stretton School
West Lodge, Albemarle Road,
Norwich, Norfolk NR2 2DF
Tel: 01603 451285
Principal: Mrs Y D Barnett
Age range: 1–8
No. of pupils: 80
Fees: Day £1,020–£7,500

Taverham Hall Preparatory School
Taverham, Norwich,
Norfolk NR8 6HU
Tel: 01603 868206
Headmaster: Mr Mike A
Crossley NPQH, BEd(Hons)
Age range: 2–13
Fees: Day £9,975–£11,400
WB £17,775 FB £17,775

Thetford Grammar School
Bridge Street, Thetford,
Norfolk IP24 3AF
Tel: 01842 752840
Headmaster: Mr G J Price MA
Age range: 4–18
No. of pupils: 298 VIth20
Fees: Day £10,191–£12,327

Thorpe House Langley Preparatory School
7 Yarmouth Road, Norwich,
Norfolk NR7 0EA
Tel: 01603 433055
Headmaster: Simon Marfleet
Age range: 2–11
No. of pupils: 144
Fees: Day £2,100–£2,540

Town Close House Preparatory School
14 Ipswich Road, Norwich,
Norfolk NR2 2LR
Tel: 01603 620180
Headmaster: Mr Graeme Lowe BEd
Age range: 3–13
No. of pupils: 455
Fees: Day £7,080–£11,085

Suffolk

Arbor Preparatory School & Cherry Trees Montessori Nursery
Flempton Road, Risby, Bury St
Edmunds, Suffolk IP28 6QJ
Tel: 01284 760531
Headmistress: Mrs W E S Compson
BSc(Hons), MontDipAdv
Age range: 0–11
No. of pupils: 240
Fees: Day £4,800–£5,850

Barnardiston Hall Prep School
Barnardiston, Haverhill,
Suffolk CB9 7TG
Tel: 01440 786316
Headmaster: Lt Col K A Boulter
MA(Cantab), PGCE
Age range: 2–13
No. of pupils: 250
Fees: Day £8,925–£11,430
WB £15,810 FB £17,145

Brandeston Hall
Brandeston, Suffolk IP13 7AH
Tel: 01728 685331
Headmaster: Mr M K Myers-
Allen BSc(Hons), PGCE
Age range: 2–13
No. of pupils: 254
Fees: Day £6,681–£11,625
WB £18,693 FB £18,693

Culford Preparatory School
Culford, Bury St Edmunds,
Suffolk IP28 6TX
Tel: 01284 385383
Headmaster: Mr Mike Schofield
Age range: 7–13
No. of pupils: 214
Fees: Day £9,795–£13,200
FB £18,780–£20,340

Culford Pre-Preparatory School
Fieldgate House, Bury St
Edmunds, Suffolk IP28 6TX
Tel: 01284 385412
Headmistress: Mrs Sarah Preston BA
Age range: 3–7
Fees: Day £2,380–£8,745

Fairstead House School
Fordham Road, Newmarket,
Suffolk CB8 7AA
Tel: 01638 662318
Headmaster: Gareth Williams
Age range: 3–11
Fees: Day £7,860–£8,460

Finborough School
The Hall, Great Finborough,
Stowmarket, Suffolk IP14 3EF
Tel: 01449 773600
Principal: Mr J Sinclair
Age range: 2–18
No. of pupils: 226 VIth20
Fees: Day £5,220–£8,580 WB
£10,860–£14,280 FB £13,200–£17,010

Framlingham College
Framlingham, Suffolk IP13 9EY
Tel: 01728 723789
Headmaster: Mr P B Taylor BA(Hons)
Age range: 13–18
No. of pupils: 418 VIth195
Fees: Day £15,237 WB
£23,706 FB £23,706

Ipswich High School GDST
Woolverstone, Ipswich,
Suffolk IP9 1AZ
Tel: 01473 780201
Head: Oona Carlin
Age range: G3–18
No. of pupils: 650 VIth100
Fees: Day £6,987–£9,627

Ipswich Preparatory School
3 Ivry Street, Ipswich,
Suffolk IP1 3QW
Tel: 01473 282800
Headteacher: Mrs A H Childs
Age range: 3–11
No. of pupils: 311
Fees: Day £8,358–£9,201

Moreton Hall Preparatory School
Mount Road, Bury St
Edmunds, Suffolk IP32 7BJ
Tel: 01284 753532
Headmaster: Mr Simon
Head MA, PGCE
Age range: 2–13
No. of pupils: 104
Fees: Day £7,035–£11,715
WB £15,735 FB £17,595

Old Buckenham Hall School
Brettenham, Ipswich, Suffolk IP7 7PH
Tel: 01449 740252
Headmaster: Mr J A Brett MA
Age range: 3–13
No. of pupils: 228
Fees: Day £15,300 WB
£20,070 FB £20,070

Old School Henstead
Toad Row, Beccles,
Suffolk NR34 7LG
Tel: 01502 741150
Head: Mr W J McKinney
Age range: 4–11
No. of pupils: 123
Fees: Day £4,500–£6,300

Orwell Park School
Nacton, Ipswich, Suffolk IP10 0ER
Tel: 01473 659225
Headmaster: Mr Adrian
Brown MA(Cantab)
Age range: 2–13
No. of pupils: 280

Saint Felix School
Halesworth Road, Southwold,
Suffolk IP18 6SD
Tel: 01502 722175
Headmaster: Mr. James Harrison
Age range: 2–18
No. of pupils: 312 VIth65
Fees: Day £6,900–£14,970 WB
£16,440–£20,970 FB £21,630–£26,160

South Lee Preparatory School
Nowton Road, Bury St Edmunds, Suffolk IP33 2BT
Tel: 01284 754654
Headmaster: Mr Mervyn Watch BEd (Hons)
Age range: 2–13
Fees: Day £7,575–£9,375

St Joseph's College
Birkfield, Belstead Road, Ipswich, Suffolk IP2 9DR
Tel: 01473 690281
Principal: Mrs Danielle Clarke
Age range: 3–18
No. of pupils: 564
Fees: Day £5,310–£13,305 WB £21,945–£24,000 FB £22,980–£29,685

Stoke College
Stoke-by-Clare, Sudbury, Suffolk CO10 8JE
Tel: 01787 278141
Head: Mr Chris Lumb
Age range: 3–16
Fees: Day £6,732–£10,482 WB £14,586–£16,926

Summerhill School
Leiston, Suffolk IP16 4HY
Tel: 01728 830540
Principal: Mrs Zoe Readhead
Age range: 5–17
Fees: Day £4,500–£10,119 FB £10,230–£17,091

Woodbridge School
Marryott House, Burkitt Road, Woodbridge, Suffolk IP12 4JH
Tel: 01394 615000
Headmaster: Mr N P Tetley MA(Cantab), PGCE
Age range: 4–18
No. of pupils: VIth200
Fees: FB £26,700

East Midlands

KEY TO SYMBOLS

- (♦) *Boys' school*
- (♦) *Girls' school*
- (🌐) *International school*
- (16) *Tutorial or sixth form college*
- (A) *A levels*
- (⚑) *Boarding accommodation*
- (£) *Bursaries*
- (IB) *International Baccalaureate*
- (✎) *Learning support*
- (16) *Entrance at 16+*
- (✺) *Vocational qualifications*
- (IAPS) *Independent Association of Prep Schools*
- (HMC) *The Headmasters' & Headmistresses' Conference*
- (ISA) *Independent Schools Association*
- (GSA) *Girls' School Association*
- (BSA) *Boarding Schools' Association*
- (S) *Society of Heads*

Unless otherwise indicated, all schools are coeducational day schools. Single-sex and boarding schools will be indicated by the relevant icon.

Derbyshire

Barlborough Hall School
Barlborough, Chesterfield,
Derbyshire S43 4TJ
Tel: 01246 810511
Headteacher: Mrs Nic Boys
Age range: 3–11
No. of pupils: 198
Fees: Day £6,420–£8,553
£ ✎

**Dame Catherine
Harpur's School**
Rose Lane, Ticknall, Derby,
Derbyshire DE73 7JW
Tel: 01332 862792
Head: Ms Whyte
Age range: 3–11
No. of pupils: 28
Fees: Day £3,375

Derby Grammar School
Rykneld Hall, Rykneld
Road, Littleover, Derby,
Derbyshire DE23 4BX
Tel: 01332 523027
Headmaster: Mr Richard D Paine
Age range: B7–18 G16–18
No. of pupils: 298 VIth66
Fees: Day £7,779–£10,779
⚥ Ⓐ £ ✎

Derby High School
Hillsway, Littleover, Derby,
Derbyshire DE23 3DT
Tel: 01332 514267
Headmaster: Mr C T Callaghan
Age range: B3–11 G3–18
No. of pupils: 576 VIth74
Fees: Day £7,050–£9,510
Ⓐ £ ✎

Emmanuel School
Juniper Lodge, 43 Kedleston Road,
Derby, Derbyshire DE22 1FP
Tel: 01332 340505
Headteacher: Mrs C Pearson
Age range: 3–16
No. of pupils: 65
Fees: Day £1,698–£2,706
✎

Foremarke Hall
Milton, Derby, Derbyshire DE65 6EJ
Tel: 01283 707100
Headmaster: Mr R Merriman
MA, BSc(Hons), FCollP
Age range: 3–13
Fees: Day £7,875–£15,237
WB £20,235 FB £20,235
⚐ Ⓐ £ ✎

Gateway Christian School
Moor Lane, Dale Abbey,
Ilkeston, Derbyshire DE7 4PP
Tel: 0115 9440609
Head Teacher: Mrs Corinna Walters
Age range: 3–11
No. of pupils: 31
Fees: Day £2,400
✎

**Michael House
Steiner School**
The Field, Shipley, Heanor,
Derbyshire DE75 7JH
Tel: 01773 718050
Age range: 3–16
No. of pupils: 150
Fees: Day £1,500–£4,200

**Normanton House
Primary School**
Normanton House, Village Street,
Derby, Derbyshire DE23 8DF
Tel: 01332 769333
Headteacher: Mr Nighat
Sultana Khan
Age range: 5–10
No. of pupils: 97

Ockbrook School
The Settlement, Ockbrook,
Derby, Derbyshire DE72 3RJ
Tel: 01332 673532
Head: Mr Tom Brooksby
Age range: B2–14 G2–18
No. of pupils: 399 VIth50
Fees: Day £7,203–£10,613
WB £5,685 FB £6,174
⚐ Ⓐ ⚐ £ ✎

Old Vicarage School
11 Church Lane, Darley Abbey,
Derby, Derbyshire DE22 1EW
Tel: 01332 557130
Headmaster: Mr M J Adshead
Age range: 3–13
No. of pupils: 95
Fees: Day £6,135–£6,810
£ ✎

S. Anselm's School
Stanedge Road, Bakewell,
Derbyshire DE45 1DP
Tel: 01629 812734
Headmaster: Peter Phillips BA
(Hons), MA, PGCE (SPLD), NPQH
Age range: 3–13
No. of pupils: 215
Fees: Day £7,680–£14,940 FB £17,550
⚐ £ ✎

St Peter & St Paul School
Brambling House, Hady Hill,
Chesterfield, Derbyshire S41 0EF
Tel: 01246 278522
Headmaster: Mr John Clark
Age range: 3 months–11 years
No. of pupils: 129
Fees: Day £6,132–£6,432
£ ✎

St Wystan's School
High Street, Repton,
Derbyshire DE65 6GE
Tel: 01283 703258
Headmaster: Phillip Soutar
Age range: 3–11
£ ✎

Leicestershire

Al-Aqsa Schools Trust
The Wayne Way, Leicester,
Leicestershire LE5 4PP
Tel: 0116 2760953
Headteacher: Mrs Amina Wiltshire
Age range: 5–16
No. of pupils: 231
✎

Brooke House Day School
Croft Road, Cosby, Leicester,
Leicestershire LE9 1SE
Tel: 0116 286 7372
Head: Mrs Joy Parker
Age range: 3–14

**Darul Arqam
Educational Institute**
2 Overton Road, Leicester,
Leicestershire LE5 0JA
Tel: 0116 2741626
Headteacher: Mr Ahmed
Abdul Dadipatel
Age range: B5–16
No. of pupils: 75
⚥

**Fairfield Preparatory
School**
Leicester Road, Loughborough,
Leicestershire LE11 2AE
Tel: 01509 215172
Headmaster: Mr A Earnshaw
BA Lancaster NPQH
Age range: 4–11
No. of pupils: 489
✎

Grace Dieu Manor School
Grace Dieu, Thringstone,
Leicestershire LE67 5UG
Tel: 01530 222276
Headmaster: Mr C E Foulds BA
Age range: 3–13
No. of pupils: 315
Fees: Day £7,935–£11,313
£ ✎

Jame'ah Girls Academy
33 Woodhill, Leicester,
Leicestershire LE5 3SP
Tel: 0116 2627745
Headteacher: Mrs S Patel
Age range: G6–16
No. of pupils: 142
⚥

**LEICESTER GRAMMAR
JUNIOR SCHOOL**
For further details see p. 48
London Road, Grea Glen,
Leicester, Leicestershire LE8 9FL
Tel: 0116 259 1950
Email:
friell@leicestergrammar.org.uk
Website:
www.leicestergrammar.org.uk/
junior-school-home
Head of School: Mrs C Rigby
Age range: 3–11
No. of pupils: 391
✎

**Leicester High
School for Girls**
454 London Road, Leicester,
Leicestershire LE2 2PP
Tel: 0116 2705338
Headmaster: Mr Alan Whelpdale
Age range: G3–18
No. of pupils: 435 VIth60
Fees: Day £2,250–£3,100
⚥ Ⓐ £

**Leicester International
School**
16-20 Beal Street, Leicester,
Leicestershire LE2 0AA
Tel: 0116 2515345
Principal: Mr N Hussein
Age range: 5–11
No. of pupils: 146
⚐

**Leicester Islamic
Academy**
320 London Road, Leicester,
Leicestershire LE2 2PP
Tel: 0116 2705343
Principal: Dr M H Mukadam
FRSA, BEd(Hons), PhD
Age range: 3–16
Fees: Day £1,300–£1,400

**Leicester Montessori
Grammar School**
58 Stoneygate Road, Leicester,
Leicestershire LE2 2BN
Tel: 0116 2706667
Headteacher: Mr Leyton
De Henton Smith
Age range: 4–14
No. of pupils: 84
Fees: Day £10,200
Ⓐ ✎

Leicester Prep School
2 Albert Road, Leicester,
Leicestershire LE2 2AA
Tel: 0116 2707414
Headmaster: Christopher
J Cann MA(Oxon)
Age range: 3–11
No. of pupils: 130
Fees: Day £1,530–£5,820

Manor House School
South Street, Ashby-de-la-
Zouch, Leicestershire LE65 1BR
Tel: 01530 412932
Headteacher: Mrs E A Scrine
Age range: 4–16
Fees: Day £4,302–£5,700

Our Lady's Convent School
Gray Street, Loughborough,
Leicestershire LE11 2DZ
Tel: 01509 263901
Headteacher: Mrs P Hawley
Age range: B3–11 G3–18
No. of pupils: 200
Fees: Day £8,499–£10,968

Ratcliffe College
Fosse Way, Ratcliffe on the Wreake,
Leicester, Leicestershire LE7 4SG
Tel: 01509 817000
Headmaster: Mr G Lloyd
BA, MSc, FMusTCL
Age range: 3–18
No. of pupils: 689 VIth154
Fees: Day £8,226–£14,865 WB
£18,471–£20,673 FB £23,190

St Crispin's School
6 St Mary's Road, Stoneygate,
Leicester, Leicestershire LE2 1XA
Tel: 0116 2707648
Head: Mrs D Lofthouse
Age range: 2–16

Stoneygate School
6 London Road, Great Glen,
Leicester, Leicestershire LE8 9DJ
Tel: 0116 259 2282
Headmaster: Mr John H
Morris MA(Cantab)
Age range: 3–13
Fees: Day £4,800–£6,100

The Dixie Grammar School
Station Road, Market Bosworth,
Leicestershire CV13 0LE
Tel: 01455 292244
Headmaster: J Wood MA
Age range: 3–18
No. of pupils: 520 VIth71
Fees: Day £5,760–£7,920

**Tiny Tots Pre-School
& Primary**
16-20 Beal Street, Leicester,
Leicestershire LE2 0AA
Tel: 0116 2515345
Principal: Mr N Hussein
Age range: 2–11
No. of pupils: 104

Lincolnshire

Ayscoughfee Hall School
Welland Hall, London Road,
Spalding, Lincolnshire PE11 2TE
Tel: 01775 724733
Headmistress: Mrs C E M
Ogden BA(Hons), PGCE
Age range: 3–11
Fees: Day £4,005–£5,925

**Bicker Preparatory
School & Early Years**
School Lane, Bicker, Boston,
Lincolnshire PE20 3DW
Tel: 01775 821786
Proprietor & Principal: Mrs S
A Page CertEdDist, SMPS
Age range: 3–11
No. of pupils: 80
Fees: Day £585–£5,205

**Copthill Independent
Day School**
Barnack Road, Uffington,
Stamford, Lincolnshire PE9 3AD
Tel: 01780 757506
Headmaster: Mr J A Teesdale
BA(Hons), PGCE
Age range: 2–11
No. of pupils: 309
Fees: Day £8,370–£9,180

Dudley House School
1 Dudley Road, Grantham,
Lincolnshire NG31 9AA
Tel: 01476 400184
Headmistress: Mrs Jenny Johnson
Age range: 3–11
No. of pupils: 50
Fees: Day £4,545

**Grantham Preparatory
International School**
Gorse Lane, Grantham,
Lincolnshire NG31 7UF
Tel: +44 (0)1476 593293
Headmistress: Mrs K A Korcz
Age range: 3–11
No. of pupils: 108
Fees: Day £6,900–£8,430

Greenwich House School
106 High Holme Road, Louth,
Lincolnshire LN11 0HE
Tel: 01507 609252
Headmistress: Mrs J Brindle
Age range: 9 months–11 years
No. of pupils: 50
Fees: Day £5,100

**Handel House
Preparatory School**
Northolme Road, Gainsborough,
Lincolnshire DN21 2JB
Tel: 01427 612426
Headmistress: Mrs Victoria Haigh
Age range: 2–11
Fees: Day £2,580–£3,075

Lincoln Minster School
Upper Lindum Street, Lincoln,
Lincolnshire LN2 5RW
Tel: 01522 551300
Principal: Mr Clive Rickart
Age range: 2.5–18
No. of pupils: 840 VIth144
Fees: Day £6,510–£9,672 WB
£14,289–£16,947 FB £15,417–£18,285

Locksley Christian School
Bliney House, Manby Park,
Manby, Lincolnshire LN11 8UT
Tel: 01507 327859
Headteacher: Mrs A Franklin BSc
Age range: 3–18
Fees: Day £2,004

St Hugh's School
Cromwell Avenue, Woodhall
Spa, Lincolnshire LN10 6TQ
Tel: 01526 352169
Head: C Ward BEd(Hons)
Age range: 2–13
No. of pupils: 195
Fees: Day £7,452–£12,987 FB £18,381

Stamford Junior School
Kettering Road, Stamford,
Lincolnshire PE9 2LR
Tel: 01780 484400
Principal: Mr S C Roberts
Age range: 2–11
No. of pupils: 344
Fees: Day £8,580 WB
£17,436 FB £17,544

Viking School
140 Church Road North,
Skegness, Lincolnshire PE25 2QJ
Tel: 01754 765749
Principal: Mrs S J Barker
Age range: 3–11
No. of pupils: 100
Fees: Day £1,085

**Witham Hall
Preparatory School**
Witham-on-the-Hill, Bourne,
Lincolnshire PE10 0JJ
Tel: +44(0)1778 590222
Headmaster: Mr Charles
Welch B.Ed (Hons)
Age range: 4–13
No. of pupils: 228
Fees: Day £6,645–£10,875 FB £14,850

Northamptonshire

Beachborough School
Westbury, Brackley,
Northamptonshire NN13 5LB
Tel: 01280 700071
Headmaster: Mr Jeremy Banks BEd
Age range: 2–13
No. of pupils: 260
Fees: Day £570–£10,485

Laxton Junior School
East Road, Oundle, Peterborough,
Northamptonshire PE8 4BX
Tel: 01832 277275
Head: Mr Mark Potter
MEd BEd(Hons)
Age range: 4–11
Fees: Day £9,885–£10,845

Maidwell Hall
Maidwell, Northampton,
Northamptonshire NN6 9JG
Tel: 01604 686234
Headmaster: R A
Lankester MA, PGCE
Age range: 7–13
No. of pupils: 111
Fees: Day £14,760 WB
£23,940 FB £23,940

**Northampton High
School GDST**
Newport Pagnell Road,
Hardingstone, Northampton,
Northamptonshire NN4 6UU
Tel: 01604 765765
Headmistress: Mrs S Dixon BA
Age range: G3–18
Fees: Day £9,795–£13,005

Overstone Park School
Overstone Park,
Overstone, Northampton,
Northamptonshire NN6 0DT
Tel: 01604 643787
Principal: Mrs M F Brown
BA(Hons), PGCE
Age range: 0–18
No. of pupils: 85
Fees: Day £2,267–£3,013
Ⓔ🖊

Pitsford School
Pitsford Hall, Pitsford, Northampton,
Northamptonshire NN6 9AX
Tel: 01604 880306
Headmaster: N R Toone BSc, MInstP
Age range: 4–18
No. of pupils: Vlth60
Fees: Day £7,752–£13,455
Ⓐ Ⓔ 🖊

Quinton House School
Upton Hall, Upton, Northampton,
Northamptonshire NN5 4UX
Tel: 01604 752050
Headteacher: Mr G Jones BA(Hons)
Age range: 2–18
No. of pupils: 350 Vlth43
Fees: Day £2,325–£2,710
Ⓐ Ⓔ 🖊

Spratton Hall
Smith Street, Spratton,
Northampton,
Northamptonshire NN6 8HP
Tel: 01604 847292
Head Master: Mr Simon Clarke
Age range: 4–13
No. of pupils: 396
Fees: Day £9,045–£12,600
Ⓔ 🖊

St Peter's Independent School
Lingswood Park,
Blackthorn, Northampton,
Northamptonshire NN3 8TA
Tel: 01604 411745
Head: Tim Cooper
Age range: 4–18
No. of pupils: 130
Fees: Day £3,600
Ⓐ

St Peter's School
52 Headlands, Kettering,
Northamptonshire NN15 6DJ
Tel: 01536 512066
Headmistress: Mrs Maria Chapman
Age range: 2–11
No. of pupils: 161
Fees: Day £3,765–£6,795
Ⓔ 🖊

Wellingborough School
Wellingborough,
Northamptonshire NN8 2BX
Tel: 01933 222427
Headmaster: Mr G R Bowe MA
Age range: 3–18
No. of pupils: Vlth145
Fees: Day £6,522–£11,004
Ⓐ Ⓔ 🖊

Winchester House School
High Street, Brackley,
Northamptonshire NN13 7AZ
Tel: 01280 702483
Head: Emma Goldsmith
Age range: 3–13
No. of pupils: 325
Fees: Day £690–£17,025
WB £17,820–£22,485
🏫 Ⓔ 🖊

Nottinghamshire

Colston Bassett Preparatory School
School Lane, Colston
bassett, Nottingham,
Nottinghamshire NG12 3FD
Tel: 01949 81118
Headteacher: Mrs Julie Hunt
Age range: 4–11
Fees: Day £5,925

Coteswood House School
19 Thackeray's Lane,
Woodthorpe, Nottingham,
Nottinghamshire NG5 4HT
Tel: 0115 9676551
Head: Mrs S M Fernley
Age range: 3–11
No. of pupils: 40
Fees: Day £4,200

Dagfa School Nottingham
Broadgate, Beeston, Nottingham,
Nottinghamshire NG9 2FU
Tel: 0115 913 8330
Headmaster: Dr P Woodroffe
MMath(Oxon)
Age range: 3–16
No. of pupils: 220
Fees: Day £8,640–£10,545
Ⓔ 🖊

Hazel Hurst School
400 Westdale Lane,
Mapperley, Nottingham,
Nottinghamshire NG3 6DG
Tel: 0115 9606759
Headteacher: Mrs Rosemary Eadie
Age range: 2–8
Fees: Day £5,406–£6,024

Highfields School
London Road, Newark,
Nottinghamshire NG24 3AL
Tel: 01636 704103
Headteacher: Mrs C L
Fraser BEd(Hons)
Age range: 3–11
No. of pupils: 120
Fees: Day £7,770
Ⓔ 🖊

Hollygirt School
Elm Avenue, Nottingham,
Nottinghamshire NG3 4GF
Tel: 0115 958 0596
Headmistress: Mrs Pam Hutley
BA(Hons), PGCE, MSc
Age range: B3–7 G3–16
No. of pupils: 240
Fees: Day £7,698–£10,224
🏃 Ⓔ 🖊

Iona School
310 Sneinton Dale, Nottingham,
Nottinghamshire NG3 7DN
Tel: 01159 415295
Chair of College: Richard Moore
Age range: 3–11
Fees: Day £3,816

Jamia Al-Hudaa Residential College
Forest House, Berkeley Avenue,
Mapperley Park, Nottingham,
Nottinghamshire NG3 5TT
Tel: 0115 9690800
Principal: Raza ul-Haq Siakhvy
Age range: G5–19
No. of pupils: 224
🏃 🏫

Jubilee House Christian School
226 Nottingham Road, Eastwood,
Nottinghamshire NG16 3GR
Tel: 01773 688100
Headteacher: Mrs J Marks
Age range: 3–16
No. of pupils: 70
Ⓔ

Nottingham Girls' High School GDST
9 Arboretum Street, Nottingham,
Nottinghamshire NG1 4JB
Tel: 0115 9417663
Headmistress: Mrs S M Gorham
Age range: G4–18
No. of pupils: 1117 Vlth239
Fees: Day £6,978–£9,627
🏃 Ⓐ Ⓔ

Nottingham High Infant and Junior School
Waverley Mount, Nottingham,
Nottinghamshire NG7 4ED
Tel: 0115 845 2214
Headteacher: Mrs C Bruce
Age range: 4–11
No. of pupils: 255
🖊

Nottingham Islamia School
30 Bentinck Road, Hyson
Green, Nottingham,
Nottinghamshire NG7 4AF
Tel: 0115 970 5858
Head: Dr Musharraf Hussain
Age range: 5–11

Plumtree School
Church Hill, Plumtree, Nottingham,
Nottinghamshire NG12 5ND
Tel: 0115 937 5859
Head Teacher: Ms. Jo Howarth
Age range: 3–11
Fees: Day £5,250
🖊

Salterford House School
Salterford Lane,
Calverton, Nottingham,
Nottinghamshire NG14 6NZ
Tel: 0115 9652127
Headmistress: Mrs Marlene
Venables CertEd
Age range: 2–11
No. of pupils: 124
Fees: Day £6,150
🖊

Saville House School
11 Church Street, Mansfield
Woodhouse, Mansfield,
Nottinghamshire NG19 8AH
Tel: 01623 625068
Head: Mrs S Hagues
Age range: 3–11
No. of pupils: 89
Fees: Day £4,125
🖊

St Joseph's School
33 Derby Road, Nottingham,
Nottinghamshire NG1 5AW
Tel: 0115 9418356
Head Teacher: Mr
Ashley Crawshaw
Age range: 1–11
Fees: Day £7,503
🖊

The Elms, Nursery & Junior School to Trent College
Derby Road, Long
Eaton, Nottingham,
Nottinghamshire NG10 4AD
Tel: 0115 8494942
Head: Mr Keith Morrow BA(Hons)
QTS, PGCPS(Ed), NPQH (EMTA)
Age range: 0–11
No. of pupils: 340
Fees: Day £7,200–£7,500

The Lammas School
Lammas Road, Sutton-in-Ashfield,
Nottinghamshire NG17 2AD
Tel: 01623 516879
Head: Mrs P Sessions
Age range: 4–16
Fees: Day £5,125–£6,650
🖊

The Orchard School
South Leverton, Retford,
Nottinghamshire DN22 0DJ
Tel: 01427 880395
Principal: Mrs S M Fox BA, PGCE
Age range: 5–16
No. of pupils: 200
Fees: Day £3,795–£6,180

Wellow House School
Wellow, Newark,
Nottinghamshire NG22 0EA
Tel: 01623 861054
Headmaster: Peter Cook BEd(Hons)
Age range: 3–13
No. of pupils: 152
Fees: Day £7,500–£11,985
WB £13,845
🏫 Ⓔ 🖊

**WORKSOP COLLEGE
PREPARATORY SCHOOL,
RANBY HOUSE**
For further details see p. 49
Retford, Nottinghamshire
DN22 8HX
Tel: 01777 714387 (Admissions)
Email: admissionsprep@
wsnl.co.uk
Website: www.wsnl.co.uk
Headmaster: C S J Pritchard
MA, BA(Hons), QTS
Age range: 3–13 years
No. of pupils: 240
Fees: Day £4,064–£4,274

Rutland

Brooke Priory School
Station Approach, Oakham,
Rutland LE15 6QW
Tel: 01572 724778
Headmistress: Mrs E Bell BEd
Age range: 2–11
No. of pupils: 180
Fees: Day £8,655

Greater London

*See also East (D99) for schools in Essex and Hertfordshire; South-East (D139) for schools in Kent and Surrey

KEY TO SYMBOLS

- (♦) *Boys' school*
- (♦) *Girls' school*
- (🌐) *International school*
- (16) *Tutorial or sixth form college*
- (A) *A levels*
- (🏫) *Boarding accommodation*
- (£) *Bursaries*
- (IB) *International Baccalaureate*
- (✎) *Learning support*
- (16) *Entrance at 16+*
- (👜) *Vocational qualifications*
- (IAPS) *Independent Association of Prep Schools*
- (HMC) *The Headmasters' & Headmistresses' Conference*
- (ISA) *Independent Schools Association*
- (GSA) *Girls' School Association*
- (BSA) *Boarding Schools' Association*
- (S) *Society of Heads*

Unless otherwise indicated, all schools are coeducational day schools. Single-sex and boarding schools will be indicated by the relevant icon.

Essex

Al-Noor Primary School
619-625 Green Lane, Goodmayes,
Ilford, Essex IG3 9RP
Tel: 020 8597 7576
Head: Mrs Someera Butt
Age range: 4–10
No. of pupils: 175
Fees: Day £2,550–£2,750

Avon House School
490-492 High Road, Woodford
Green, Essex IG8 0PN
Tel: 020 8504 1749
Headteacher: Mrs A Campbell
Age range: 3–11
Fees: Day £8,355–£8,925

Bancroft's School
High Road, Woodford
Green, Essex IG8 0RF
Tel: 020 8505 4821
Head: Mary E Ireland
Age range: 7–18
No. of pupils: 1131 VIth240
Fees: Day £12,255–£15,048

Beehive Preparatory School
233 Beehive Lane, Redbridge,
Ilford, Essex IG4 5ED
Tel: 020 8550 3224
Headmaster: Mr C J Beasant BEd
Age range: 4–11
Fees: Day £4,900

Cranbrook College
Mansfield Road, Ilford,
Essex IG1 3BD
Tel: 020 8554 1757
Executive Principal: Mr.
David Morrison
Age range: B4–16
No. of pupils: 200
Fees: Day £6,405–£8,235

Eastcourt Independent School
1 Eastwood Road, Goodmayes,
Ilford, Essex IG3 8UW
Tel: 020 8590 5472
Headmistress: Mrs Christine
Redgrave BSc(Hons), DipEd, MEd
Age range: 3–11
Fees: Day £6,300

Gidea Park College
2 Balgores Lane, Gidea Park,
Romford, Essex RM2 5JR
Tel: 01708 740381
Headmistress: Mrs Susan-
Jayne Gooding BA
Age range: 3–11
No. of pupils: 177
Fees: Day £1,275–£2,500

Goodrington School
17 Walden Road, Hornchurch,
Essex RM11 2JT
Tel: 01708 448349
Head Teacher: Mrs J R Ellenby
Age range: 3–11
Fees: Day £5,400

Ilford Grammar School
785 High Road, Seven Kings,
Ilford, Essex IG3 8RW
Tel: 020 8599 8822
Headmistress: B P M Wiggs
BSc(Hons), PGCE
Age range: 3–16
Fees: Day £5,250–£7,200

Ilford Ursuline R C Preparatory School
2 Coventry Road, Ilford,
Essex IG1 4QR
Tel: 020 8518 4050
Headmistress: Mrs C Spinner
Age range: G3–11
No. of pupils: 159
Fees: Day £5,697

Immanuel School
Havering Grange Centre,
Havering Road North,
Romford, Essex RM1 4HR
Tel: 01708 764449
Principal: Miss Norcross
Age range: 3–16

Maytime Montessori Nursery - Cranbrook Road
341 Cranbrook Road,
Ilford, Essex IG1 4UF
Tel: 020 8554 3079

Maytime Montessori Nursery - Eastwood Road
2 Eastwood Road,
Goodmayes, Essex IG3 8XB
Tel: 020 8599 3744

Maytime Montessori Nursery - York Road
87 York Road, Ilford, Essex IG1 3AF
Tel: 020 8553 1524
Headteacher: Mrs M O'Mahoney
Age range: 0–6

Oakfields Montessori School
Harwood Hall, Harwood Hall Lane,
Corbets Tey, Essex RM14 2YG
Tel: 01708 220117
Headmistress: Mrs K Malandreniotis
Age range: 2–11
Fees: Day £2,508–£4,260

Park School for Girls
20 Park Avenue, Ilford, Essex IG1 4RS
Tel: 020 8554 2466
Headmistress: Mrs N O'Brien BA
Age range: G7–18
No. of pupils: 230 VIth19
Fees: Day £4,755–£6,285

Raphael Independent School
Park Lane, Hornchurch,
Essex RM11 1XY
Tel: 01708 744735
Head of School: Mr Jack Luis
Age range: 4–16
No. of pupils: 135
Fees: Day £5,200–£7,800

St Aubyn's School
Bunces Lane, Woodford
Green, Essex IG8 9DU
Tel: 020 8504 1577
Headmaster: Leonard Blom
BEd(Hons) BA NPQH
Age range: 3–13
No. of pupils: 510
Fees: Day £4,610–£10,449

St Mary's Hare Park School & Nursery
South Drive, Gidea Park,
Romford, Essex RM2 6HH
Tel: 01708 761220
Head Teacher: Mrs K Karwacinski
Age range: 2–11
No. of pupils: 180
Fees: Day £4,485

WOODFORD GREEN PREPARATORY SCHOOL
For further details see p. 52
Glengall Road, Woodford
Green, Essex IG8 0BZ
Tel: 020 8504 5045
Email: admin@wgprep.co.uk
Website: www.wgprep.co.uk
Headmaster: Mr J P Wadge
Age range: 3–11
No. of pupils: 375
Fees: Day £2,995

Hertfordshire

Lyonsdown School
3 Richmond Road, New Barnet,
Barnet, Hertfordshire EN5 1SA
Tel: 020 8449 0225
Head: Mrs L Maggs-Wellings BEd
Age range: B3–7 G3–11
No. of pupils: 203 B38 G165
Fees: Day £3,456–£8,790

Norfolk Lodge Montessori Nursery & Pre-Prep School
Dancers Hill Road, Barnet,
Hertfordshire EN5 4RP
Tel: 020 8447 1565
Head Teacher: Mrs Mary Wales
Age range: 6 months–7 years
No. of pupils: 140
Fees: Day £2,200–£2,400

The Royal Masonic School for Girls
Rickmansworth Park,
Rickmansworth,
Hertfordshire WD3 4HF
Tel: 01923 725337
Headmistress: Miss Linda
Beckett BEd(Hons)
Age range: 4–11

Kent

Ashgrove School
116 Widmore Road,
Bromley, Kent BR1 3BE
Tel: 020 8460 4143
Principal: Patricia Ash CertEd,
BSc(Hons), PhD, CMath, FIMA
Age range: 4–11
Fees: Day £8,190

Babington House School
Grange Drive, Chislehurst,
Kent BR7 5ES
Tel: 020 8467 5537
Headmaster: Mr Tim Lello
Age range: B3–11 G3–18
No. of pupils: 319
Fees: Day £2,880–£4,888

Benedict House Preparatory School
1-5 Victoria Road, Sidcup,
Kent DA15 7HD
Tel: 020 8300 7206
Headmistress: Mrs Gemma Chikola
Age range: 3–11
Fees: Day £2,145–£2,395

Bickley Park School
24 Page Heath Lane, Bickley,
Bromley, Kent BR1 2DS
Tel: 020 8467 2195
Headmaster: Mr Paul Ashley
Age range: B3–13 G3–4
No. of pupils: 370
Fees: Day £6,525–£11,925

Bishop Challoner School
228 Bromley Road, Shortlands,
Bromley, Kent BR2 0BS
Tel: 020 8460 3546
Headteacher: Ms Paula Anderson
Age range: 3–18
No. of pupils: 412 VIth32
Fees: Day £6,441–£9,036

Breaside Preparatory School
41-43 Orchard Road,
Bromley, Kent BR1 2PR
Tel: 020 8460 0916
Headmistress: Mrs Karen Nicholson
BEd, NPQH, Diploma in Early Years
Age range: 2–11
No. of pupils: 304
Fees: Day £9,450–£9,525

BROMLEY HIGH SCHOOL GDST
For further details see p. 50
Blackbrook Lane, Bickley,
Bromley, Kent BR1 2TW
Tel: 020 8781 7000/1
Email: bhs@bro.gdst.net
Website:
www.bromleyhigh.gdst.net
Head: Mrs A M Drew
BA(Hons), MBA (Dunelm)
Age range: G4–18
No. of pupils: 912 VIth125
Fees: Day £12,423–£15,405

Farringtons Junior School
Perry Street, Chislehurst,
Kent BR7 6LR
Tel: 020 8467 0256
Head: Mrs C E James MA
Age range: 3–11
No. of pupils: 287
Fees: Day £8,760

Merton Court Preparatory School
38 Knoll Road, Sidcup,
Kent DA14 4QU
Tel: 020 8300 2112
Headmaster: Mr Dominic
Price BEd, MBA
Age range: 3–11
Fees: Day £8,115–£8,910

St Christopher's The Hall School
49 Bromley Road,
Beckenham, Kent BR3 5PA
Tel: 020 8650 2200
Headmaster: Mr A Velasco
MEd, BH(Hons), PGCE
Age range: 3–11
No. of pupils: 305
Fees: Day £2,250–£6,630

St David's College
Beckenham Road, West
Wickham, Kent BR4 0QS
Tel: 020 8777 5852
Principal: Mrs J Foulger
Age range: 4–11
No. of pupils: 155
Fees: Day £6,015–£6,165

West Lodge School
36 Station Road, Sidcup,
Kent DA15 7DU
Tel: 020 8300 2489
Head Teacher: Mrs Susan Webb
Age range: 3–11
No. of pupils: 161
Fees: Day £4,995–£8,355

Wickham Court School
Schiller International,
Layhams Road, West
Wickham, Kent BR4 9HW
Tel: 020 8777 2942
Head: Mrs Barbara Hunter
Age range: 2–16
No. of pupils: 121
Fees: Day £4,481–£6,900

Middlesex

ACS Hillingdon International School
Hillingdon Court, 108 Vine
Lane, Hillingdon, Uxbridge,
Middlesex UB10 0BE
Tel: +44 (0) 1895 259 771
Head of School: Linda LaPine
Age range: 4–18
No. of pupils: 520
Fees: Day £17,090–£22,550

Alpha Preparatory School
21 Hindes Road, Harrow,
Middlesex HA1 1SH
Tel: 020 8427 1471
Head: C.J.W Trinidad
BSc(Hons), PGCE
Age range: 3–11
No. of pupils: 170
Fees: Day £3,150–£9,900

Ashton House School
50-52 Eversley Crescent,
Isleworth, Middlesex TW7 4LW
Tel: 020 8560 3902
Headteacher: Mrs M
Grundberg MA, PGCE
Age range: 3–11
Fees: Day £9,300–£10,200

Athelstan House School
36 Percy Road, Hampton,
Middlesex TW12 2LA
Tel: 020 8979 1045
Headmistress: Elsa Woolf
Age range: 3–7

Buckingham College Preparatory School
458 Rayners Lane, Pinner,
Middlesex HA5 5DT
Tel: 020 8866 2737
Headmaster: Mr L S Smith BA(Hons),
MSc, LCP, PGDE, CertEd
Age range: B4–11
Fees: Day £7,560–£9,900

Buxlow Preparatory School
5/6 Castleton Gardens,
Wembley, Middlesex HA9 7QJ
Tel: 020 8904 3615
Headmistress: Mrs Ann Baines
Age range: 4–11
Fees: Day £6,885

Denmead School
41-43 Wensleydale Road,
Hampton, Middlesex TW12 2LP
Tel: 020 8979 1844
Headmaster: Mr M T
McKaughan BEd
Age range: 3–11
Fees: Day £4,995–£11,580

Holland House School
1 Broadhurst Avenue, Edgware,
Middlesex HA8 8TP
Tel: 020 8958 6979
Headmistress: Mrs Irinia
Tyk BA(Hons)
Age range: 4–11
Fees: Day £2,170

Jack and Jill School
30 Nightingale Road, Hampton,
Middlesex TW12 3HX
Tel: 020 8979 3195
Principal: Miss K Papirnik BEd(Hons)
Age range: B2–5 G2–7
No. of pupils: 155
Fees: Day £2,409–£9,597

Newland House School
32-34 Waldegrave Park,
Twickenham, Middlesex TW1 4TQ
Tel: 020 8865 1234
Headmaster: Mr D A Alexander
Age range: B4–13 G4–11
Fees: Day £9,300–£10,440

North London Collegiate School
Canons, Canons Drive,
Edgware, Middlesex HA8 7RJ
Tel: +44 (0)20 8952 0912
Headmistress: Mrs Bernice McCabe
Age range: G4–18
No. of pupils: 1080
Fees: Day £5,214–£6,169

Northwood College for Girls GDST
Maxwell Road, Northwood,
Middlesex HA6 2YE
Tel: 01923 825446
Head Mistress: Miss Jacqualyn
Pain MA, MA, MBA
Age range: G3–18
No. of pupils: 750 VIth100
Fees: Day £8,400–£13,800

Orley Farm School
South Hill Avenue, Harrow,
Middlesex HA1 3NU
Tel: 020 8869 7600
Headmaster: Tim Calvey
Age range: 4–13
No. of pupils: 496
Fees: Day £12,834–£14,811
£ 🏊

Quainton Hall
School & Nursery
91 Hindes Road, Harrow,
Middlesex HA1 1RX
Tel: 020 8861 8861
Headmaster: S Ford BEd
(Hons), UWE Bristol
Age range: B2–13 G2–11
Fees: Day £9,075–£9,975
£

Radnor House
Pope's Villa, Cross Deep,
Twickenham, Middlesex TW1 4QG
Tel: 020 8891 6264
Head of School: Mr.
David Paton MA
🏊

Reddiford School
36–38 Cecil Park, Pinner,
Middlesex HA5 5HH
Tel: 020 8866 0660
Headteacher: Mrs J
Batt CertEd, NPQH
Age range: 3–11
No. of pupils: 320
Fees: Day £3,480–£8,340

Roxeth Mead School
Buckholt House, 25 Middle Road,
Harrow, Middlesex HA2 0HW
Tel: 020 8422 2092
Headmistress: Mrs A Isaacs
Age range: 3–7
No. of pupils: 54
Fees: Day £9,450

St Catherine's School
Cross Deep, Twickenham,
Middlesex TW1 4QJ
Tel: 020 8891 2898
Headmistress: Sister Paula
Thomas BEd(Hons), MA
Age range: G3–18
No. of pupils: 430
Fees: Day £9,915–£13,680
👤 A £ 🏊

St Christopher's School
71 Wembley Park Drive,
Wembley, Middlesex HA9 8HE
Tel: 020 8902 5069
Headteacher: Mrs Alison McNeill
Age range: 4–11
No. of pupils: 72
Fees: Day £2,435–£2,560

St Helen's College
Parkway, Hillingdon, Uxbridge,
Middlesex UB10 9JX
Tel: 01895 234371
Joint Headteachers: Mr D A
Crehan & Mrs G R Crehan
Age range: 3–11
No. of pupils: 351
Fees: Day £5,160–£9,090

St Helen's School
Eastbury Road, Northwood,
Middlesex HA6 3AS
Tel: +44 (0)1923 843210
Headmistress: Dr Mary
Short BA, PhD
Age range: G3–18
No. of pupils: 1135 VIth153
👤 🌐 A £ IB

St John's School
Potter Street Hill, Northwood,
Middlesex HA6 3QY
Tel: 020 8866 0067
Headmaster: Mr M S Robinson BSc
Age range: B3–13 years
No. of pupils: 350
Fees: Day £9,000–£13,250
👤 £

St Martin's School
40 Moor Park Road, Northwood,
Middlesex HA6 2DJ
Tel: 01923 825740
Headmaster: Mr D T
Tidmarsh BSc(Wales)
Age range: B3–13
No. of pupils: 400
Fees: Day £1,450–£4,066
👤 £ 🏊

Staines Preparatory School
3 Gresham Road, Staines upon
Thames, Middlesex TW18 2BT
Tel: 01784 450909
Head of School: Samantha
Sawyer BEd (Hons)
Age range: 3–11
No. of pupils: 396
Fees: Day £9,150–£10,500
£ 🏊

Tashbar of Edgeware
47-49 Mowbray Road, Edgware,
Middlesex HA8 8JL
Tel: 020 8958 5162
Headteacher: Mr N Jaffe
Age range: B3–11
No. of pupils: 88
👤

The Falcons Preparatory
School for Boys
41 Few Foot Road, Richmond,
Middlesex TW9 2SS
Tel: 0844 225 2211
Headmaster: Mr Gordon Milne
Age range: B7–13
No. of pupils: 100
Fees: Day £12,660
👤 🏊

The Hall Pre-Preparatory
School & Nursery
The Grange Country House,
Rickmansworth Road,
Northwood, Middlesex HA6 2RB
Tel: 01923 822807
Headmistress: Mrs S M Goodwin
Age range: 1–7
Fees: Day £3,120–£10,350
🏊

The Lady Eleanor
Holles School (Junior
Department)
177 Uxbridge Road, Hampton
Hill, Middlesex TW12 1BD
Tel: 020 8979 2173
Headmistress: Mrs G Low MA(Oxon)
Age range: G7–11
No. of pupils: 190
Fees: Day £13,050
👤 🏊

The Mall School
185 Hampton Road, Twickenham,
Middlesex TW2 5NQ
Tel: 020 8614 1082
Headmaster: Mr D C Price BSc, MA
Age range: B4–13
No. of pupils: 320
Fees: Day £10,281–£11,934
👤 £ 🏊

The Noam Primary School
8-10 Forty Avenue, Wembley,
Middlesex HA9 8JW
Tel: 020 8908 9491
Headteacher: Mrs Sarah Simmonds
Age range: 3–11
No. of pupils: 154
👤

The St Michael
Steiner School
Park Road, Hanworth Park,
London TW13 6PN
Tel: 0208 893 1299
Age range: 3–16 (17 from Jul 2014)
No. of pupils: 101
Fees: Day £5,800–£8,900
£ 🏊

Twickenham
Preparatory School
Beveree, 43 High Street,
Hampton, Middlesex TW12 2SA
Tel: 020 8979 6216
Head: Mr D Malam BA(Hons)
(Southampton), PGCE(Winchester)
Age range: B4–13 G4–11
No. of pupils: 272
Fees: Day £9,345–£10,110
£ 🏊

Surrey

Al-Khair School
109-117 Cherry Orchard Road,
Croydon, Surrey CR0 6BE
Tel: 020 8662 8664
Headteacher: Mr Usman Qureshi
Age range: 5–16
No. of pupils: 126

Broomfield House School
Broomfield Road, Kew Gardens,
Richmond, Surrey TW9 3HS
Tel: 020 8940 3884
Headteacher: Mr N O York
BA(Hons), MA, MPhil, FRSA
Age range: 3–11
No. of pupils: 160
Fees: Day £5,054–£11,787
🏊

Collingwood School
3 Springfield Road, Wallington,
Surrey SM6 0BD
Tel: 020 8647 4607
Headmaster: Mr Chris Fenwick
Age range: 3–11
No. of pupils: 120
Fees: Day £3,600–£6,750
🏊

CROYDON HIGH
SCHOOL GDST
For further details see p. 51
Old Farleigh Road, Selsdon,
South Croydon, Surrey CR2 8YB
Tel: 020 8260 7500
Email: admissions@cry.gdst.net
Website:
www.croydonhigh.gdst.net
Head of Junior School:
Mrs Sophie Bradshaw
Age range: G3–18
No. of pupils: 600 VIth110
👤 A £ 🏊

Cumnor House School
168 Pampisford Road, South
Croydon, Surrey CR2 6DA
Tel: 020 8660 3445
Head Master: Mr P J Clare-
Hunt MA(Ed) Cert Ed
Age range: B2–13
No. of pupils: 440
Fees: Day £2,945–£3,735
👤 🏊

Cumnor House
School for Girls
1 Woodcote Lane, Purley,
Surrey CR8 3HB
Tel: 020 8660 3445
Headmaster: Mr Peter Kelly
Age range: G2–11
No. of pupils: 180
Fees: Day £2,945–£3,735
👤

Educare Small School
12 Cowleaze Road, Kingston upon Thames, Surrey KT2 6DZ
Tel: 020 8547 0144
Head Teacher: Mrs E Steinthal
Age range: 3–11
No. of pupils: 46
Fees: Day £4,800

Elmhurst School
44-48 South Park Hill Rd, South Croydon, Surrey CR2 7DW
Tel: 020 8688 0661
Headmaster: Mr M J Apsley BA(Hons), PGCE
Age range: B4–11
No. of pupils: 207
Fees: Day £6,300–£7,545

Folly's End Christian School
Folly's End Church, 5-9 Surrey Street, Croydon, Surrey CR0 1RG
Tel: 020 8649 9121
Senior Leaders: Dave & Ze Markee
Age range: 3–11
Fees: Day £4,740

Holy Cross Preparatory School
George Road, Kingston upon Thames, Surrey KT2 7NU
Tel: 020 8942 0729
Headteacher: Mrs S Hair BEd(Hons)
Age range: G4–11
No. of pupils: 250
Fees: Day £9,960

Homefield Preparatory School
Western Road, Sutton, Surrey SM1 2TE
Tel: 020 8642 0965
Acting Headteacher: Ms Sabine White
Age range: B3–13
No. of pupils: 400
Fees: Day £4,800–£11,130

Kew College
24-26 Cumberland Road, Kew, Surrey TW9 3HQ
Tel: 020 8940 2039
Headteacher: Mrs Marianne Austin BSc(Hons) MA(Hons) ACA PGCE
Age range: 3–11
No. of pupils: 296
Fees: Day £5,850–£9,150

Kew Green Preparatory School
Layton House, Ferry Lane, Kew Green, Richmond, Surrey TW9 3AF
Tel: 020 8948 5999
Headmaster: Mr J Peck
Age range: 4–11
No. of pupils: 260
Fees: Day £15,606

King's House School
68 King's Road, Richmond, Surrey TW10 6ES
Tel: 020 8940 1878
Head: Mr Mark Turner BA, PGCE, NPQH
Age range: B3–13 G3–4
No. of pupils: 449
Fees: Day £6,300–£14,910

Laleham Lea School
29 Peaks Hill, Purley, Surrey CR8 3JJ
Tel: 020 8660 3351
Headteacher: Mrs J Staunton
Age range: 3–11
Fees: Day £2,128–£6,405

Oakwood Independent School
Godstone Road, Purley, Surrey CR8 2AN
Tel: 020 8668 8080
Headmaster: Mr Ciro Candia BA(Hons), PGCE
Age range: 3–11
No. of pupils: 176
Fees: Day £5,280–£7,644

Old Palace of John Whitgift School
Old Palace Road, Croydon, Surrey CR0 1AX
Tel: 020 8686 7347
Head: Mrs. C Jewell
Age range: B3 months–4 years G3 months–19 years
No. of pupils: 780 VIth140
Fees: Day £9,792–£13,104

Old Vicarage School
48 Richmond Hill, Richmond, Surrey TW10 6QX
Tel: 020 8940 0922
Headmistress: Mrs G D Linthwaite
Age range: G4–11
No. of pupils: 200
Fees: Day £12,630

Park Hill School
8 Queens Road, Kingston upon Thames, Surrey KT2 7SH
Tel: 020 8546 5496
Principal: Mrs Marie Christie
Age range: 2–7
No. of pupils: 100
Fees: Day £4,320–£8,130

Reedham Park School
71A Old Lodge Lane, Purley, Surrey CR8 4DN
Tel: 020 8660 6357
Headteacher: Ms Louise Shaw BA(Hons), DipEurHum
Age range: 4–11
No. of pupils: 122
Fees: Day £3,540–£4,110

Rokeby School
George Road, Kingston upon Thames, Surrey KT2 7PB
Tel: 020 8942 2247
Head: Mr J R Peck
Age range: B4–13
No. of pupils: 370
Fees: Day £3,974–£4,948

Royal Russell Junior School
Coombe Lane, Croydon, Surrey CR9 5BX
Tel: 020 8651 5884
Junior School Headmaster: Mr James C Thompson
Age range: 3–11
No. of pupils: 300
Fees: Day £3,660–£10,155

Seaton House School
67 Banstead Road South, Sutton, Surrey SM2 5LH
Tel: 020 8642 2332
Headmistress: Mrs Debbie Morrison Higher Diploma in Education (RSA)
Age range: B3–5 G3–11
No. of pupils: 164
Fees: Day £2,187–£8,955

Shrewsbury House School
107 Ditton Road, Surbiton, Surrey KT6 6RL
Tel: 020 8399 3066
Headmaster: Mr K Doble BA, PDM, PGCE
Age range: B7–13
No. of pupils: 320
Fees: Day £13,680

St David's School
23/25 Woodcote Valley Road, Purley, Surrey CR8 3AL
Tel: 020 8660 0723
Headmistress: Mrs Lindsay Nash BEd(Hons)
Age range: 3–11
No. of pupils: 167
Fees: Day £2,985–£5,940

Surbiton High School
13-15 Surbiton Crescent, Kingston upon Thames, Surrey KT1 2JT
Tel: 020 8546 5245
Principal: Ann Haydon BSc(Hons)
Age range: G4–18
No. of pupils: 1210 VIth186
Fees: Day £6,390–£10,857

The Study School
57 Thetford Road, New Malden, Surrey KT3 5DP
Tel: 020 8942 0754
Head of School: Ms Donna Brackstone-Drake
Age range: 3–11
No. of pupils: 134
Fees: Day £3,984–£8,973

Treetops Nursery
91 Pampisford Road, South Croydon, London CR2 6DH
Tel: +44 (0)20 8660 3445
Manager: Mrs Charlotte Figueira BEd(Hons)
Age range: 2–4
No. of pupils: 200
Fees: Day £1,370–£2,945

Unicorn School
238 Kew Road, Richmond, Surrey TW9 3JX
Tel: 020 8948 3926
Headmaster: Mr Kit Thompson
Age range: 3–11
Fees: Day £6,000–£11,010

Westbury House
80 Westbury Road, New Malden, Surrey KT3 5AS
Tel: 020 8942 5885
Head of School: Rosalyn Holiday
Age range: 3–11
Fees: Day £1,045–£2,507

London

KEY TO SYMBOLS

- (†) Boys' school
- (‡) Girls' school
- (🌐) International school
- (16) Tutorial or sixth form college
- (A) A levels
- (🏫) Boarding accommodation
- (£) Bursaries
- (IB) International Baccalaureate
- (✎) Learning support
- (16) Entrance at 16+
- (💼) Vocational qualifications
- (IAPS) Independent Association of Prep Schools
- (HMC) The Headmasters' & Headmistresses' Conference
- (ISA) Independent Schools Association
- (GSA) Girls' School Association
- (BSA) Boarding Schools' Association
- (S) Society of Heads

Unless otherwise indicated, all schools are coeducational day schools. Single-sex and boarding schools will be indicated by the relevant icon.

Central London

Charterhouse Square School
40 Charterhouse Square,
London EC1M 6EA
Tel: 020 7600 3805
Head of School: Mrs Caroline
Lloyd BEd (Hons)
Age range: 3–11
No. of pupils: 196
Fees: Day £4,575

City of London School for Girls
St Giles' Terrace, Barbican,
London EC2Y 8BB
Tel: 020 7847 5500
Headmistress: Mrs E Harrop
Age range: G7–18
Fees: Day £14,409
(symbols)

Dallington School
8 Dallington Street, Islington,
London EC1V 0BW
Tel: 020 7251 2284
Headteacher: Mrs M C Hercules
Age range: 3–11
No. of pupils: 116
Fees: Day £9,216–£11,742

ST PAUL'S CATHEDRAL SCHOOL
For further details see p. 65
2 New Change,
London EC4M 9AD
Tel: 020 7248 5156
Email: admissions@
spcs.london.sch.uk
Website: www.spcslondon.com
Headmaster: Mr Neil
Chippington MA, MEd, FRCO
Age range: 4–13
No. of pupils: 252
Fees: Day £12,939–
£13,932 FB £8,057
(symbols)

The Lyceum
6 Paul Street, London EC2A 4JH
Tel: 020 7247 1588
Joint Headteachers: Mr Jeremy
Rowe & Mrs Lynn Hannay
Age range: 4–11
No. of pupils: 100
Fees: Day £8,700–£13,800

East London

Al-Falah Primary School
48 Kenninghall Road,
Clapton, London E5 8BY
Tel: 020 8985 1059
Headteacher: Mr M A Hussain
Age range: 5–11
No. of pupils: 83
Fees: Day £1,600

Al-Mizan School
46 Whitechapel Road,
London E1 1JX
Tel: 020 7650 3070
Head: Mr Ziaurr Ahman
Age range: B7–18
No. of pupils: 200 VIth13
Fees: Day £2,400
(symbols)

Beis Trana Girls' School
186 Upper Clapton Road,
London E5 9DH
Tel: 020 8815 8003
Age range: G3–16
No. of pupils: 270
(symbol)

Faraday School
Trinity Buoy Wharf, 64 Orchard
Place, London E14 0JW
Tel: 020 8965 7374
Head Teacher: Mr M McElhone
Age range: 4–11
Fees: Day £6,480
(symbol)

FOREST SCHOOL
For further details see p. 55
College Place, Snaresbrook,
London E17 3PY
Tel: 020 8520 1744
Email: info@forest.org.uk
Website: www.forest.org.uk
Warden: Mr Antony Faccinello
Age range: 4–18
No. of pupils: 1355
Fees: Day £11,049–£16,335
(symbols)

Gatehouse School
Sewardstone Road, Victoria
Park, London E2 9JG
Tel: 020 8980 2978
Headmistress: Mrs Belinda Canham
JP, BA(Hons), PGCE(Froebel)
Age range: 3–11
No. of pupils: 320
Fees: Day £6,920–£8,502
(symbols)

Grangewood Independent School
Chester Road, Forest
Gate, London E7 8QT
Tel: 020 8472 3552
Headteacher: Mrs B A Roberts
Age range: 3–11
No. of pupils: 61
(symbol)

Green Gables Montessori Primary School
The Institute, 302 The Highway,
Wapping, London E1W 3DH
Tel: 020 7488 2374
Head: Mrs V Hunt
Age range: 0–8
No. of pupils: 45
Fees: Day £740–£10,480

Hyland House School
Holcombe Road, Tottenham,
, London N17 9AD
Tel: 020 8520 4186
Headmistress: Mrs T Thorpe
Age range: 3–11
Fees: Day £2,520

Lubavitch House School (Junior Boys)
135 Clapton Common,
London E5 9AE
Tel: 020 8800 1044
Head: Rabbi D Golomb
Age range: B5–11
No. of pupils: 101
Fees: Day £520–£3,100
(symbol)

Normanhurst School
68-74 Station Road,
Chingford, London E4 7BA
Tel: 020 8529 4307
Headmistress: Mrs Claire Osborn
Age range: 2–16
No. of pupils: 250
Fees: Day £7,470–£11,235
(symbol)

Paragon Christian Academy
233-241 Glyn Road, London E5 0JP
Tel: 020 8985 1119
Headteacher: Mrs J A Lynch
Age range: 5–16
No. of pupils: 34

Pillar Box Montessori Nursery & Pre-Prep School
107 Bow Road, London E3 2AN
Tel: 020 8980 0700
Age range: 0–7
Fees: Day £250–£500

Promised Land Academy
St Cedds Hall, Webb Gardens,
Plaistow, London E13 8SR
Tel: 0207 473 3229
Head: Mr A Coote
Age range: 4–16

Quwwat-ul Islam Girls School
16 Chaucer Road, Forest
Gate, London E7 9NB
Tel: 020 8548 4736
Headteacher: Mrs B Khan
Age range: G4–11
No. of pupils: 150
(symbol)

River House Montessori School
3-4 Shadwell Pierhead, Glamis
Road, London E1W 3TD
Tel: 020 7538 9886
Headmistress: Miss S Greenwood
Age range: 3–12
Fees: Day £2,700–£9,000
(symbol)

Snaresbrook Preparatory School
75 Woodford Road, South
Woodford, London E18 2EA
Tel: 020 8989 2394
Head of School: Mr Christopher Curl
Age range: 3–11
No. of pupils: 164
Fees: Day £6,696–£8,952
(symbol)

St Joseph's Convent School For Girls
59 Cambridge Park,
Wanstead, London E11 2PR
Tel: 020 8989 4700
Headteacher: Ms C Glover
Age range: G3–11
No. of pupils: 171
Fees: Day £5,355
(symbols)

Talmud Torah Machikei Hadass School
96-98 Clapton Common,
London E5 9AL
Tel: 020 8800 6599
Headteacher: Rabbi C Silbiger
Age range: B4–11
No. of pupils: 271
(symbol)

Winston House Preparatory School
140 High Road, London E18 2QS
Tel: 020 8505 6565
Head Teacher: Mrs Marian Kemp
Age range: 3–11
Fees: Day £5,850–£7,050

North London

Annemount School
18 Holne Chase, Hampstead
Garden Suburb, London N2 0QN
Tel: 020 8455 2132
Principal: Mrs G Maidment
BA(Hons), MontDip
Age range: 2–7
No. of pupils: 100
Fees: Day £2,500–£4,500

Avenue Nursery & Pre-Preparatory School
2 Highgate Avenue, London N6 5RX
Tel: 020 8348 6815
Principal: Mrs. Mary Fysh
Age range: 3 1/2–7 1/2
No. of pupils: 79

Beis Aharon School
97-99 Bethune Road,
London N16 5ED
Tel: 020 88007 368
Head: Y Pomerantz
Age range: B2–12
No. of pupils: 177

Beis Chinuch Lebonos Girls School
Woodberry Down Centre,
Woodberry Down, London N4 2SH
Tel: 020 88097 737
Headmistress: Mrs Bertha Schneck
Age range: G2–16
No. of pupils: 421

Beis Malka Girls School
93 Alkham Road, London N16 6XD
Tel: 020 8806 2070
Headmaster: M Dresdner
Age range: G5–16
No. of pupils: 339

Beis Rochel D'Satmar Girls School
51-57 Amhurst Park, London N16 5DL
Tel: 020 8800 9060
Headmistress: Mrs A Scher
Age range: G2–17
No. of pupils: 788

Bnois Jerusalem School
79-81 Amhurst Park, London N16 5DL
Tel: 020 8802 7470
Head: Mrs Sonnenschein
Age range: G3–16

Channing School
The Bank, Highgate, London N6 5HF
Tel: 020 8340 2328
Head: Mrs B M Elliott
Age range: G4–18
No. of pupils: 746 VIth108
Fees: Day £14,085–£15,255

Dwight School London
6 Friern Barnet Lane, London N11 3LX
Tel: +44 (0)20 8920 0600
Head: Mr David Rose
MA(Ed), BA, CertEd, FRSA
Age range: 2–18+

Finchley & Acton Yochien School
6 Hendon Avenue, Finchley,
London N3 1UE
Tel: 020 8343 2191
Headteacher: Mr
Katsumasa Kitagaki
Age range: 2–6
No. of pupils: 145

Getters Talmud Torah
86 Amhurst Park, London N16 5AR
Tel: 020 8802 2512
Headteacher: Mr David Kahana
Age range: B4–11
No. of pupils: 171

Grange Park Preparatory School
13 The Chine, Grange Park,
Winchmore Hill, London N21 2EA
Tel: 020 8360 1469
Headteacher: Mrs B McLaughlin
Age range: G4–11
No. of pupils: 90
Fees: Day £9,900

Highgate
North Road, Highgate,
London N6 4AY
Tel: 020 8340 1524
Head Master: Mr A S Pettitt MA
Age range: 3–18
No. of pupils: 1541 VIth312
Fees: Day £15,135–£17,475

Highgate Junior School
Cholmeley House, 3 Bishopswood
Road, London N6 4PL
Tel: 020 8340 9193
Principal: Mr S M James BA
Age range: 7–11
Fees: Day £10,695–£11,955

Highgate Pre-Preparatory School
7 Bishopswood Road,
London N6 4PH
Tel: 020 8340 9196
Principal: Mrs Diane Hecht
Age range: 3–7
No. of pupils: 140
Fees: Day £16,200

Keble Preparatory School
Wades Hill, London N21 1BG
Tel: 020 8360 3359
Headmaster: Mr G McCarthy
Age range: B4–13
Fees: Day £9,390–£11,670

Kerem School
Norrice Lea, London N2 0RE
Tel: 020 8455 0909
Acting Head Teacher:
Miss Alyson Burns
Age range: 3–11
Fees: Day £8,250–£6,675

Montessori House
5 Princes Avenue, Muswell
Hill, London N10 3LS
Tel: 020 8444 4399
Head: Ms Lisa Christoforou
Age range: 6 months–7 years
No. of pupils: 100
Fees: Day £5,355–£9,450

Mustard School
Parish Hall, Nuttall Street,
London N1 5LR
Tel: 020 7739 3499
Headteacher: Mr A F Johnson
Age range: 3–18
No. of pupils: 47 VIth3
Fees: Day £3,060

Norfolk House School
10 Muswell Avenue, Muswell
Hill, London N10 2EG
Tel: 020 8883 4584
Head Teacher: Ms Sam Habgood
Age range: 4–11
No. of pupils: 130
Fees: Day £9,855

North London Muslim School
131-133 Fore Street, Edmonton,
London N18 2XF
Tel: 020 8345 7008
Headteacher: Mr W Abdulla
Age range: 4–10
No. of pupils: 21

North London Rudolf Steiner School
1-3 The Campsbourne,
London N8 7PN
Tel: 020 8341 3770
Age range: 2.5–7
No. of pupils: 40

Palmers Green High School
Hoppers Road, Winchmore
Hill, London N21 3LJ
Tel: 020 8886 1135
Headmistress: Mrs Christine
Edmundson BMus(Hons),
MBA, PGCE, LRAM, ARCM
Age range: G3–16
No. of pupils: 300
Fees: Day £5,985–£10,785

Rosemary Works Independent School
1 Branch Place, London N1 5PH
Tel: 020 7739 3950
Head: Dorothy Davey
Age range: 3–11
No. of pupils: 104
Fees: Day £6,195

Salcombe Preparatory School
224-226 Chase Side, Southgate,
, London N14 4PL
Tel: 020 8441 5356
Headmistress: Mrs Sarah-Jane
Davies BA(Hons) QTS MEd
Age range: 4–11
No. of pupils: 236
Fees: Day £7,890

St Paul's Steiner School
1 St Paul's Road, Islington,
London N1 2QH
Tel: 020 7226 4454
College of Teachers:
College of Teachers
Age range: 2–14
No. of pupils: 136

Sunrise Day Nursery
1 Cazenove Road, Hackney,
London N16 6PA
Tel: 020 8806 6279/8885 3354
Principal: Didi Ananda Manika
Age range: 2–11
No. of pupils: 50
Fees: Day £3,900–£4,976

Sunrise Primary School
55 Coniston Road, Tottenham,
London N17 0EX
Tel: 020 8806 6279 (Office); 020
8885 3354 (School)
Head: Mrs Mary-Anne
Lovage MontDipEd, BA
Age range: 2–11
No. of pupils: 30
Fees: Day £3,900

Talmud Torah Bobov Primary School
87 Egerton Road, London N16 6UE
Tel: 020 8809 1025
Headteacher: Rabbi A Just
Age range: B3–13
No. of pupils: 320

Talmud Torah Chaim Meirim School
26 Lampard Grove, London N16 6XB
Tel: 020 8806 0017
Principal: Rabbi S Hoffman
Age range: B6–13

Talmud Torah Yetev Lev School
111-115 Cazenove Road,
London N16 6AX
Tel: 020 8806 3834
Headteacher: Mr J Stauber
Age range: B2–11
No. of pupils: 567

Tayyibah Girls School
88 Filey Avenue, Stamford
Hill, London N16 6JJ
Tel: 020 8880 0085
Headmistress: Mrs N B Qureishi MSc
Age range: G5–15
No. of pupils: 270
Fees: Day £1,630

The Children's House Upper School
King Henry's Walk, London N1 4PB
Tel: 020 7249 6273
Headteacher: Mrs J Rothwell
Age range: 4–7
No. of pupils: 60
Fees: Day £3,250

The Gower School Montessori Nursery
18 North Road, Islington, London N7 9EY
Tel: 020 7700 2445
Principal: Miss Emma Gowers
Age range: 3 months–5 years
No. of pupils: 237

The Gower School Montessori Primary
10 Cynthia Street, Barnsbury, London N1 9JF
Tel: 020 7278 2020
Principal: Miss Emma Gowers
Age range: 4–11
No. of pupils: 237
Fees: Day £4,680–£19,129

TTTYY School
14 Heathland Road, London N16 5NH
Tel: 020 8802 1348
Headmaster: Mr S B Gluck
Age range: B2–13
No. of pupils: 187

Vita et Pax School
Priory Close, Southgate, London N14 4AT
Tel: 020 8449 8336
Headmistress: Mrs M O'Connor BEd(Hons)
Age range: 3–11
Fees: Day £6,150

Yesodey Hatorah School
2-4 Amhurst Park, London N16 5AE
Tel: 020 8826 5500
Headteacher: Rabbi Pinter
Age range: 3–16
No. of pupils: 920

North-West London

Abercorn School
Infant Department, 28 Abercorn Place, London NW8 9XP
Tel: 020 7286 4785
High Mistress: Mrs Andrea Greystoke BA(Hons)
Age range: 2–13
No. of pupils: 360
Fees: Day £7,245–£13,425

Al-Sadiq & Al-Zahra Schools
134 Salusbury Road, London NW6 6PF
Tel: 020 7372 7706
Headteacher: Dr M Movahedi
Age range: 4–16
No. of pupils: 389

Arnold House School
1 Loudoun Road, St John's Wood, London NW8 0LH
Tel: 020 7266 4840
Headmaster: Mr Vivian Thomas
Age range: B5–13
No. of pupils: 270
Fees: Day £5,300

Beis Soroh Schneirer
Arbiter House, Wilberforce Road, London NW9 6AT
Tel: 020 8343 1190
Head: Mrs R Weiss
Age range: G2–11
No. of pupils: 150

Belmont, Mill Hill Preparatory School
The Ridgeway, London NW7 4ED
Tel: 020 8906 7270
Headmaster: Mr Leon Roberts MA
Age range: 7–13
No. of pupils: 472
Fees: Day £15,500

Chalcot Montessori School AMI
9 Chalcot Gardens, London NW3 4YB
Tel: 020 7722 1386
Principal: Ms Joanna Morfey AMI Dip
Age range: 2–6
No. of pupils: 28
Fees: Day £6,960–£7,260

DEVONSHIRE HOUSE PREPARATORY SCHOOL
For further details see p. 54
2 Arkwright Road, Hampstead, London NW3 6AE
Tel: 020 7435 1916
Email: enquiries@devonshire houseprepschool.co.uk
Website: www.devonshire houseschool.co.uk
Headmistress: Mrs S. Piper BA(Hons)
Age range: B2–13 G2–11
No. of pupils: 620
Fees: Day £9,060–£16,635

Golders Hill School
666 Finchley Road, London NW11 7NT
Tel: 020 8455 2589
Headmistress: Mrs A T Eglash BA(Hons)
Age range: 2–7
No. of pupils: 180
Fees: Day £831–£6,870

Goodwyn School
Hammers Lane, Mill Hill, London NW7 4DB
Tel: 020 8959 3756
Principal: Struan Robertson
Age range: 3–11
No. of pupils: 223
Fees: Day £3,645–£7,673.40

Gower House School & Nursery
Blackbird Hill, London NW9 8RR
Tel: 020 8205 2509
Headmaster: Mr M Keane
Age range: 2–11
No. of pupils: 200
Fees: Day £5,010–£5,835

Grimsdell, Mill Hill Pre-Preparatory School
Winterstoke House, Wills Grove, Mill Hill, London NW7 1QR
Tel: 020 8959 6884
Head: Mrs Kate Simon BA, PGCE
Age range: 3–7
No. of pupils: 182
Fees: Day £1,971–£4,285

Hampstead Hill Pre-Prep & Nursery School
St Stephen's Hall, Pond Street, Hampstead, London NW3 2PP
Tel: 020 7435 6262
Principal: Mrs Andrea Taylor
Age range: B2–7+ G2–7+
Fees: Day £11,000–£14,000

Heathside Preparatory School
16 New End, Hampstead, London NW3 1JA
Tel: +44 (0)20 7794 5857
Headteacher: Ms Melissa Remus Elliot MSc
Age range: 2–13
No. of pupils: 370
Fees: Day £9,300–£14,250

Hendon Preparatory School
20 Tenterden Grove, Hendon, London NW4 1TD
Tel: 020 8203 7727
Headmaster: Mr David Baldwin
Age range: 2–13
Fees: Day £7,650–£9,945

Hereward House School
14 Strathray Gardens, London NW3 4NY
Tel: 020 7794 4820
Headmaster: Mr T W Burden
Age range: B4–13
No. of pupils: 170
Fees: Day £13,065–£14,205

International Community School
4 York Terrace East, Regents Park, London NW1 4PT
Tel: +44 20 7935 1206
Head of School: Ms Rose Threlfall
Age range: 3–18
No. of pupils: 260
Fees: Day £16,650–£22,100

L'Ile Aux Enfants
22 Vicar's Road, London NW5 4NL
Tel: 020 7267 7119
Headmistress: Mrs Chailleux
Age range: 3–11
No. of pupils: 192
Fees: Day £3,270

LYNDHURST HOUSE PREP SCHOOL
For further details see p. 59
24 Lyndhurst Gardens, Hampstead, London NW3 5NW
Tel: 020 7435 4936
Email: pmg@ lyndhursthouse.co.uk
Website: www.lyndhursthouse.co.uk
Headmaster: Andrew Reid MA(Oxon)
Age range: B4–13
No. of pupils: 165
Fees: Day £5,515–£6,160

Maple Walk School
62A Crownhill Road, London NW10 4EB
Tel: 020 8963 3890
Headteacher: Sarah Knollys
Age range: 4–11
Fees: Day £6,300

Maria Montessori School - Hampstead
26 Lyndhurst Gardens, Hampstead, London NW3 5NW
Tel: +44 (0)20 7435 3646
Director of School: Mrs L Lawrence
Age range: 2–11
No. of pupils: 60
Fees: Day £5,400

Naima Jewish Preparatory School
21 Andover Place, London NW6 5ED
Tel: 020 7328 2802
Headteacher: Mr Michael Cohen MA, NPQH
Age range: 3–11
Fees: Day £5,997–£7,470

Nancy Reuben Primary School
Finchley Lane, Hendon, London NW4 1DJ
Tel: 020 82025646
Head: D A David
Age range: 3–11
No. of pupils: 207

North Bridge House Junior School
8 Netherhall Gardens,
London NW3 5RR
Tel: 0207 267 6266
Head Teacher: Mrs J Hockley
Age range: 5–6
No. of pupils: 208
Fees: Day £14,700

NORTH BRIDGE HOUSE PREPARATORY SCHOOL
For further details see p. 61
1 Gloucester Avenue,
London NW1 7AB
Tel: 020 7267 6266
Email: admissions@
northbridgehouse.com
Website: www.northbridge
house.com/prep
Head: Brodie Bibby
Age range: 7–13
No. of pupils: 486
Fees: Day £15,585

OYH Primary School
Finchley Lane, Hendon,
London NW4 1DJ
Tel: 020 8202 5646
Headteacher: D A David
Age range: 3–11
No. of pupils: 180

Rainbow Montessori School
13 Woodchurch Road,
Hampstead, London NW6 3PL
Tel: 020 7328 8986
Head Mistress: Maggy
Miller MontDip
Age range: 5–12
Fees: Day £3,250–£3,297

Saint Christina's R C Preparatory School
25 St Edmunds Terrace, Regent's
Park, London NW8 7PY
Tel: 020 7722 8784
Headteacher: Mrs P Mortimer
Age range: B3–7 G3–11
No. of pupils: 224
Fees: Day £11,076

Sarum Hall
15 Eton Avenue, London NW3 3EL
Tel: 020 7794 2261
Headmistress: Mrs Christine Smith
Age range: G3–11
No. of pupils: 170
Fees: Day £6,048–£10,065

South Hampstead High School GDST
3 Maresfield Gardens,
London NW3 5SS
Tel: 020 7435 2899
Headmistress: Mrs J E Stephen BSc
Age range: G4–18
No. of pupils: 852 VIth162
Fees: Day £9,342–£12,006

Southbank International School - Hampstead
16 Netherhall Gardens,
London NW3 5TH
Tel: 020 7243 3803
Principal: Shirley Harwood
Age range: 3–11

St Anthony's School
90 Fitzjohn's Avenue, Hampstead,
London NW3 6NP
Tel: 020 7431 1066
Headmaster: Chris McGovern
Age range: B5–13
No. of pupils: 295
Fees: Day £12,345–£12,690

St Christopher's School
32 Belsize Lane, Hampstead,
London NW3 5AE
Tel: 020 7435 1521
Head: Mrs S A West
BA(Hons), PGCE, MA
Age range: G4–11
No. of pupils: 235
Fees: Day £12,450

St Johns Wood Pre-Preparatory School
St Johns Hall, Lords
Roundabout, Prince Albert
Road, London NW8 7NE
Tel: 020 7722 7149
Headmistress: Ms D Louskas
Age range: 3–7
No. of pupils: 70
Fees: Day £7,620–£12,090

St Margaret's School
18 Kidderpore Gardens,
Hampstead, London NW3 7SR
Tel: 020 7435 2439
Principal: Mr M Webster BSc, PGCE
Age range: G4–16
No. of pupils: 156
Fees: Day £10,410–£12,060

St Martin's School
22 Goodwyn Avenue, Mill
Hill, London NW7 3RG
Tel: 020 8959 1965
Head: Mrs Angela Wilson DipEd
Age range: 3–11
No. of pupils: 125
Fees: Day £6,500

St Mary's School Hampstead
47 Fitzjohn's Avenue, Hampstead,
London NW3 6PG
Tel: 020 7435 1868
Head Teacher: Miss Angela
Rawlinson BA, MA(1st Class
Honours), DipTchng, NPQH
Age range: B2 years 9 months–7
years G2 years 9 months–11 years
No. of pupils: 300
Fees: Day £6,975–£12,915

St Nicholas School
22 Salmon Street, London NW9 8PN
Tel: 020 8205 7153
Headmistress: Mrs Alyce
Gregory CertEd
Age range: 5–11
No. of pupils: 80
Fees: Day £5,760

Swaminarayan School
260 Brentfield Road, Neasden,
London NW10 8HE
Tel: 020 8965 8381
Headteacher: Nilesh Manani
Age range: 2–18
No. of pupils: 452 VIth36
Fees: Day £7,818–£10,707

Talmud Torah Torat Emet
27 Green Lane, London NW4 2NL
Tel: 020 8201 7770
Headteacher: Rabbi M Nissim
Age range: B5–9

The Academy School
3 Pilgrims Place, Rosslyn Hill,
Hampstead, London NW3 1NG
Tel: 020 7435 6621
Headteacher: Mr Garth Evans
Age range: 6–14

The American School in London
One Waverley Place,
London NW8 0NP
Tel: 020 7449 1221
Head: Mrs Coreen Hester
Age range: 4–18
No. of pupils: 1350
Fees: Day £21,950–£25,650

The Cavendish School
31 Inverness Street, Camden
Town, London NW1 7HB
Tel: 020 7485 1958
Headmistress: Mrs T Dunbar
BSc(Hons), PGCE, NPQH
Age range: G3–11
No. of pupils: 218
Fees: Day £11,550

The Hall School
23 Crossfield Road, Hampstead,
London NW3 4NU
Tel: 020 7722 1700
Headmaster: P Lough MA
Age range: B4–13
No. of pupils: 440
Fees: Day £9,300–£11,400

The King Alfred School
Manor Wood, North End
Road, London NW11 7HY
Tel: 020 8457 5200
Head: Mrs Dawn Moore
MA(London)
Age range: 4–18
No. of pupils: 615 VIth70
Fees: Day £12,624–£15,219

The Mulberry House School
7 Minster Road, West
Hampstead, London NW2 3SD
Tel: 020 8452 7340
Headteacher: Ms Julie Kirwan
Age range: 2–8
No. of pupils: 184
Fees: Day £8,460–£15,698

The Phoenix School
36 College Crescent,
London NW3 5LF
Tel: 020 7722 4433
Headmistress: Mrs Lisa
Mason-Jones
Age range: 3–7
No. of pupils: 130
Fees: Day £2,585–£3,795

The School of the Islamic Republic of Iran
100 Carlton Vale, London NW6 5HE
Tel: 020 7372 8051
Headteacher: Mr Farzad Farzan
Age range: 6–16
No. of pupils: 53

The Village School
2 Parkhill Road, Belsize
Park, London NW3 2YN
Tel: 020 7485 4673
Headmistress: Miss C E F
Gay BSc(Hons), PGCE
Age range: G3–11
No. of pupils: 100
Fees: Day £14,490

Torah Vodaas
Julian Headon House,
West Hendon Broadway,
London NW9 7AL
Tel: 02036704670
Head of School: Mr Mark Shelton
Age range: B2–11

Trevor-Roberts School
55-57 Eton Avenue,
London NW3 3ET
Tel: 020 7586 1444
Headmaster: Simon
Trevor-Roberts BA
Age range: 5–13
Fees: Day £12,270–£14,070

University College School (Junior)
11 Holly Hill, London NW3 6QN
Tel: 020 7435 3068
Headmaster: Mr Lewis Hayward
MA (Oxon Lit. Hum), MA (OU,
ED. Management), PGCE
Age range: B7–11
No. of pupils: 250
Fees: Day £5,105

South-East London

Alleyn's School
Townley Road, Dulwich,
London SE22 8SU
Tel: 020 8557 1500
Headmaster: Dr G Savage
MA, PhD, FRSA
Age range: 4–18
No. of pupils: 1223 VIth291
Fees: Day £14,139–£16,587
Ⓐ Ⓔ 🖉

Blackheath High School GDST
Vanbrugh Park, Blackheath,
London SE3 7AG
Tel: 020 8853 2929
Head: Mrs Carol Chandler-Thompson BA (Hons)
Exeter, PGCE Exeter
Age range: G3–18
No. of pupils: 780
🖐 Ⓐ Ⓔ 🖉

Blackheath Nursery & Preparatory School
4 St Germans Place,
Blackheath, London SE3 0NJ
Tel: 020 8858 0692
Headmistress: Mrs P J Thompson
Age range: 3–11
Fees: Day £5,670–£10,305
Ⓔ 🖉

Colfe's Preparatory School
Horn Park Lane, Lee,
London SE12 8AW
Tel: 020 8463 8240
Head: Mrs Sarah Marsh
Age range: 3–11
No. of pupils: 355
Fees: Day £8,730–£10,134
🖉

Dulwich College
London SE21 7LD
Tel: 020 8693 3601
Master: Dr J A F Spence
Age range: B7–18
No. of pupils: 1589 VIth470
Fees: Day £18,231 WB
£35,679 FB £38,052
🖐 🌐 Ⓐ 🏫 Ⓔ 🖉

Dulwich College Kindergarten & Infants School
Eller Bank, 87 College
Road, London SE21 7HH
Tel: 020 8693 1538
Head: Mrs H M Friell
Age range: 3 months–7 years
No. of pupils: 251

Dulwich College Preparatory School
42 Alleyn Park, Dulwich,
London SE21 7AA
Tel: 020 8766 5500
Headmaster: Mr M W
Roulston MBE, MEd
Age range: B3–13 G3–5
No. of pupils: 817
Fees: Day £4,350–£13,542
WB £18,213–£19,662
🖐 🏫 Ⓔ 🖉

Eltham College
Grove Park Road, Mottingham,
London SE9 4QF
Tel: 020 8857 1455
Headmaster: Mr P J
Henderson BA, FRSA
Age range: B7–18 G16–18
No. of pupils: 830 VIth220
Fees: Day £10,800–£12,525
🖐 Ⓐ Ⓔ 🖉

Eltham College Junior School
Grove Park Road, London SE9 4QF
Tel: 020 8857 1455
Headmaster: Keith John BSc, PGCE
Age range: B7–11
No. of pupils: 213
Fees: Day £10,320
🖐

Greenwich Steiner School
Woodlands, 90 Mycenae Road,
Blackheath, London SE3 7SE
Tel: 020 8858 4404
Age range: 3–14
No. of pupils: 180
Fees: Day £5,310–£8,004

Heath House Preparatory School
37 Wemyss Road, Blackheath,
London SE3 0TG
Tel: 020 8297 1900
Head Teacher: Mrs Sophia
Laslett CertEd PGDE
Age range: 3–11
No. of pupils: 120
Fees: Day £9,585–£13,185
Ⓔ

HERNE HILL SCHOOL
For further details see p. 56
The Old Vicarage, 127 Herne
Hill, London SE24 9LY
Tel: 020 7274 6336
Email: enquiries@
hernehillschool.co.uk
Website:
www.hernehillschool.co.uk
Headteacher: Mrs Ngaire Telford
Age range: 2+ to–7
No. of pupils: 275
Fees: Day £1,790–£4,435

James Allen's Girls' School
East Dulwich Grove, Dulwich,
London SE22 8TE
Tel: 020 8693 1181
Headmistress: Mrs Marion Gibbs
BA(Hons), PGCE, MLitt, FRSA
Age range: G4–18
No. of pupils: VIth200
Fees: Day £12,540–£14,103
🖐 Ⓐ Ⓔ

Kings Kids Christian School
New Testament Church of
God, Bawtree Road, New
Cross, London SE14 6ET
Tel: 020 8691 5813
Headteacher: Mrs M Okenwa
Age range: 5–11
No. of pupils: 36

London Christian School
40 Tabard Street, London SE1 4JU
Tel: 020 3130 6430
Headmistress: Miss Georgina Hale
Age range: 3–11
No. of pupils: 105
Fees: Day £7,725

Oakfield Preparatory School
125-128 Thurlow Park Road, West
Dulwich, London SE21 8HP
Tel: 020 8670 4206
Head of School: Ms. Jane Stevens
Age range: 2–11 years
No. of pupils: 420
Fees: Day £9,750

Octavia House School, Vauxhall
Vauxhall Primary School, Vauxhall
Street, London SE11 5LG
Tel: 02036 514396
Executive Head: Mr James Waite
Age range: 5–14
No. of pupils: 65

Octavia House School, Walworth
Larcom House, Larcom
Street, London SE17 1RT
Tel: 02036 514396
Head of School: Mr James Waite

Riverston School
63-69 Eltham Road, Lee
Green, London SE12 8UF
Tel: 020 8318 4327
Headmistress: Mrs S E Salathiel
Age range: 9 months–19 years
No. of pupils: 215
Ⓔ 🖉

Rosemead Preparatory School, Dulwich
70 Thurlow Park Road,
London SE21 8HZ
Tel: 020 8670 5865
Headmaster: Arthur Bray CertEd
Age range: 3–11
No. of pupils: 351
Fees: Day £10,272–£10,854
Ⓔ 🖉

Springfield Christian School
145 Perry Hill, Catford,
London SE6 4LP
Tel: 020 8291 4433
Principal: Mr B Oludimu BSc
Age range: 2–11
No. of pupils: 85
Fees: Day £2,550–£4,710
🖉

St Dunstan's College
Stanstead Road, London SE6 4TY
Tel: 020 8516 7200
Headmistress: Mrs J D Davies BSc
Age range: 3–18
No. of pupils: 870
🌐 Ⓐ Ⓔ IB

St Olave's Preparatory School
106 Southwood Road, New
Eltham, London SE9 3QS
Tel: 020 8294 8930
Head: Mr J Tilly
Age range: 3–11
No. of pupils: 220
Fees: Day £5,414–£8,700
🖉

Sydenham High School GDST
19 Westwood Hill, London SE26 6BL
Tel: 020 8557 7000
Headteacher: Kathryn Pullen MA
Age range: G4–18
No. of pupils: 630 VIth70
Fees: Day £11,466–£14,592
🖐 Ⓐ Ⓔ 🖉

The Pointer School
19 Stratheden Road,
Blackheath, London SE3 7TH
Tel: 020 8293 1331
Headmaster: Mr R J S Higgins
MA, BEd, CertEd, FCollP
Age range: 3–11
No. of pupils: 370
Fees: Day £6,912–£13,782
Ⓔ 🖉

The Villa Pre-Preparatory School & Nursery
54 Lyndhurst Grove, Peckham,
London SE15 5AH
Tel: 020 7703 6216
Head Teacher: Suzy Prebble
Age range: 2–7
No. of pupils: 210

Virgo Fidelis Preparatory School
Central Hill, Upper Norwood,
London SE19 1RS
Tel: 020 8653 2169
Head Teacher: Mrs Meg Baines
Age range: 3–11
Fees: Day £2,520–£6,930
Ⓔ 🖉

South-West London

Al-Muntada Islamic School
7 Bridges Place, Parsons Green, London SW6 4HW
Tel: 020 7471 8283
Headteacher: Salma Ullah
Age range: 4–11
No. of pupils: 165
Fees: Day £2,500

Al-Risalah Secondary School
145 Upper Tooting Road, London SW17 7TJ
Tel: 020 8767 6057
Headmaster: Nasir Qurashi
Age range: 3–16
No. of pupils: 250

Beechwood School
55 Leigham Court Road, Streatham, London SW16 2NJ
Tel: 020 8677 8778
Headmistress: Mrs M Marshall
Age range: 0–11
No. of pupils: 100
Fees: Day £6,726–£7,875

Bertrum House School
290 Balham High Road, London SW17 7AL
Tel: 020 8767 4051
Principal: Miss. Kirsty Pirrie
Age range: 2–7
No. of pupils: 94
Fees: Day £1,630–£4,090

Broomwood Hall School
68-74 Nightingale Lane, London SW12 8NR
Tel: 020 8682 8830
Head of School: Mrs Carole Jenkinson
Age range: B4–8 G4–13
No. of pupils: 670
Fees: Day £13,680–£16,815

Cameron House
4 The Vale, Chelsea, London SW3 6AH
Tel: 020 7352 4040
Headmistress: Mrs Lucie Moore BEd(Hons)
Age range: 4–11
No. of pupils: 120
Fees: Day £16,875

Colet Court (St Paul's Preparatory School)
Colet Court, Lonsdale Road, London SW13 9JT
Tel: 020 8748 3461
Headmaster: Mr T A Meunier MA(Cantab)
Age range: B7–13
No. of pupils: 436
Fees: Day £15,729

Dolphin School
106 Northcote Road, London SW11 6QW
Tel: 020 7924 3472
Principal: Mr James Savile BA(Hons), FCollT, FCIEA
Age range: 2–11
No. of pupils: 323
Fees: Day £10,185–£11,085

Donhead
33 Edge Hill, London SW19 4NP
Tel: 020 8946 7000
Headmaster: Mr G C McGrath BA(Hons), PGCE, MBA(Ed)
Age range: B4–11
No. of pupils: 280
Fees: Day £7,800–£8,325

Eaton House Belgravia
3-5 Eaton Gate, London SW1W 9BA
Tel: 020 7924 6000
Headmistress: Mrs Annabel Abbott
Age range: B4–8
Fees: Day £14,670

Eaton House The Manor Girls School
58 Clapham Common Northside, London SW4 9RU
Tel: 020 7924 6000
Head: Mrs Sarah Segrave
Age range: G4–11
Fees: Day £14,244

Eaton House The Manor Pre Prep School
58 Clapham Common Northside, London SW4 9RU
Tel: 020 7924 6000
Head of School: Mr Huw May
Age range: B4–8
No. of pupils: 220
Fees: Day £14,244

Eaton House The Manor Prep School
58 Clapham Common Northside, London SW4 9RU
Tel: 020 7924 6000
Head: Mr Jeremy Edwards
Age range: B8–13
No. of pupils: 165
Fees: Day £17,424

Eaton House The Vale
2 Elvaston Place, London SW7 5QH
Tel: 020 7924 6000
Head: Mr Robin Greenwood
Age range: 3–11
Fees: Day £7,416–£14,670

Eaton Square School
79 Eccleston Square, London SW1V 1PP
Tel: 020 7931 9469
Headmaster: Mr Sebastian Hepher BEd(Hons)
Age range: 2–13
No. of pupils: 529
Fees: Day £4,080–£19,050

Eveline Day & Nursery Schools
14 Trinity Crescent, Upper Tooting, London SW17 7AE
Tel: 020 8672 4673
Headmistress: Ms Eveline Drut
Age range: 3 months–11 years
No. of pupils: 80
Fees: Day £11,059

Falkner House
19 Brechin Place, South Kensington, London SW7 4QB
Tel: 020 7373 4501
Headteacher: Mrs Anita Griggs BA(Hons), PGCE
Age range: B3–4 G3–11
Fees: Day £8,025–£16,050

Finton House School
171 Trinity Road, London SW17 7HL
Tel: 020 8682 0921
Headmaster: Adrian Floyd BSc, PGCE
Age range: 4–11
No. of pupils: 305
Fees: Day £11,880–£12,885

Francis Holland School, Sloane Square, SW1
39 Graham Terrace, London SW1W 8JF
Tel: 020 7730 2971
Head: Mrs Lucy Elphinstone MA(Cantab)
Age range: G4–18
No. of pupils: 500 VIth70
Fees: Day £16,350–£18,450

Garden House School
Boys' School & Girls' School, Turk's Row, London SW3 4TW
Tel: 020 7730 1652
Boys Head: C Warland BA(Hons)
Age range: B3–8 G3–11
No. of pupils: 449
Fees: Day £9,300–£15,885

Glendower School
86/87 Queen's Gate, London SW7 5JX
Tel: 020 7370 1927
Headmistress: Mrs Sarah Knollys BA, PGCE
Age range: G4–11+
No. of pupils: 206
Fees: Day £14,280

Hall School Wimbledon
Beavers Holt, Stroud Crescent, Putney Vale, London SW15 3EQ
Tel: 020 8788 2370
Headmaster: Timothy J Hobbs MA
Age range: 4–16
No. of pupils: 520
Fees: Day £9,999–£13,224

Hill House International Junior School
17 Hans Place, Chelsea, London SW1X 0EP
Tel: 020 7584 1331
Headmaster: Richard Townend FLSM(Chm)
Age range: 4–13
No. of pupils: 980
Fees: Day £10,350–£14,100

Hornsby House School
Hearnville Road, Balham, London SW12 8RS
Tel: 020 8673 7573
Headmaster: Mr Edward Rees
Age range: 4–11
Fees: Day £12,375–£13,305

Hurlingham School
122 Putney Bridge Road, Putney, London SW15 2NQ
Tel: 020 8874 7186
Headteacher: Mr Jonathan Brough
Age range: 4–11
No. of pupils: 320
Fees: Day £14,400–£15,030

Ibstock Place School
Clarence Lane, London SW15 5PY
Tel: 020 8876 9991
Head: Mrs Anna Sylvester-Johnson BA(Hons), PGCE
Age range: 4–18
No. of pupils: 970
Fees: Day £4,755–£6,130

Kensington Prep School GDST
596 Fulham Road, London SW6 5PA
Tel: 0207 731 9300
Head: Mrs P Lynch MA (St Andrews) PGCE
Age range: G4–11
No. of pupils: 289
Fees: Day £11,103

King's College Junior School
Southside, Wimbledon Common, London SW19 4TT
Tel: 020 8255 5335
Headmaster: Dr. G A Silverlock
Age range: B7–13
No. of pupils: 460

Knightsbridge School
67 Pont Street, Knightsbridge, London SW1X 0BD
Tel: 020 7590 5900
Head: Mr Magoo Giles
Age range: 4–13
No. of pupils: 390
Fees: Day £16,224–£17,265

L'Ecole de Battersea
Trott Street, Battersea, London SW11 3DS
Tel: 020 7371 8350
Director: Mrs F Brisset
Age range: 3–11
No. of pupils: 252
Fees: Day £10,550–£10,800

L'Ecole des Petits
2 Hazlebury Road, Fulham, London SW6 2NB
Tel: 020 7371 8350
Director: Mrs F Brisset
Age range: 3–6
No. of pupils: 136
Fees: Day £10,400–£10,700

Lion House School
The Old Methodist Hall, Gwendolen Avenue, London SW15 6EH
Tel: 020 8780 9446
Head: Miss H J Luard MontDip
Age range: 2–7
No. of pupils: 115

Lycee Francais Charles de Gaulle
35 Cromwell Road, London SW7 2DG
Tel: 020 7584 6322
Headteacher: Mr Olivier Rauch
Age range: 3–18
No. of pupils: 4007
Fees: Day £4,521–£10,791

NEWTON PREP
For further details see p. 60
149 Battersea Park Road, London SW8 4BX
Tel: 020 7720 4091
Email: admin@newtonprep.co.uk
Website: www.newtonprepschool.co.uk
Headmistress: Mrs Alison Fleming BA, MA Ed, PGCE
Age range: 3–13
No. of pupils: 640
Fees: Day £8,310–£17,625

Northcote Lodge School
26 Bolingbroke Grove, London SW11 6EL
Tel: 020 8682 8888
Head of School: Mr Mark Smith
Age range: B8–13
No. of pupils: 220
Fees: Day £16,815

Oliver House Preparatory School
7 Nightingale Lane, London SW4 9AH
Tel: 020 8772 1911
Headteacher: Ms Maureen Fields
Age range: 2–13
No. of pupils: 144
Fees: Day £4,200–£9,300

Parkgate House School
80 Clapham Common North Side, London SW4 9SD
Tel: +44 (0)20 7350 2461
Principal: Miss Catherine Shanley
Age range: 2.5–11 years
No. of pupils: 245
Fees: Day £5,355–£14,010

Parsons Green Prep School
1 Fulham Park Road, Fulham, London SW6 4LJ
Tel: 020 7371 9009
Headteacher: Ms. Helen Stavert
Age range: 3–11
No. of pupils: 180
Fees: Day £3,962–£4,212

PROSPECT HOUSE SCHOOL
For further details see p. 63
75 Putney Hill, London SW15 3NT
Tel: 020 8780 0456 Registrar: 020 8246 4897
Email: registrar@prospecths.org.uk
Website: www.prospecths.org.uk
Headmistress: Mrs Dianne Barratt MEd (Newcastle-upon-Tyne)
Age range: 3–11
No. of pupils: 300
Fees: Day £7,890–£16,440

Putney High School GDST
35 Putney Hill, London SW15 6BH
Tel: 020 8788 4886
Headmistress: Dr Denise Lodge BSc, MSc, PhD
Age range: G4–18
No. of pupils: VIth150

QUEEN'S GATE SCHOOL
For further details see p. 64
133 Queen's Gate, London SW7 5LE
Tel: 020 7589 3587
Email: registrar@queensgate.org.uk
Website: www.queensgate.org.uk
Principal: Mrs R M Kamaryc BA, MSc, PGCE
Age range: G4–18
No. of pupils: 523 VIth90

Ravenstone Preparatory School
24 Elvaston Place, South Kensington, London SW7 5NL
Tel: 020 7225 3131
Head of School: Dr Ronald Pritchard
Age range: 2–11
No. of pupils: 110
Fees: Day £11,280–£16,875

Redcliffe School Trust Ltd
47 Redcliffe Gardens, Chelsea, London SW10 9JH
Tel: 020 7352 9247
Head: Mrs Susan Bourne BSc, PGCE
Age range: B3–8 G3–11
Fees: Day £13,920

Sinclair House Montessori Nursery
159 & 196 Munster Road, Fulham, London SW6 6AU
Tel: 0207 736 9182
Principal: Mrs Carlotta T M O'Sullivan

Sinclair House Preparatory School
59 Fulham High Street, Fulham, London SW6 3JJ
Tel: 0207 736 9182
Principal: Mrs Carlotta T M O'Sullivan
Age range: 2–13
No. of pupils: 120
Fees: Day £10,950

St Nicholas Preparatory School
23 Princes Gate, Kensington, London SW7 1PT
Tel: 020 7225 1277
Headmaster: Mr Tony Lewis
Age range: 3–11
No. of pupils: 280
Fees: Day £11,475–£13,110

St Philip's School
6 Wetherby Place, London SW7 4NE
Tel: 020 7373 3944
Headmaster: H J Biggs-Davison MA(Cantab)
Age range: B7–13
No. of pupils: 110
Fees: Day £12,750

Streatham & Clapham High School GDST
42 Abbotswood Road, London SW16 1AW
Tel: 020 8677 8400
Headmaster: Dr Millan Sachania
Age range: B3–5 G3–18
No. of pupils: 603 VIth70
Fees: Day £5,886–£9,810

Sussex House School
68 Cadogan Square, Knightsbridge, London SW1X 0EA
Tel: 020 7584 1741
Headmaster: Mr N P Kaye MA(Cantab), ACP, FRSA
Age range: B8–13
No. of pupils: 182
Fees: Day £16,200

Swedish School
82 Lonsdale Road, London SW13 9JS
Tel: 020 8741 1751
Head of School: Ms. Annika Simonsson Bergqvist
Age range: 3–18
No. of pupils: 242
Fees: Day £6,600

THE HAMPSHIRE SCHOOL, CHELSEA
For further details see p. 66
15 Manresa Road, Chelsea, London SW3 6NB
Tel: 020 7352 7077
Email: o.baskett@thehampshireschoolchelsea.co.uk
Website: www.thehampshireschoolchelsea.co.uk
Principal: Mr Dónal Brennan
Age range: 3–13
No. of pupils: 307
Fees: Day £14,925–£16,440

The Harrodian School
Lonsdale Road, London SW13 9QN
Tel: 020 8748 6117
Headmaster: James R Hooke
Age range: 5–18
No. of pupils: 890 VIth95
Fees: Day £10,407–£15,219

The Merlin School
4 Carlton Drive, Putney Hill, London SW15 2BZ
Tel: 020 8788 2769
Principal: Mrs Kate Prest
Age range: 4–8
No. of pupils: 170

The Montessori Pavilion - The Kindergarten School
Vine Road, Barnes, London SW13 0NE
Tel: 020 8878 9695
Age range: 3–8
No. of pupils: 50
Fees: Day £1,950–£3,600

The Norwegian School
28 Arterberry Road, Wimbledon, London SW20 8AH
Tel: 020 8947 6617
Head: Mr Geir Johansen
Age range: 3–16

The Roche School
11 Frogmore, London SW18 1HW
Tel: 020 8877 0823
Headmistress: Mrs V Adams BA(Hons), PGCE, MA
Age range: 2–11 years
No. of pupils: 239
Fees: Day £10,320–£11,130

The Rowans School
19 Drax Avenue, Wimbledon, London SW20 0EG
Tel: 020 8946 8220
Head Teacher: Mrs S Wingrove
Age range: 3–8
Fees: Day £5,460–£10,725

The Study Preparatory School
Wilberforce House, Camp Road, Wimbledon Common, London SW19 4UN
Tel: 020 8947 6969
Headmistress: Mrs Susan Pepper MA Oxon, PGCE
Age range: G4–11
No. of pupils: 315

The Waldorf School of South West London
PO Box 8541, London SW16 1ZB
Tel: 0208 772 3504
Age range: 3–14
No. of pupils: 80
Fees: Day £4,515–£6,217

The White House Preparatory School & Woodentops Kindergarten
24 Thornton Road, London SW12 0LF
Tel: 020 8674 9514
Principal: Ms Mary McCahery
Age range: 2–11
Fees: Day £9,800–£12,300

Thomas's Preparatory School - Battersea
28-40 Battersea High Street,
London SW11 3JB
Tel: 020 7978 0900
Head: Ben V R Thomas MA
Age range: 4–13
No. of pupils: 538
Fees: Day £11,085–£16,245

Thomas's Preparatory School - Clapham
Broomwood Road,
London SW11 6JZ
Tel: 020 7326 9300
Headmaster: Mr Philip
Ward BEd(Hons)
Age range: 4–13
Fees: Day £10,365–£11,730

Thomas's Preparatory School - Fulham
Hugon Road, London SW6 3ES
Tel: 020 7751 8200
Head: Miss Annette Dobson
BEd(Hons), PGCertDys
Age range: 4–11

Tower House School
188 Sheen Lane, London SW14 8LF
Tel: 020 8876 3323
Head: Mr Gregory Evans
Age range: B4–13
No. of pupils: 180
Fees: Day £11,073–£12,558

Ursuline Preparatory School
18 The Downs, London SW20 8HR
Tel: 020 8947 0859
Headmistress: Mrs Anne Farnish
BA (Hons) MA, NPQH, PGCE
Age range: B3–4 G3–11
Fees: Day £5,607–£9,183

Wandsworth Preparatory School
The Old Library, 2 Allfarthing
Lane, London SW18 2PQ
Tel: 0208 870 4133

Westminster Abbey Choir School
Dean's Yard, London SW1P 3NY
Tel: 0207 654 4918
Headmaster: Jonathan Milton BEd
Age range: B8–13
No. of pupils: 35
Fees: FB £7,404

Westminster Cathedral Choir School
Ambrosden Avenue,
London SW1P 1QH
Tel: 020 7798 9081
Headmaster: Mr Neil McLaughlan
Age range: B8–13
No. of pupils: 150
Fees: Day £13,656 FB £6,945

Westminster Under School
Adrian House, 27 Vincent
Square, London SW1P 2NN
Tel: 020 7821 5788
Headteacher: Mrs E A Hill MA
Age range: B7–13
No. of pupils: 265
Fees: Day £14,676

Willington School
Worcester Road, Wimbledon,
London SW19 7QQ
Tel: 020 8944 7020
Head: Mr Michael Chanter
Age range: B4–13
No. of pupils: 250
Fees: Day £9,345–£11,385

Wimbledon Common Preparatory
113 Ridgway, Wimbledon,
London SW19 4TA
Tel: 020 8946 1001
Head Teacher: Mrs Tracey Buck
Age range: B4–8
No. of pupils: 160
Fees: Day £10,725

Wimbledon High School GDST
Mansel Road, Wimbledon,
London SW19 4AB
Tel: 020 8971 0900
Headmistress: Mrs H Hanbury
Age range: G4–18
No. of pupils: 900 VIth155
Fees: Day £11,445–£15,024

West London

Avenue House School
70 The Avenue, Ealing,
London W13 8LS
Tel: 020 8998 9981
Headteacher: Mr Sheppard
Age range: 3–11
No. of pupils: 135
Fees: Day £5,070–£8,670

Barbara Speake Stage School
East Acton Lane, East
Acton, London W3 7EG
Tel: 020 8743 1306
Principal: Miss B M Speake
MBE, ARAD, MISTD, MIDTA
Age range: 3–16
Fees: Day £6,000–£6,300

Bute House Preparatory School for Girls
Bute House, Luxemburg
Gardens, London W6 7EA
Tel: 020 7603 7381
Head: Mrs Helen Lowe
Age range: G4–11
No. of pupils: 306
Fees: Day £13,317

Chepstow House School
19 Pembridge Villas,
London W11 3EP
Tel: 0207 243 0243
Headteacher: Angela Barr
Age range: 4–7

Chiswick & Bedford Park Prep School
Priory House, Priory Avenue,
London W4 1TX
Tel: 020 8994 1804
Headmistress: Mrs C A Sunderland
Age range: B4–7+ G4–11
No. of pupils: 180
Fees: Day £8,850

Clifton Lodge
8 Mattock Lane, Ealing,
London W5 5BG
Tel: 020 8579 3662
Head: Mr. Floyd Steadman
Age range: 3–13
No. of pupils: 145
Fees: Day £11,055–£11,940

Connaught House School
47 Connaught Square,
London W2 2HL
Tel: 020 7262 8830
Principals: Mrs J A Hampton
& Mr F Hampton MA, RCA
Age range: B4–8 G4–11
No. of pupils: 75
Fees: Day £13,200–£14,700

Durston House
12-14 Castlebar Road,
Ealing, London W5 2DR
Tel: 020 8991 6530
Headmaster: Mr Ian
Kendrick MA, BEd(Hons)
Age range: B4–13
No. of pupils: 415
Fees: Day £9,810–£12,570

Ecole Francaise Jacques Prevert
59 Brook Green, London W6 7BE
Tel: 020 7602 6871
Principal: P Possenti
Age range: 4–11

Fulham Prep School
200 Greyhound Road,
London W14 9SD
Tel: 020 7386 2448
Principal: Mrs J Emmett
Age range: 4–13
No. of pupils: 596
Fees: Day £14,400–£15,975

Great Beginnings Montessori School
The Welsh Church Hall, 82a
Chiltern Street, Marylebone,
London W1H 5JE
Tel: 020 7486 2276
Age range: 2–6
Fees: Day £1,095–£1,650

Greek Primary School of London
3 Pierrepoint Road, Acton,
London W3 9JR
Tel: 020 8992 6156
Age range: 1–11

Harvington School
20 Castlebar Road, Ealing,
London W5 2DS
Tel: 020 8997 1583
Headmistress: Mrs Anna Evans
Age range: B3–4 G3–16
No. of pupils: 210
Fees: Day £7,560–£9,840

Heathfield House School
Turnham Green Church
Hall, Heathfield Gardens,
Chiswick, London W4 4JU
Tel: 020 8994 3385
Headteacher: Mrs Goodsman
Age range: 4–11
Fees: Day £6,300–£6,900

Holland Park Pre Prep School and Day Nursery
5 & 9 Holland Road, Kensington,
London W14 8HJ
Tel: 020 7602 9066/020
7602 9266
Principal: Mrs Kitty Mason
Age range: 3 months–8 years
No. of pupils: 128
Fees: Day £4,650–£10,935

House Schools Group
42 Hartington Road, London W4 3TX
Tel: 020 8580 9626

Instituto Espanol Canada Blanch
317a Portobello Road,
Kensington, London W10 5SZ
Tel: +44 (0) 20 8969 2664
Principal: Mr A Vitria
Age range: 4–19
No. of pupils: 405

International School of London (ISL) London
139 Gunnersbury Avenue,
Ealing, London W3 8LG
Tel: +44 (0)20 8992 5823
**Middle & Lower School
Principal:** Andrew Mitchell
Age range: 3–18 years
No. of pupils: 480
Fees: Day £18,000–£24,600

King Fahad Academy
Bromyard Avenue, Acton,
London W3 7HD
Tel: 020 8743 0131
**Acting Head of Primary
School:** Ms Julie Benafif
Age range: 3–18
No. of pupils: 446
Fees: Day £3,000

La Petite Ecole Francais
73 Saint Charles Square,
London W10 6EJ
Tel: +44 208 960 1278
Principal: Ms A Stones
Age range: 2–6

Latymer Prep School
36 Upper Mall, Hammersmith,
London W6 9TA
Tel: 0845 638 5700
Principal: Mr Stuart Dorrian
BA(Hons), PGCE
Age range: 7–11
No. of pupils: 159
Fees: Day £14,490

Le Herisson
River Court Methodist
Church, Rover Court Road,
Hammersmith, London W6 9JT
Tel: 020 8563 7664
Head Teacher: C Behroozi
Age range: 2–6
Fees: Day £8,730–£8,970

L'Ecole Bilingue
St David's Welsh Church, St
Mary's Terrace, London W2 1SJ
Tel: 020 7224 8427
Headteacher: Ms
Veronique Ferreira
Age range: 3–11
No. of pupils: 68
Fees: Day £6,000–£6,600

Norland Place School
162-166 Holland Park Avenue,
London W11 4UH
Tel: 020 7603 9103
Headmaster: Mr Patrick Mattar MA
Age range: B4–8 years G4–11 years
Fees: Day £13,590–£16,389

Notting Hill & Ealing High School GDST
2 Cleveland Road, West
Ealing, London W13 8AX
Tel: 020 8991 2165
Headmistress: Ms Lucinda Hunt
Age range: G4–18
No. of pupils: 870 VIth130
Fees: Day £9,387–£12,063

Notting Hill Preparatory School
95 Lancaster Road,
London W11 1QQ
Tel: 020 7221 0727
Headmistress: Mrs Jane Cameron
Age range: 4–13
No. of pupils: 285
Fees: Day £4,890

One World Montessori Nursery & Pre-Prep
69-71 Brock Green, Hammersmith,
London W6 7BE
Tel: 020 7603 6065
Headteacher: Ms N Greer
Age range: 2–8
No. of pupils: 21

One World Preparatory School
10 Stanley Gardens,
Acton, London W3 7SZ
Tel: 020 87433300
Head: Ms Lisa Manser
Age range: 3–11
No. of pupils: 52
Fees: Day £3,000

ORCHARD HOUSE SCHOOL
For further details see p. 62
16 Newton Grove, Bedford
Park, London W4 1LB
Tel: 020 8742 8544 Registrar:
020 8987 9886
Email: registrar@
orchardhs.org.uk
Website: www.orchardhs.org.uk
Headmistress: Mrs M V Edwards
BEd (Bedford), CertEd (Man)
Age range: 3–11
No. of pupils: 290
Fees: Day £7,890–£16,440

Pembridge Hall
18 Pembridge Square,
London W2 4EH
Tel: 020 7229 0121
Headteacher: Mr Henry
Keighley-Elstub
Age range: G4–11
No. of pupils: 413

Ravenscourt Park Preparatory School
16 Ravenscourt Avenue,
London W6 0SL
Tel: 020 8846 9153
Headmaster: Mr Carl Howes
Age range: 4–11
No. of pupils: 340
Fees: Day £15,606

Ravenstone Pre-Preparatory School
The Long Garden, St
George's Fields, Albion
Street, London W2 2AX
Tel: 020 7262 1190
Head of School: Mrs Karen Dapson
Age range: 2–7
No. of pupils: 74
Fees: Day £11,280–£16,875

Southbank International School - Kensington
36-38 Kensington Park
Road, London W11 3BU
Tel: 020 7243 3803
Principal: Siobhan McGrath
Age range: 3–11

St Augustine's Priory
Hillcrest Road, Ealing,
London W5 2JL
Tel: 020 8997 2022
Headteacher: Mrs.
Sarah Raffray MA
Age range: G3–18
No. of pupils: 470
Fees: Day £3,180–£13,572

St Benedict's Junior School and Nursery
5 Montpelier Avenue,
Ealing, , London W5 2XP
Tel: 020 8862 2254
Headmaster: Mr R G Simmons
Age range: 3–11
No. of pupils: 286
Fees: Day £10,560–£11,760

St James Junior School
Earsby Street, London W14 8SH
Tel: 020 7348 1777
Headmistress: Mrs Catherine
Thomlinson BA(Hons)
Age range: B4–11 G4–10
Fees: Day £10,650

Tabernacle School
32 St Anns Villas, Holland
Park, London W11 4RS
Tel: 020 7602 6232
Headteacher: Mrs P Wilson
Age range: 3–16
Fees: Day £4,500

The Falcons School for Boys
2 Burnaby Gardens,
Chiswick, London W4 3DT
Tel: 020 8747 8393
Headmaster: Mr Gordon Milne
Age range: B3–7
No. of pupils: 225
Fees: Day £3,875–£11,625

The Falcons School for Girls
15 Gunnersbury Avenue,
Ealing, London W5 3XD
Tel: 020 8992 5189
Headteacher: Miss
Joan McGillewie
Age range: G4–11
No. of pupils: 102
Fees: Day £3,625

The Japanese School
87 Creffield Road, Acton,
London W3 9PU
Tel: 020 8993 7145
Headteacher: Mrs Kiyoe Tsuruoka
Age range: 6–16
No. of pupils: 500

The Lloyd Williamson School
12 Telford Road, London W10 5SH
Tel: 020 8962 0345
Co-Principals: Ms Lucy Meyer
& Mr Aaron Williams
Age range: 4 months–14 years
Fees: Day £12,600

Thomas's Preparatory School - Kensington
17-19 Cottesmore Gardens,
London W8 5PR
Tel: 020 7361 6500
Headmistress: Miss Joanna Ebner
MA, BEd(Hons)(Cantab), NPQH
Age range: 4–11
Fees: Day £14,505–£15,795

Wetherby Preparatory School
48 Bryanston Square,
London W1H 2EA
Tel: 020 7535 3520
Headteacher: Mr Nick Baker
Age range: B8–13
No. of pupils: 192
Fees: Day £4,665

Wetherby Pre-Preparatory School
11 Pembridge Square,
London W2 4ED
Tel: 020 7727 9581
Headmaster: Mr Mark Snell
Age range: B2 1/2–8
No. of pupils: 340
Fees: Day £19,620

Ysgol Gymraeg Llundain London Welsh School
Hanwell Community Centre,
Westcott Crescent, London W7 1PD
Tel: 020 8575 0237
Head Teacher: Mrs Julie Griffiths
Age range: 3–11
No. of pupils: 30
Fees: Day £1,950

North-East

KEY TO SYMBOLS

(♀) *Boys' school*
(♀) *Girls' school*
(🌐) *International school*
(16) *Tutorial or sixth form college*
(A) *A levels*
(♨) *Boarding accommodation*
(£) *Bursaries*
(IB) *International Baccalaureate*
(✎) *Learning support*
(16) *Entrance at 16+*
(💼) *Vocational qualifications*
(IAPS) *Independent Association of Prep Schools*
(HMC) *The Headmasters' & Headmistresses' Conference*
(ISA) *Independent Schools Association*
(GSA) *Girls' School Association*
(BSA) *Boarding Schools' Association*
(S) *Society of Heads*

Unless otherwise indicated, all schools are coeducational day schools. Single-sex and boarding schools will be indicated by the relevant icon.

Durham

Barnard Castle Preparatory School
Westwick Road, Barnard
Castle, Durham DL12 8UW
Tel: 01833 696032
Headmaster: C F Rycroft
Age range: 4–11
No. of pupils: 180
Fees: Day £7,671 FB £14,832

Bow, Durham School
South Road, Durham DH1 3LS
Tel: 0191 384 8233
Headmaster: R N Baird
BA(Hons), PGCE
Age range: 3–11
No. of pupils: 150
Fees: Day £5,370–£7,938

Diamond Junior School
Grange Road, Darlington,
Durham DL1 5PA
Tel: 01325 463383
Head of School: Mrs A P J Foster
Dept of Ed, TCert(Dunelm)
Age range: 2–11
No. of pupils: 182
Fees: Day £6,150–£8,550 WB
£16,755–£16,755 FB £17,355–£17,355

Durham High School for Girls
Farewell Hall, Durham DH1 3TB
Tel: 0191 384 3226
Headmistress: Mrs Lynne Renwick
Age range: G3–18
No. of pupils: 555 VIth99
Fees: Day £6,270–£9,945

The Chorister School
The College, Durham DH1 3EL
Tel: 0191 384 2935
Headmistress: Mrs Y F S Day
Age range: 3–13 years
No. of pupils: 214
Fees: Day £8,340–£11,235 WB
£17,460 FB £10,170–£19,440

Northumberland

Longridge Towers School
Longridge Towers, Berwick-upon-
Tweed, Northumberland TD15 2XH
Tel: 01289 307584
Headmaster: Mr T M Manning BSc
Age range: 3–18
No. of pupils: VIth46
Fees: Day £7,896–£12,336 WB
£18,153–£19,506 FB £23,811–£25,128

Mowden Hall School
Newton, Stocksfield,
Northumberland NE43 7TP
Tel: 01661 842147
Headmaster: Mr Ben
Beardmore-Gray
Age range: 3–13
Fees: Day £7,920–£13,770 FB £17,790

Stockton-on-Tees

Red House School
36 The Green, Norton,
Stockton-on-Tees TS20 1DX
Tel: 01642 553370
Headmaster: Mr A R W Taylor
BSc, MSc, PGCE, CBiol, MSB
Age range: 3–16
No. of pupils: 415
Fees: Day £6,810–£10,020

Teesside High School
The Avenue, Eaglescliffe,
Stockton-on-Tees TS16 9AT
Tel: 01642 782095
Headmaster: Mr Thomas
Packer BSc, MSc, FInstP
Age range: G3–18
No. of pupils: 390 VIth70

Yarm Preparatory School
Grammar School Lane, Yarm,
Stockton-on-Tees TS15 9ES
Tel: 01642 781447
Headteacher: Mr Bill Sawyer
Age range: 3–11
No. of pupils: 360
Fees: Day £4,308–£8,859

Tyne & Wear

Argyle House School
19/20 Thornhill Park, Tunstall Road,
Sunderland, Tyne & Wear SR2 7LA
Tel: 0191 510 0726
Headmaster: Mr C Johnson
Age range: 3–16
Fees: Day £6,090–£7,260

Dame Allan Junior School
Hunters Road, Spital Tongues,
Newcastle upon Tyne,
Tyne & Wear NE2 4NG
Tel: 0191 275 0608
Head: Mr A J Edge
Age range: 3–11
No. of pupils: 140
Fees: Day £6,345–£8,310

Gateshead Jewish Primary School
18-20 Gladstone Terrace,
Gateshead, Tyne & Wear NE8 4EA
Tel: 0191 477 2154 / 0191 478 5841
Headmasters: A
Hammond & Y Spitzer
Age range: 5–11
No. of pupils: 446
Fees: Day £2,392–£3,016

Newcastle High School for Girls GDST
Eskdale Terrace, Jesmond,
Newcastle upon Tyne,
Tyne & Wear NE2 4DS
Tel: 0191 281 1768
Head: Mrs H J French
MA, MEd, NPQH
Age range: G3–18
No. of pupils: G960 VIth200
Fees: Day £7,695–£12,036

Newcastle Preparatory School
6 Eslington Road, Jesmond,
Newcastle upon Tyne,
Tyne & Wear NE2 4RH
Tel: 0191 281 1769
Head Teacher: Mrs
Margaret Coates
No. of pupils: 273
Fees: Day £7,779–£8,742

Newcastle School for Boys
30 West Avenue, Gosforth,
Newcastle upon Tyne,
Tyne & Wear NE3 4ES
Tel: 0191 255 9300
Headmaster: Mr D J Tickner
Age range: B3–18
No. of pupils: 400
Fees: Day £6,900–£9,270

Royal Grammar School
Eskdale Terrace, Newcastle upon
Tyne, Tyne & Wear NE2 4DX
Tel: 0191 281 5711
Headmaster: Dr Bernard
St J Trafford
Age range: 7–18
No. of pupils: 1275 VIth334
Fees: Day £9,810–£11,643

Sunderland High School
Mowbray Road, Sunderland,
Tyne & Wear SR2 8HY
Tel: 0191 567 4984
Head: Dr Angela J Slater BA, PhD
Age range: 2–18
No. of pupils: VIth75
Fees: Day £5,022–£7,194

Westfield School
Oakfield Road, Gosforth,
Newcastle upon Tyne,
Tyne & Wear NE3 4HS
Tel: 0191 255 3980
Headmistress: Mrs M Farndale
BA(Hons)(Lon), PGCE(Oxon), FRSA
Age range: G3–18
No. of pupils: 315 VIth50
Fees: Day £1,372–£3,688

North-West

KEY TO SYMBOLS

- (♦) *Boys' school*
- (♣) *Girls' school*
- (🌐) *International school*
- (16) *Tutorial or sixth form college*
- (A) *A levels*
- (⚓) *Boarding accommodation*
- (£) *Bursaries*
- (IB) *International Baccalaureate*
- (✎) *Learning support*
- (16) *Entrance at 16+*
- (👥) *Vocational qualifications*
- (IAPS) *Independent Association of Prep Schools*
- (HMC) *The Headmasters' & Headmistresses' Conference*
- (ISA) *Independent Schools Association*
- (GSA) *Girls' School Association*
- (BSA) *Boarding Schools' Association*
- (S) *Society of Heads*

Unless otherwise indicated, all schools are coeducational day schools. Single-sex and boarding schools will be indicated by the relevant icon.

Cheshire

Abbey Gate College
Saighton Grange, Saighton,
Chester, Cheshire CH3 6EN
Tel: 01244 332077
Head: Mrs Tracy Pollard
Age range: 4–18
No. of pupils: 514 VIth92
Fees: Day £7,440–£10,875
(A)(£)(✎)

Abbey Gate Prep School
Clare Avenue, Hoole, Chester,
Cheshire CH2 3HR
Tel: 01244 319649
Headteacher: Mrs Sally
Ann Rhodes-Leader
Age range: 3–11
No. of pupils: 59
Fees: Day £7,125–£7,605
(£)(✎)

Alderley Edge School for Girls
Wilmslow Road, Alderley
Edge, Cheshire SK9 7QE
Tel: 01625 583028
Headmistress: Mrs Susan Goff
Age range: G2–18
No. of pupils: 500 VIth60
Fees: Day £5,070–£9,201
(♫)(A)(£)(IB)(✎)

Beech Hall School
Beech Hall Drive, Tytherington,
Macclesfield, Cheshire SK10 2EG
Tel: 01625 422192
Headmistress: Mrs G Yandell BA
Age range: 6 months–16 years
No. of pupils: 230
Fees: Day £6,285–£8,940
(£)(✎)

Bowdon Preparatory School for Girls
Ashley Road, Altrincham,
Cheshire WA14 2LT
Tel: 0161 928 0678
Headmistress: Mrs J H Tan BA, DipEd
Age range: G3–11
No. of pupils: 200
Fees: Day £4,986
(♫)

Brabyns Preparatory School
34-36 Arkwright Road, Marple,
Stockport, Cheshire SK6 7DB
Tel: 0161 427 2395
Headteacher: Mr Lee Sanders
Age range: 2–11
No. of pupils: 134
Fees: Day £1,313–£1,779
(£)(✎)

Cransley School
Belmont Hall, Great Budworth,
Northwich, Cheshire CW9 6HN
Tel: 01606 891747
Headmistress: Mrs G Gaunt
Age range: B3–11 G3–16
Fees: Day £1,173–£2,673
(£)(✎)

Greater Grace School of Christian Education
Church Lane, Backford,
Chester, Cheshire CH2 4BE
Tel: 01244 851 797
Head Teacher: Mrs A Mulligan
Age range: 5–18
Fees: Day £1,900

Green Meadow Independent Primary School
Robson Way, Lowton, Warrington,
Cheshire WA3 2RD
Tel: 01942 671138
Head: Mrs S Green
Age range: 4–11
Fees: Day £6,390

Pownall Hall School
Carrwood Road, Pownall Park,
Wilmslow, Cheshire SK9 5DW
Tel: 01625 523141
Headmaster: Mr David Goulbourn
Age range: 2–11
Fees: Day £2,475–£5,385
(✎)

Terra Nova School
Jodrell Bank, Holmes Chapel,
Crewe, Cheshire CW4 8BT
Tel: 01477 571251
Headmaster: Mr M Mitchell
Age range: 3–13
No. of pupils: 295
Fees: Day £4,050–£12,990
(♫)(£)(✎)

The Firs School
Newton Lane, Upton, Chester,
Cheshire CH2 2HJ
Tel: 01244 322443
Headmistress: Mrs M Denton CertEd
Age range: 3–11
No. of pupils: 226
Fees: Day £6,720
(✎)

The Grange School
Bradburns Lane, Hartford,
Northwich, Cheshire CW8 1LU
Tel: 01606 74007 or 77447
Headmaster: Mr C P
Jeffery BA, FRSA
Age range: 4–18
No. of pupils: 1185 VIth193
Fees: Day £7,080–£9,480
(A)(£)(✎)

The Hammond School
Mannings Lane, Chester,
Cheshire CH2 4ES
Tel: 01244 305350
Principal: Ms Maggie Evans BA
(Hons) MA, PGCE, NPQH, FRSA
Age range: 4–19
No. of pupils: 265
Fees: Day £10,875–£17,745
FB £18,840–£25,710
(♫)(A)(♫)(£)(✎)

The King's School
Wrexham Road, Chester,
Cheshire CH4 7QL
Tel: 01244 689500
Headmaster: C D Ramsey MA
Age range: 4–18
No. of pupils: 1050 VIth218
Fees: Day £8,100–£12,423
(A)(£)(✎)

The King's School
Cumberland Street, Macclesfield,
Cheshire SK10 1DA
Tel: 01625 260000
Headmaster: Dr Simon Hyde
Age range: 3–18
No. of pupils: 1200 VIth250
Fees: Day £7,740–£10,770
(A)(£)(✎)

The Queen's School
City Walls Road, Chester,
Cheshire CH1 2NN
Tel: 01244 312078
Headmistress: Mrs E S Clark
Age range: G4–18
No. of pupils: 610 VIth100
Fees: Day £7,455–£10,650
(♫)(A)(£)

The Ryleys School
Ryleys Lane, Alderley Edge,
Cheshire SK9 7UY
Tel: 01625 583241
Headteacher: Claire Hamilton
BSc(Hons), PGCE
Age range: 3–13
No. of pupils: 251
Fees: Day £9,261–£10,752
(£)(✎)

Wilmslow Preparatory School
Grove Avenue, Wilmslow,
Cheshire SK9 5EG
Tel: 01625 524246
Headteacher: Mrs Helen Rigby
Age range: 2–11
No. of pupils: 110
Fees: Day £1,375–£9,240
(£)(✎)

Yorston Lodge School
18 St John's Road, Knutsford,
Cheshire WA16 0DP
Tel: 01565 633177
Headmistress: Mrs J
Dallimore BEd(Hons)
Age range: 3–11
Fees: Day £5,160

Cumbria

Austin Friars School
Etterby Scaur, Carlisle,
Cumbria CA3 9PB
Tel: 01228 528042
Headmaster: Mr Christopher
Lumb BSc, MEd
Age range: 3–18
No. of pupils: 507 VIth70
Fees: Day £4,470–£9,210
(A)(£)(✎)

Casterton, Sedbergh Preparatory School
Casterton, Carnforth,
Cumbria LA6 2SG
Tel: 01524 279200
Headmaster: Mr Scott
Carnochan BEd
Age range: 3–13
No. of pupils: 200
(♫)(£)(✎)

Hunter Hall School
Frenchfield, Penrith,
Cumbria CA11 8UA
Tel: 01768 891291
Head Teacher: Mrs Donna Vinsome
Age range: 3–11
No. of pupils: 133
Fees: Day £6,534
(£)(✎)

Lime House School
Holm Hill, Dalston, Carlisle,
Cumbria CA5 7BX
Tel: 01228 710225
Headmaster: Mr N A Rice
BA, CertEd, MA(EdMem)
Age range: 3–18+
No. of pupils: 138 VIth38
Fees: Day £4,500–£10,350
WB £21,000–£24,000 FB
£21,000–£25,500
(♫)(A)(♫)(£)(✎)

Windermere Preparatory School
Ambleside Road, Windermere,
Cumbria LA23 1AP
Tel: 015394 43308
Head: Mr Ben Freeman
BEd(Hons), PG Dip
Age range: 2–11
No. of pupils: 120
Fees: Day £6,459–£13,617 WB
£20,271–£23,166 FB £21,414–£24,378
(♫)(£)(✎)

Greater Manchester

Abbotsford Preparatory School
211 Flixton Road, Urmston, Manchester, Greater Manchester M41 5PR
Tel: 0161 748 3261
Head Teacher: Mrs Pamela Shiels
Age range: 3–11
No. of pupils: 106
Fees: Day £5,065–£5,469

Altrincham Preparatory School
Marlborough Road, Bowdon, Altrincham, Greater Manchester WA14 2RR
Tel: 0161 928 3366
Headmaster: Mr Andrew C Potts
Age range: B3–11
No. of pupils: 310
Fees: Day £6,180–£6,840

Beech House School
184 Manchester Road, Rochdale, Greater Manchester OL11 4JQ
Tel: 01706 646309
Headmaster: K Sartain BSc(Hons), PGCE, DipSp, CBiol, FIBiol
Age range: 2–16
Fees: Day £3,945–£4,938

Beis Rochel School
1-7 Seymour Road, Crumpsall, Manchester, Greater Manchester M8 5BQ
Tel: 0161 795 1830
Headmistress: Mrs E Krausz
Age range: G3–16
No. of pupils: 200

Bnos Yisroel School
Foigel Esther Shine House, Leicester Road, Manchester, Greater Manchester M7 4DA
Tel: 0161 792 3896
Headmaster: Rabbi R Spitzer
Age range: G2–16
No. of pupils: 489

Bolton School (Boys' Division)
Chorley New Road, Bolton, Greater Manchester BL1 4PA
Tel: 01204 840201
Headmaster: Philip J Britton MBE
Age range: B7–18
No. of pupils: VIth210
Fees: Day £9,024–£11,280

Bolton School (Girls' Division)
Chorley New Road, Bolton, Greater Manchester BL1 4PB
Tel: 01204 840201
Headmistress: Miss Sue Hincks MA(Oxon)
Age range: B0–7 G0–18
No. of pupils: VIth210
Fees: Day £9,024–£11,280

Branwood Preparatory School
Stafford Road, Monton, Eccles, Manchester, Greater Manchester M30 9HN
Tel: 0161 789 1054
Head: Mrs C Follett NPQSL, MA, BEd(Hons), Dip
Age range: 3–11
No. of pupils: 156
Fees: Day £5,925

Bridgewater School
Drywood Hall, Worsley Road, Worsley, Manchester, Greater Manchester M28 2WQ
Tel: 0161 794 1463
Head Teacher: Mrs J A T Nairn CertEd(Distinction)
Age range: 3–18
No. of pupils: 467
Fees: Day £6,750–£9,000

Bury Catholic Preparatory School
Arden House, Manchester Road, Bury, Greater Manchester BL9 9BH
Tel: 0161 764 2346
Headteacher: Mrs A C Dean
Age range: 3–11
Fees: Day £4,500

Bury Grammar School Boys
Tenterden Street, Bury, Greater Manchester BL9 0HN
Tel: 0161 797 2700
Headmaster: Mr R N Marshall MSc
Age range: B7–18
No. of pupils: 602 VIth92
Fees: Day £6,750–£9,084

Bury Grammar School for Girls
Bridge Road, Bury, Greater Manchester BL9 0HH
Tel: 0161 797 2808
Headmistress: Mrs R S Georghiou
Age range: B4–7 G4–18
No. of pupils: VIth120
Fees: Day £6,750–£9,084

Cheadle Hulme School
Claremont Road, Cheadle Hulme, Cheadle, Greater Manchester SK8 6EF
Tel: 0161 488 3330
Head: Miss Lucy Pearson
Age range: 4–18
No. of pupils: 1416 VIth277
Fees: Day £7,695–£10,656

Chetham's School of Music
Long Millgate, Manchester, Greater Manchester M3 1SB
Tel: 0161 834 9644
Head of School: Mr Alun Jones
Age range: 8–18
No. of pupils: 298
Fees: Day £25,573 FB £31,713

Clarendon Cottage School
Ivy Bank House, Half Edge Lane, Eccles, Manchester, Greater Manchester M30 9BJ
Tel: 0161 950 7868
Headteacher: Mrs E L Howard
Age range: 3–11
No. of pupils: 81
Fees: Day £3,210–£3,840

Clevelands Preparatory School
425 Chorley New Road, Bolton, Greater Manchester BL1 5DH
Tel: 01204 843898
Headteacher: Mrs Lesley Parlane
Age range: 2–11
No. of pupils: 141
Fees: Day £6,240

Covenant Christian School
The Hawthorns, 48 Heaton Moor Road, Stockport, Greater Manchester SK4 4NX
Tel: 0161 432 3782
Head: Dr Roger Slack
Age range: 5–16
No. of pupils: 32

Farrowdale House Preparatory School
Farrow Street, Shaw, Oldham, Greater Manchester OL2 7AD
Tel: 01706 844533
Headteacher: Miss K Brook BSc(Mathematics), QTS
Age range: 3–11
No. of pupils: 140
Fees: Day £4,995

Firwood Manor Preparatory School
Broadway, Chadderton, Oldham, Greater Manchester OL9 0AD
Tel: 0161 6206570
Headteacher: Mrs P M Wild
Age range: 2–11
Fees: Day £5,400

Forest Park School
Lauriston House, 27 Oakfield, Sale, Greater Manchester M33 6NB
Tel: 0161 973 4835
Headteacher: Mrs Helen Gee BEd(Hons)
Age range: 3–11
No. of pupils: 145
Fees: Day £4,515–£4,950

Forest Preparatory School
Moss Lane, Timperley, Altrincham, Greater Manchester WA15 6LJ
Tel: 0161 980 4075
Headmaster: Rick Hyde
Age range: 2–11
No. of pupils: 197
Fees: Day £1,940–£2,190

Grafton House Preparatory School
1 Warrington Street, Ashton-under-Lyne, Greater Manchester OL6 6XB
Tel: 0161 343 3015
Head: Mrs Pamela Oaks
Age range: 2–11
No. of pupils: 110

Greenbank Preparatory School
Heathbank Road, Cheadle Hulme, Cheadle, Greater Manchester SK8 6HU
Tel: 0161 485 3724
Headmistress: Mrs J L Lowe
Age range: 3–11
Fees: Day £7,095

Hale Preparatory School
Broomfield Lane, Hale, Altrincham, Greater Manchester WA15 9AS
Tel: 0161 928 2386
Headmaster: John Connor
Age range: 4–11
Fees: Day £6,150

Hulme Hall Grammar School (Junior School)
75 Hulme Hall Road, Cheadle Hulme, Cheadle, Greater Manchester SK8 6LA
Tel: 0161 486 9970
Headmaster: Mr Philip Marland BSc(Hons), MA, PGCE
Age range: 2–11
No. of pupils: 122
Fees: Day £4,143–£5,482

King of Kings School
142 Dantzic Street, Manchester, Greater Manchester M4 4DN
Tel: 0161 834 4214
Head Teacher: Mrs B Lewis
Age range: 3–18
No. of pupils: 29

Lady Barn House School
Langlands, Schools Hill, Cheadle, Greater Manchester SK8 1JE
Tel: 0161 428 2912
Headmistress: Mrs S Marsh
Age range: 3–11
No. of pupils: 463
Fees: Day £5,469–£6,246

Lighthouse Christian School
193 Ashley Lane, Moston, Manchester, Greater Manchester M9 4NQ
Tel: 0161 205 0957
Head: Mr A I Akinyele
Age range: 3–11
No. of pupils: 18
Fees: Day £2,880

Loreto Preparatory School
Dunham Road, Altrincham,
Greater Manchester WA14 4GZ
Tel: 0161 928 8310
Headteacher: Mrs R A Hedger
Age range: B3–7 G3–11
No. of pupils: 163
Fees: Day £4,650

Manchester High School for Girls
Grangethorpe Road, Manchester,
Greater Manchester M14 6HS
Tel: 0161 224 0447
Head Mistress: Mrs A C Hewitt
Age range: G4–18
No. of pupils: 923 VIth193
Fees: Day £7,053–£9,900

Manchester Junior Girls School
64 Upper Park Road, Salford,
Greater Manchester M7 4JA
Tel: 0161 740 0566
Headmistress: Mrs Lieberman
Age range: G3–11
No. of pupils: 200

Manchester Muslim Preparatory School
551 Wilmslow Road, Withington,
Manchester, Greater
Manchester M20 4BA
Tel: 0161 445 5452
Head Teacher: Mrs A Ali
Age range: 3–11
No. of pupils: 186
Fees: Day £4,200–£4,400

Monton Village School
Francis Street, Monton,
Eccles, Manchester, Greater
Manchester M30 9PR
Tel: 0161 789 0472
Head: Mrs K S McWilliams
Age range: 1–7
No. of pupils: 109

Moor Allerton School
131 Barlow Moor Road, West
Didsbury, Manchester, Greater
Manchester M20 2PW
Tel: 0161 445 4521
Head of School: Ruth Adams
Age range: 3–11
Fees: Day £6,660–£7,185

Oldham Hulme Grammar School
Chamber Road, Oldham,
Greater Manchester OL8 4BX
Tel: 0161 630 6104
Principal: Mr CJD Mairs
Age range: 3–18
No. of pupils: 840 VIth160
Fees: Day £7,335–£10,035

OYY Lubavitch Girls School
Beis Menachem, Park Lane, Salford,
Greater Manchester M7 4JD
Tel: 0161 795 0002
Headmistress: Mrs J Hanson
Age range: 2–16
No. of pupils: 82

Prestwich Preparatory School
St Margaret's Building, 400 Bury
Old Road, Prestwich, Manchester,
Greater Manchester M25 1PZ
Tel: 0161 773 1223
Headmistress: Miss P Shiels
Age range: 2–11
No. of pupils: 122
Fees: Day £3,336

Ramillies Hall School
Cheadle Hulme, Cheadle,
Greater Manchester SK8 7AJ
Tel: 0161 485 3804
Principal: Miss D M Patterson
BA, PGCE & Mrs A L Poole
Age range: 0–16
No. of pupils: 166
Fees: Day £6,000–£8,550

Saddleworth School
High Street, Uppermill, Oldham,
Greater Manchester OL3 6BU
Tel: 01457 872072
Headmistress: Mrs L K Hirst
Age range: 3–7

St Ambrose Preparatory School
Hale Barns, Altrincham, Greater
Manchester WA15 0HE
Tel: 0161 903 9193
Headmaster: F J Driscoll
Age range: B3–11 G3–4
No. of pupils: 150
Fees: Day £6,195

Staleydene Preparatory School
Wellington Parade, Dukinfield,
Greater Manchester SK16 4LE
Tel: 07904 693660
Head of School: Miss Kirsty Best
Age range: 3–11
No. of pupils: 23

Stella Maris Junior School
St Johns Road, Heaton
Mersey, Stockport, Greater
Manchester SK4 3BR
Tel: 0161 432 0532
Headmaster: Mr A Whittell
Age range: 3–11
No. of pupils: 63
Fees: Day £4,890

Stockport Grammar School
Buxton Road, Stockport,
Greater Manchester SK2 7AF
Tel: 0161 456 9000
Headmaster: Mr A H
Chicken BA, MEd, FRSA
Age range: 3–18
No. of pupils: 1402 VIth257
Fees: Day £7,695–£9,981

Tashbar School
20 Upper Park Road, Salford,
Greater Manchester M7 4HL
Tel: 0161 7208254
Headteacher: Mr Pinczewski
Age range: B5–11
No. of pupils: 325

The Manchester Grammar School
Old Hall Lane, Fallowfield,
Manchester, Greater
Manchester M13 0XT
Tel: 0161 224 7201
High Master: Dr Martin Boulton
Age range: B7–18
Fees: Day £11,400

Trinity Christian School
Birbeck Street, Stalybridge,
Greater Manchester SK15 1SH
Tel: 0161 303 0674
Headteacher: Mr W Ross Evans
Age range: 3–16
Fees: Day £2,964–£4,146

Withington Girls' School
Wellington Road, Fallowfield,
Manchester, Greater
Manchester M14 6BL
Tel: 0161 224 1077
Headmistress: Mrs S E Marks MA
Age range: G7–18
No. of pupils: 650 VIth167
Fees: Day £9,300

Isle of Man

The Buchan School
West Hill, Castletown,
Isle of Man IM9 1RD
Tel: 01624 820481
Headteacher: Mrs Alison
Hope Hedley
Age range: 4–11
No. of pupils: 195
Fees: Day £2,849–£3,716

Lancashire

Al-Asr Primary School
58-60 St Silas Road, Blackburn,
Lancashire BB2 6JX
Tel: 01254 696933
Headteacher: Mrs Hameed
Age range: 4–10
Fees: Day £1,200

Arnold KEQMS (AKS)
Clifton Drive South, Lytham St
Annes, Lancashire FY8 1DT
Tel: 01253 784100
Headmaster: Mr. Mike Walton
BA, MA (Ed), PGCE, NPQH
Age range: 2–18
No. of pupils: 800 VIth165
Fees: Day £6,537–£8,541

Ashbridge Independent School
Lindle Lane, Hutton, Preston,
Lancashire PR4 4AQ
Tel: 01772 619900
Headteacher: Mrs H Sharples
Age range: 0–11
No. of pupils: 315
Fees: Day £6,318

Heathland School
Broadoak, Sandy Lane,
Accrington, Lancashire BB5 2AN
Tel: 01254 234284
Principal: Mrs J Harrison
BA(Hons), CertEd, FRSA
Age range: 4–16
Fees: Day £4,515

Highfield Priory School

Fulwood Row, Fulwood,
Preston, Lancashire PR2 5RW
Tel: 01772 709624
Headmaster: Mr Jeremy
Duke BEd(Hons)
Age range: 6 months–11
Fees: Day £6,210
£

Kingsfold Christian School

Moss Lane, Hesketh Bank,
Preston, Lancashire PR4 6AA
Tel: 01772 813824
Age range: 4–16

Kingswood College at Scarisbrick School

Southport Road, Scarisbrisk,
Ormskirk, Lancashire L40 9RQ
Tel: 01704 880200
Principal: E J Borowski
Age range: 2–16
Fees: Day £3,000–£6,225
£ 🖊

KIRKHAM GRAMMAR JUNIOR SCHOOL
For further details see p. 67
Ribby Road, Kirkham, Preston,
Lancashire PR4 2BH
Tel: 01772 684264
Email:
info@kirkhamgrammar.co.uk
Website:
www.kirkhamgrammar.co.uk
Head: Mrs Annette Roberts
No. of pupils: 250
🖊 £ 🖊

Lancaster Steiner School

Lune Road, Lancaster,
Lancashire LA1 5QU
Tel: 01524 841351
Headteacher: Mrs Denise Randal
Age range: 0–14

Moorland School

Ribblesdale Avenue, Clitheroe,
Lancashire BB7 2JA
Tel: 01200 423833
Principal: Mr T Smith
BSc(Hons), PGCE
Age range: 3 months–16 years
Fees: Day £4,650–£5,190 WB
£10,800–£12,750 FB £11,250–£13,500
🖊 £

Oakhill College

Wiswell Lane, Whalley,
Clitheroe, Lancashire BB7 9AF
Tel: 01254 823546
Principal: Michael A
Kennedy BSc, MA
Age range: 2–16
No. of pupils: 268
Fees: Day £4,767–£7,389
🖊 £ 🖊

Rossall School

Broadway, Fleetwood,
Lancashire FY7 8JW
Tel: +44 (0)1253 774201
Head: Ms Elaine Purves
Age range: 2–18
No. of pupils: 629 VIth186
Fees: Day £7,650–£12,450 WB
£13,200–£21,450 FB £19,620–£35,550
🖊 A 🖊 £ IB 🖊

St Anne's College Grammar School

293 Clifton Drive South, Lytham
St Annes, Lancashire FY8 1HN
Tel: +44 (0)1253 725815
Principal: Mrs S M Welsby
Age range: 3–18
No. of pupils: VIth15
Fees: Day £4,500–£6,300
WB £5,000 FB £7,000
A £ 🖊

St Joseph's School, Park Hill

Park Hill, Padiham Road,
Burnley, Lancashire BB12 6TG
Tel: 01282 455622
Headmistress: Mrs
Annette Robinson
Age range: 3–11
Fees: Day £5,600

St Pius X Preparatory School

Oak House, 200 Garstang
Road, Fulwood, Preston,
Lancashire PR2 8RD
Tel: 01772 719937
Headmistress: Miss B M Banks MA
Age range: 2–11
No. of pupils: 260
Fees: Day £6,975–£7,325
🖊

STONYHURST ST MARY'S HALL
For further details see p. 68
Stonyhurst, Lancashire BB7 9PU
Tel: 01254 827073
Email: admissions@
stonyhurst.ac.uk
Website: www.stonyhurst.ac.uk
Headmaster: Mr Ian Murphy
BA (Hons), PGCE Durham
Age range: 3–13
No. of pupils: 262
Fees: Day £8,013–£14,907
WB £19,449 FB £22,950
🖊 £ 🖊

The Bennett House School

332 Eaves Lane, Chorley,
Lancashire PR6 0DX
Tel: 01257 267393
Headmistress: Mrs C A Mills MA
Age range: 0–5

Westholme School

Meins Road, Blackburn,
Lancashire BB2 6QU
Tel: 01254 506070
Principal: Mrs Lillian Croston
BSc(Hons)(Dunelm),
PGCE(Cantab), ALCM
Age range: B2–13 G2–18
No. of pupils: 1070 VIth140
Fees: Day £5,571–£8,850
🖊 🖊 A £ 🖊

Merseyside

Avalon Preparatory School

Caldy Road, West Kirby, Wirral,
Merseyside CH48 2HE
Tel: 0151 625 6993
Head of School: Ms
Joanna Callaway
Age range: 2–11
No. of pupils: 178
Fees: Day £1,860–£5,205
🖊

Belvedere Preparatory School

23 Belvidere Road, Princes
Park, Aigburth, Liverpool,
Merseyside L8 3TF
Tel: 0151 471 1137
Head of School: Ms Clare Burnham
Age range: 3–11
No. of pupils: 180

Birkenhead School

The Lodge, 58 Beresford Road,
Birkenhead, Merseyside CH43 2JD
Tel: 0151 652 4014
Headmaster: Mr David
John Clark MA
Age range: 3 months–18 years
No. of pupils: VIth103
Fees: Day £6,645–£9,606
A £ 🖊

Carleton House Preparatory School

145 Menlove Avenue, Liverpool,
Merseyside L18 3EE
Tel: 0151 722 0756
Head: Mr Peter Andrew
Age range: 4–11
No. of pupils: 145
Fees: Day £5,928
🖊

Christian Fellowship School

Overbury Street, Edge Hill,
Liverpool, Merseyside L7 3HL
Tel: 0151 709 1642
Headteacher: Miss Barbara Lord
Age range: 4–16
No. of pupils: 191
Fees: Day £1,752–£3,528
🖊

Kingsmead School

Bertram Drive, Hoylake, Wirral,
Merseyside CH47 0LL
Tel: 0151 632 3156
Headmaster: Mr M G Gibbons
BComm, MSc, QTS
Age range: 3–16
Fees: Day £2,625–£9,105 WB
£13,050–£15,345 FB £13,755–£16,050
🖊 🖊 🖊 £ 🖊

Prenton Preparatory School

Mount Pleasant, Oxton, Wirral,
Merseyside CH43 5SY
Tel: 0151 652 3182
Head: Mr Jones
Age range: 2–11
Fees: Day £4,650
🖊

Redcourt St Anselm's

Redcourt, Devonshire Place,
Birkenhead, Merseyside CH43 1TX
Tel: 0151 652 5228
Headmaster: Mr K S Davey
Age range: 3–11
No. of pupils: 320
Fees: Day £2,500–£3,000

Runnymede St Edward's School

North Drive, Sandfield Park,
Liverpool, Merseyside L12 1LE
Tel: 0151 281 2300
Headmaster: Mr Bradley Slater
Age range: 3–11
No. of pupils: 270
Fees: Day £6,276–£6,617
£ 🖊

St Mary's College

Everest Road, Crosby, Liverpool,
Merseyside L23 5TW
Tel: 0151 924 3926
Principal: Mr Michael Kennedy
Age range: 0–18
No. of pupils: 880 VIth132
Fees: Day £4,815–£7,533
A £ 🖊

Streatham House School

Victoria Road West, Blundellsands,
Liverpool, Merseyside L23 8UQ
Tel: 0151 924 1514
Executive Headteacher:
Mrs Debby Rigby BA(Hons),
PGCE, CertEd(Man)
Age range: B3 months–11
G3 months–16
Fees: Day £1,200
🖊 £ 🖊

Tower College

Mill Lane, Rainhill, Prescot,
Merseyside L35 6NE
Tel: 0151 426 4333
Principal: Miss R J Oxley NNEB, RSH
Age range: 3–16
No. of pupils: 486
Fees: Day £5,013–£5,895
🖊

South-East

*See also Greater London (D113)
for schools in Kent and Surrey

KEY TO SYMBOLS

- (†) Boys' school
- (‡) Girls' school
- (🌐) International school
- (16) Tutorial or sixth form college
- (A) A levels
- (🏫) Boarding accommodation
- (£) Bursaries
- (IB) International Baccalaureate
- (✎) Learning support
- (16+) Entrance at 16+
- (💼) Vocational qualifications
- (IAPS) Independent Association of Prep Schools
- (HMC) The Headmasters' & Headmistresses' Conference
- (ISA) Independent Schools Association
- (GSA) Girls' School Association
- (BSA) Boarding Schools' Association
- (S) Society of Heads

*Unless otherwise indicated, all schools are
coeducational day schools. Single-sex and boarding
schools will be indicated by the relevant icon.*

Berkshire

Alder Bridge School
Bridge House, Mill Lane, Padworth,
Reading, Berkshire RG7 4JU
Tel: 0118 971 4471
Age range: 1–11
No. of pupils: 58
Fees: Day £3,420–£4,470

Brigidine School Windsor
Queensmead, King's Road,
Windsor, Berkshire SL4 2AX
Tel: 01753 863779
Headmistress: Mrs
Elizabeth Robinson
Age range: B2–7 G3–18
No. of pupils: 300
Fees: Day £3,945–£11,865

Caversham School
16 Peppard Road, Caversham,
Reading, Berkshire RG4 8JZ
Tel: 01189 478 684
Head: Mrs Jacqueline Lawson
Age range: 4–11
No. of pupils: 60
Fees: Day £6,750

Claires Court Junior Boys
Maidenhead Thicket,
Maidenhead, Berkshire SL6 3QE
Tel: 01628 411490
Head: J M E Spanswick
Age range: B4–11
No. of pupils: 248
Fees: Day £7,965–£13,860

Claires Court Nursery, Girls and Sixth Form
1 College Avenue, Maidenhead,
Berkshire SL6 6AW
Tel: 01628 411480
Head: Mr Paul Bevis
Age range: B16–18 G3–18
No. of pupils: 495 VIth111
Fees: Day £5,715–£14,580

Crosfields School
Shinfield, Reading,
Berkshire RG2 9BL
Tel: 0118 987 1810
Headmaster: Mr J P Wansey
Age range: 3–13
No. of pupils: 510
Fees: Day £6,600–£10,710

Dolphin School
Waltham Road, Hurst, Reading,
Berkshire RG10 0FR
Tel: 0118 934 1277
Head: Mr Tom Lewis
Age range: 3–13
Fees: Day £8,340–£11,190

Eagle House School
Sandhurst, Berkshire GU47 8PH
Tel: 01344 772134
Headmaster: Mr A P N
Barnard BA(Hons), PGCE
Age range: 3–13
No. of pupils: 395
Fees: Day £10,590–
£16,575 FB £22,245

Elstree School
Woolhampton, Reading,
Berkshire RG7 5TD
Tel: 0118 971 3302
Headmaster: Mr S Inglis
Age range: B3–13 G3–7
No. of pupils: 248
Fees: Day £17,775 FB £22,800

Eton End PNEU School
35 Eton Road, Datchet,
Slough, Berkshire SL3 9AX
Tel: 01753 541075
Headmistress: Mrs V M
Pilgerstorfer BA(Hons), PGCE
Age range: B3–7 G3–11
No. of pupils: 245
Fees: Day £5,850–£6,900

Hemdean House School
Hemdean Road, Caversham,
Reading, Berkshire RG4 7SD
Tel: 0118 947 2590
Headmistress: Mrs J Harris BSc
Age range: B3–11 G3–16
Fees: Day £5,280–£7,200

Herries Preparatory School
Dean Lane, Cookham
Dean, Berkshire SL6 9BD
Tel: 01628 483350
Headmistress: Sophie Green
Age range: 3–11
Fees: Day £6,645–£8,985

Highfield Preparatory School
2 West Road, Maidenhead,
Berkshire SL6 1PD
Tel: 01628 624918
Headteacher: Ms A Lee
Age range: B3–5 G3–11
Fees: Day £822–£8,490

Holme Grange School
Heathlands Road, Wokingham,
Berkshire RG40 3AL
Tel: 0118 978 1566
Headteacher: Mrs C Robinson
Age range: 3–13
Fees: Day £4,965–£11,745

Hurst Lodge
Bagshot Road, Ascot,
Berkshire SL5 9JU
Tel: 01344 622154
Principal: Ms Victoria Smit
Age range: 3–18
No. of pupils: 202 VIth13
Fees: Day £6,420–£25,200
WB £19,905–£34,005

Lambrook School
Winkfield Row, Bracknell,
Berkshire RG42 6LU
Tel: 01344 882717
Headmaster: Mr Jonathan Perry
Age range: 3–13
No. of pupils: 440
Fees: Day £9,078–£15,180 WB
£16,803–£18,009 FB £17,433–£18,639

Long Close School
Upton Court Road, Upton,
Slough, Berkshire SL3 7LU
Tel: 01753 520095
Head: Mr David Brazier
Age range: 2–16
No. of pupils: 283
Fees: Day £5,715–£10,080

LUDGROVE
For further details see p. 71
Wokingham, Berkshire RG40 3AB
Tel: 0118 978 9881
Email: registrar@
ludgroveschool.co.uk
Website: www.ludgrove.net
Head of School: Mr Simon Barber
Age range: B8–13
No. of pupils: 190

LVS Ascot (Licensed Victuallers' School)
London Road, Ascot,
Berkshire SL5 8DR
Tel: 01344 882770
Headmistress: Mrs Christine
Cunniffe BA(Hons), MMus
Age range: 4–18
No. of pupils: 901 VIth150
Fees: Day £8,220–£15,435
FB £21,015–£24,900

Meadowbrook Montessori School
Malt Hill Road, Warfield,
Bracknell, Berkshire RG42 6JQ
Tel: 01344 890869
Head of School: Mrs S Gunn
Age range: 2–12
Fees: Day £670–£2,215

Newbold School
Popeswood Road, Binfield,
Bracknell, Berkshire RG42 4AH
Tel: 01344 421088
Headteacher: Mrs P Eastwood
Age range: 3–11
Fees: Day £3,000–£4,000

Our Lady's Preparatory School
The Avenue, Crowthorne,
Wokingham, Berkshire RG45 6PB
Tel: 01344 773394
Headmistress: Mrs Helene Robinson
Age range: 3 months–11 years
No. of pupils: 100
Fees: Day £5,328–£10,464

Papplewick School
Windsor Road, Ascot,
Berkshire SL5 7LH
Tel: 01344 621488
Head: Mr T W Bunbury BA, PGCE
Age range: B6–13
No. of pupils: 195

Reddam House Bearwood
Bearwood Road, Wokingham,
Berkshire RG41 5BG
Tel: 0118 974 8300
Headmaster: Mr Donald Wilkinson
Age range: 0–18
No. of pupils: 487 VIth80
Fees: Day £13,890–£16,365
FB £24,360–£28,080

Redroofs School for the Performing Arts (Redroofs Theatre School)
26 Bath Road, Maidenhead,
Berkshire SL6 4JT
Tel: 01628 674092
Principal: June Rose
Age range: 8–18
No. of pupils: 100
Fees: Day £4,000

St Andrew's School
Buckhold, Pangbourne,
Reading, Berkshire RG8 8QA
Tel: 0118 974 4276
Headmaster: Dr D Livingstone
BSc, PhD, NPQH
Age range: 3–13
Fees: Day £4,050–£14,280
WB £16,950

St Bernard's Preparatory School
Hawtrey Close, Slough,
Berkshire SL1 1TB
Tel: 01753 521821
Head Teacher: Mrs M B
Smith CertEd, NPQH
Age range: 2–11

St Edward's School
64 Tilehurst Road, Reading,
Berkshire RG30 2JH
Tel: 0118 957 4342
Principal: G W Mottram
Age range: B4–13
No. of pupils: 170
Fees: Day £6,660–£8,550

St George's School Windsor Castle
Windsor, Berkshire SL4 1QF
Tel: 01753 865553
Head Master: Mr C F McDade
Age range: 3–13
Fees: Day £8,493–£14,097
WB £18,723 FB £19,203

St John's Beaumont Preparatory School
Priest Hill, Old Windsor, Berkshire SL4 2JN
Tel: 01784 432428
Headmaster: Mr G E F Delaney BA(Hons), PGCE
Age range: B3–13
No. of pupils: 310
Fees: Day £7,140–£13,320 WB £17,520 FB £20,250

St Joseph's College
Upper Redlands Road, Reading, Berkshire RG1 5JT
Tel: 0118 966 1000
Head of College (Senior School): Mr Andrew Colpus
Age range: 3–18
No. of pupils: VIth46
Fees: Day £5,634–£9,630

St Piran's Preparatory School
Gringer Hill, Maidenhead, Berkshire SL6 7LZ
Tel: 01628 594302
Headmaster: Mr J A Carroll BA(Hons), BPhilEd, PGCE, NPQH
Age range: 3–11
Fees: Day £9,900–£14,550

Sunningdale School
Dry Arch Road, Sunningdale, Berkshire SL5 9PY
Tel: 01344 620159
Headmaster: T A C N Dawson MA, PGCE
Age range: B7–13
No. of pupils: 90
Fees: Day £13,950 FB £17,985

The Abbey School
Kendrick Road, Reading, Berkshire RG1 5DZ
Tel: 0118 987 2256
Head: Mrs Rachel S E Dent
Age range: G3–18
No. of pupils: 1070
Fees: Day £15,090

The Deenway Montessori School
3-5 Sidmouth Street, Reading, Berkshire RG1 4QX
Tel: 0118 9574737
Headteacher: Mr M Karim
Age range: 3–11

The Marist Preparatory School
King's Road, Sunninghill, Ascot, Berkshire SL5 7PS
Tel: 01344 626137
Headteacher: J Finlayson
Age range: G2–11
No. of pupils: 225
Fees: Day £8,700–£9,360

The Marist Schools
King's Road, Sunninghill, Ascot, Berkshire SL5 7PS
Tel: 01344 624291
Head of Secondary School: Mr K McCloskey
Age range: G2–18
No. of pupils: 550 VIth60
Fees: Day £7,845–£10,695

The Oratory Preparatory School
Great Oaks, Goring Heath, Reading, Berkshire RG8 7SF
Tel: 0118 984 4511
Headmaster: Mr J J Smith BA, PGCE
Age range: 3–13
No. of pupils: 400
Fees: Day £3,425–£11,475 WB £14,565 FB £15,825

The Vine Christian School
SORCF Christian Centre, Basingstoke Road, Three Mile Cross, Reading, Berkshire RG7 1AT
Tel: 0118 988 6464
Head: Mrs Joan Muirhead
Age range: 5–13
No. of pupils: 9

Upton House School
115 St Leonard's Road, Windsor, Berkshire SL4 3DF
Tel: 01753 862610
Headmistress: Mrs Madeleine Collins BA(Hons), PGCE(Oxford)
Age range: B2–7 G2–11
No. of pupils: 280

Waverley School
Waverley Way, Finchampstead, Wokingham, Berkshire RG40 4YD
Tel: 0118 973 1121
Principal: Mrs Jane Sculpher
Age range: 3–11
Fees: Day £3,300–£7,362

Buckinghamshire

Caldicott
Crown Lane, Farnham Royal, Buckinghamshire SL2 3SL
Tel: 01753 649301
Headmaster: Mr S J G Doggart BA(Cantab)
Age range: B7–13
No. of pupils: 256
Fees: Day £13,080–£14,148 FB £19,227

Dair House School
Bishops Blake, Beaconsfield Road, Farnham Royal, Buckinghamshire SL2 3BY
Tel: 01753 643964
Headmaster: Mr Terry Wintle BEd(Hons)
Age range: 3–11
No. of pupils: 104
Fees: Day £2,907–£8,526

Gayhurst School
Bull Lane, Gerrards Cross, Buckinghamshire SL9 8RJ
Tel: 01753 882690
Headmaster: A J Sims MA(Cantab)
Age range: B3–13 G3–13
Fees: Day £9,882–£12,555

Heatherton House School
Copperkins Lane, Chesham Bois, Amersham, Buckinghamshire HP6 5QB
Tel: 01494 726433
Headteacher: Mrs Debbie Isaachsen
Age range: G3–11
No. of pupils: 165
Fees: Day £1,068–£12,330

Maltman's Green School
Maltman's Lane, Gerrards Cross, Buckinghamshire SL9 8RR
Tel: 01753 883022
Headmistress: Mrs Joanna Pardon MA, BSc(Hons), PGCE
Age range: G3–11
No. of pupils: 425
Fees: Day £7,725–£11,460

St Mary's School
94 Packhorse Road, Gerrards Cross, Buckinghamshire SL9 8JQ
Tel: 01753 883370
Headmistress: Mrs J A Ross BA(Hons), NPQH
Age range: G3–18
No. of pupils: 320 VIth38
Fees: Day £3,420–£12,155

Thorpe House School
Oval Way, Gerrards Cross, Buckinghamshire SL9 8QA
Tel: 01753 882474
Headmaster: Mr Terrence Ayres
Age range: B3–16
Fees: Day £9,000–£13,500

East Sussex

Ashdown House School
Forest Row, East Sussex RH18 5JY
Tel: 01342 822574
Headmaster: Haydon Moore
Age range: 7–13
No. of pupils: 125
Fees: FB £23,250

Battle Abbey School
Battle, East Sussex TN33 0AD
Tel: 01424 772385
Headmaster: Mr R C Clark BA(Hons), MA(Ed)
Age range: 2–18
No. of pupils: 286 VIth48
Fees: Day £6,630–£13,390 FB £23,190

Bricklehurst Manor Preparatory
Bardown Road, Stonegate, Wadhurst, East Sussex TN5 7EL
Tel: 01580 200448
Headteacher: Mrs C Flowers
Age range: 3–11
No. of pupils: 127
Fees: Day £980–£8,925

Brighton & Hove High School GDST
Montpelier Road, Brighton, East Sussex BN1 3AT
Tel: 01273 280280
Head: Mrs Lorna Duggleby
Age range: G3–18
No. of pupils: 680 VIth70
Fees: Day £5,028–£8,898

Brighton & Hove Montessori School
67 Stanford Avenue, Brighton,
East Sussex BN1 6FB
Tel: 01273 702485
Headteacher: Mrs Daisy
Cockburn AMI, MontDip
Age range: 2–11
Fees: Day £1,400–£5,900

Brighton College
Eastern Road, Brighton,
East Sussex BN2 0AL
Tel: 01273 704200
Head Master: Richard Cairns MA
Age range: 3–18
No. of pupils: 945 VIth340
Fees: Day £4,890–£18,675 WB
£24,729–£25,884 FB £28,575–£30,141

Brighton Steiner School
John Howard House, Roedean
Road, Brighton, East Sussex BN2 5RA
Tel: 01273 386300
**Chair of the College of
Teachers:** Carrie Rawle
Age range: 3–16
Fees: Day £6,540

Charters Ancaster College
Woodsgate Place, Gunters Lane,
Bexhill-on-Sea, East Sussex TN39 4EB
Tel: 01424 216670
Headmistress: Mrs Miriam Black
Age range: 2–13
No. of pupils: 125
Fees: Day £5,325–£6,750

Claremont Preparatory & Nursery School
Ebdens Hill, Baldslow, St Leonards-
on-Sea, East Sussex TN37 7PW
Tel: 01424 751555
Headmistress: Mrs Diane Durrant
Age range: 1–14
Fees: Day £5,000–£10,000

Darvell School
Darvell Bruderhof, Robertsbridge,
East Sussex TN32 5DR
Tel: 01580 883300
Headteacher: Mr Arnold Meier
Age range: 4–16
No. of pupils: 121

Deepdene School
195 New Church Road, Hove,
East Sussex BN3 4ED
Tel: 01273 418984
Heads: Mrs Nicola Gane
& Miss Elizabeth Brown
Age range: 6 months–11 years
Fees: Day £1,800–£6,870

Dharma School
The White House, Ladies Mile
Road, Patcham, Brighton,
East Sussex BN1 8TB
Tel: 01273 502055
Headteacher: Kevin Fossey BEd
Age range: 3–11
Fees: Day £3,000

Greenfields School
Priory Road, Forest Row,
East Sussex RH18 5JD
Tel: 01342 822189
Headteacher: Mr G Hudson
Age range: 2–19
No. of pupils: 125
Fees: Day £500–£10,800
FB £19,170–£20,850

K-BIS Theatre School
Clermont Hall, Cumberland Road,
Brighton, East Sussex BN1 6SL
Tel: 01273 566739
Principal: Mrs Marcia King LGSM
Age range: 5–18
No. of pupils: VIth7
Fees: Day £5,980

Lancing College Preparatory School at Hove
The Droveway, Hove,
East Sussex BN3 6LU
Tel: 01273 503452
Headmaster: A P Laurent
Age range: 3–13
No. of pupils: 181
Fees: Day £2,550–£10,155

Lewes New School
Talbot Terrace, Lewes,
East Sussex BN7 2DS
Tel: 01273 477074
Head Teacher: Lizzie Overton
Age range: 3–11
No. of pupils: 76
Fees: Day £3,300–£3,600

Lewes Old Grammar School
High Street, Lewes, East
Sussex BN7 1XS
Tel: 01273 472634
Headmaster: Mr Robert Blewitt
Age range: 3–18
No. of pupils: 463 VIth50
Fees: Day £5,550–£10,815

Michael Hall School
Kidbrooke Park, Forest Row,
East Sussex RH18 5JA
Tel: 01342 822275
Age range: 3–19
Fees: Day £7,900–£11,250
FB £5,400–£7,800

Moira House Girls School
Upper Carlisle Road, Eastbourne,
East Sussex BN20 7TE
Tel: 01323 644144
Principal: Mrs L A Watson
MA(Ed), MInstD
Age range: G2–18
No. of pupils: 360 VIth105
Fees: Day £6,300–£14,655 WB
£19,260–£24,060 FB £20,715–£26,550

Sacred Heart School
Mayfield Lane, Durgates,
Wadhurst, East Sussex TN5 6DQ
Tel: 01892 783414
Headteacher: Mrs H Blake
BA(Hons), PGCE
Age range: 3–11
Fees: Day £2,235–£6,225

Skippers Hill Manor Prep School
Five Ashes, Mayfield, East
Sussex TN20 6HR
Tel: 01825 830234
Headmaster: T W Lewis
BA(Exon), PGCE(London)
Age range: 3–13
Fees: Day £3,852–£12,930

St Andrew's Preparatory School
Meads, Eastbourne, East
Sussex BN20 7RP
Tel: 01323 733203
Headmaster: Gareth
Jones BA(Hons), PGCE
Age range: 1–13
Fees: Day £8,880–£15,465 FB £21,960

St Bede's Preparatory School
Duke's Drive, Eastbourne,
East Sussex BN20 7XL
Tel: 01323 734222
Head: Mr Nicholas Bevington
Age range: 3 months–13 years
No. of pupils: 395

St Christopher's School
33 New Church Road, Hove,
East Sussex BN3 4AD
Tel: 01273 735404
Headmaster: Mr Julian Withers
Age range: 4–13
Fees: Day £6,570–£8,688

The Drive Prep School
101 The Drive, Hove,
East Sussex BN3 3JE
Tel: 01273 738444
Head Teacher: Mrs S Parkinson
CertEd, CertPerfArts
Age range: 7–16
Fees: Day £3,885–£7,500

Torah Academy
31 New Church Road, Hove,
East Sussex BN3 4AD
Tel: 01273 328675
Principal: P Efune
Age range: 4–11

Vinehall School
Robertsbridge, East Sussex TN32 5JL
Tel: 01580 880413
Headmaster: Richard Follett
Age range: 2–13
No. of pupils: 260
Fees: Day £8,913–£16,620
FB £19,545–£21,675

Windlesham School
190 Dyke Road, Brighton,
East Sussex BN1 5AA
Tel: 01273 553645
Headmistress: Mrs Aoife
Bennett-Odlum
Age range: 3–11
No. of pupils: 233
Fees: Day £5,100–£7,200

Hampshire

Alton Convent School
Anstey Lane, Alton,
Hampshire GU34 2NG
Tel: 01420 82070
Head: Graham Maher
Age range: B0–11 G0–18
No. of pupils: 563 VIth53
Fees: Day £8,655–£12,285

Ballard School
Fernhill Lane, New Milton,
Hampshire BH25 5SU
Tel: 01425 626900
Headmaster: Mr Alastair Reid
Age range: 18 months–16 years
No. of pupils: 500
Fees: Day £2,370–£4,265

Boundary Oak School
Roche Court, Fareham,
Hampshire PO17 5BL
Tel: 01329 280955/820373
Head: Mrs Hazel Kellett
Age range: 2–13
No. of pupils: 120
Fees: Day £7,500–£12,510 WB
£5,370 FB £7,095–£19,605

Brockwood Park & Inwoods School
Brockwood Park, Bramdean,
Hampshire SO24 0LQ
Tel: +44 (0)1962 771744
Co-Principals: Mr Adrian Sydenham
& Dr Gopal Krishnamurthy
Age range: 4–19
No. of pupils: 92
Fees: Day £3,150 FB £17,270

Brookham School
Highfield Lane, Liphook,
Hampshire GU30 7LQ
Tel: 01428 722005
Headteacher: Mrs Sophie Baber
Age range: 3–8
No. of pupils: 141
Fees: Day £10,125–£13,350

Churcher's College
Petersfield, Hampshire GU31 4AS
Tel: 01730 263033
Headmaster: Mr Simon
Williams MA, BSc
Age range: 4–18
No. of pupils: 1067 VIth224
Fees: Day £7,605–£11,955

Daneshill School
Stratfield Turgis, Basingstoke,
Hampshire RG27 0AR
Tel: 01256 882707
Headmaster: S V Spencer
CertEd, DipPhysEd
Age range: 3–13
Fees: Day £3,900–£9,150

Ditcham Park School
Ditcham Park, Petersfield,
Hampshire GU31 5RN
Tel: 01730 825659
Headteacher: A P N Rowley
BSc (Hons), PGCE
Age range: 4–16
No. of pupils: 366
Fees: Day £6,957–£11,610

Dunhurst (Bedales Junior School)
Petersfield, Hampshire GU32 2DP
Tel: 01730 300200
Head: Jane Grubb
Age range: 8–13
No. of pupils: 199
Fees: Day £16,635 FB £21,255

Durlston Court
Becton Lane, Barton-on-Sea, New
Milton, Hampshire BH25 7AQ
Tel: 01425 610010
Head of School: Mr Richard May
Age range: 2–13
No. of pupils: 304
Fees: Day £3,540–£12,255

Farleigh School
Red Rice, Andover,
Hampshire SP11 7PW
Tel: 01264 710766
Headmaster: Father Simon Everson
Age range: 3–13
Fees: Day £3,870–£14,085
FB £16,515–£18,345

Forres Sandle Manor
Fordingbridge, Hampshire SP6 1NS
Tel: 01425 653181
Headmaster: Mr M N
Hartley BSc(Hons)
Age range: 3–13
No. of pupils: 264
Fees: Day £3,150–£14,205
WB £19,380 FB £19,380

GEMS Sherfield School
Sherfield-on-Loddon, Hook,
Hampshire RG27 0HU
Tel: +44 (0)1256 284 800
Headmaster: Mr Dick Jaine
Age range: 3 months–18 years
No. of pupils: 445 VIth16
Fees: Day £7,350–£13,890 FB £20,946

Glenhurst School
16 Beechworth Road, Havant,
Hampshire PO9 1AX
Tel: 023 9248 4054
Principal: Mrs E M Haines
Age range: 3 months–8 years
Fees: Day £4,500

Hampshire Collegiate School
Embley Park, Romsey,
Hampshire SO51 6ZE
Tel: 01794 512206
Principal: Mrs Emma-Kate Henry
Age range: 2–18
No. of pupils: 683

Highfield School
Liphook, Hampshire GU30 7LQ
Tel: 01428 728000
Headmaster: Mr Philip Evitt MA
Age range: 8–13
Fees: Day £17,025–£19,575
FB £21,450–£23,550

Kingscourt School
Catherington Lane, Catherington,
Hampshire PO8 9NJ
Tel: 023 9259 3251
Headmistress: Mrs J L Easton
Age range: 2–11
Fees: Day £5,430

Mayville High School
35/37 St Simon's Road, Southsea,
Portsmouth, Hampshire PO5 2PE
Tel: 023 9273 4847
Headteacher: Mrs L Owens B.Ed
Age range: 6 months–16 years
No. of pupils: 479
Fees: Day £5,481–£8,040

Meoncross School
Burnt House Lane, Stubbington,
Fareham, Hampshire PO14 2EF
Tel: 01329 662182
Headmistress: Mrs Sarah
Ebery BSc (Hons), MEd
Age range: 2–18
No. of pupils: 405
Fees: Day £7,365–£10,485

Moyles Court School
Moyles Court, Ringwood,
Hampshire BH24 3NF
Tel: 01425 472856
Headmaster: Mr Dean
Age range: 3–16
Fees: Day £3,285–£4,650
FB £6,690–£7,740

New Forest Small School
1 Southampton Road, Lyndhurst,
Hampshire SO43 7BU
Tel: 02380 284 415
Headteacher: Mr Nicholas Alp
Age range: 3–16

Portsmouth High School GDST
Kent Road, Southsea, Portsmouth,
Hampshire PO5 3EQ
Tel: 023 9282 6714
Headmistress: Mrs Jane
Prescott BSc NPQH
Age range: G3–18
No. of pupils: 421
Fees: Day £2,542–£4,248

Prince's Mead School
Worthy Park House, Kings Worthy,
Winchester, Hampshire SO21 1AN
Tel: 01962 888000
Headmistress: Miss Penelope Kirk
Age range: 4–11
No. of pupils: 270
Fees: Day £9,600–£14,640

Ringwood Waldorf School
Folly Farm Lane, Ashley,
Ringwood, Hampshire BH24 2NN
Tel: 01425 472664
Age range: 3–18
No. of pupils: 235
Fees: Day £3,622–£7,825

Rookwood School
Weyhill Road, Andover,
Hampshire SP10 3AL
Tel: 01264 325900
Headmistress: Mrs L Whetstone MA
Age range: 3–16
Fees: Day £7,770–£12,780
FB £19,545–£22,875

Sherborne House School
Lakewood Road, Chandlers Ford,
Eastleigh, Hampshire SO53 1EU
Tel: 023 8025 2440
Head Teacher: Mrs
Heather Hopson-Hill
Age range: 3–11
No. of pupils: 293
Fees: Day £1,044–£8,730

St John's College
Grove Road South, Southsea,
Portsmouth, Hampshire PO5 3QW
Tel: 023 9281 5118
Head of College: Mr. T J Bayley
Age range: 2–18
No. of pupils: 599 VIth86
Fees: Day £8,460–£11,100
FB £23,970–£25,770

St Mary's College
57 Midanbury Lane, Bitterne Park,
Southampton, Hampshire SO18 4DJ
Tel: 023 8067 1267
Head of School: Mrs. Owen
Age range: 3–16
No. of pupils: 470
Fees: Day £1,750–£2,350

St Neot's School
St Neot's Road, Eversley, Hook,
Hampshire RG27 0PN
Tel: 0118 973 2118
Head of School: Mrs
Deborah Henderson
Age range: 3 months–13 years
No. of pupils: 300
Fees: Day £1,494–£14,850

St Nicholas' School
Redfields House, Redfields
Lane, Church Crookham,
Fleet, Hampshire GU52 0RF
Tel: 01252 850121
Headmistress: Mrs A V
Whatmough BA, CertEd
Age range: B3–7 G3–16
No. of pupils: 370

St Swithun's Junior School
Alresford Road, Winchester,
Hampshire SO21 1HA
Tel: 01962 835750
Headmistress: Mrs P
Grimes BA(Hons)
Age range: B3–7 G3–11
No. of pupils: 183
Fees: Day £1,415–£3,650

St Winifred's School
17-19 Winn Road, Southampton,
Hampshire SO17 1EJ
Tel: 023 8055 7352
Head Teacher: Mr M Brogan
BEd,CertSpNeeds
Age range: 3–11
Fees: Day £6,330

Stockton House School
Stockton Avenue, Fleet,
Hampshire GU51 4NS
Tel: 01252 616323
Early Years Manager: Mrs
Jenny Bounds BA EYPS
Age range: 2–5
Fees: Day £25.50–£70

The Children's House and Grantham Farm Montessori School
Grantham Farm, Baughurst,
Tadley, Hampshire RG26 5JS
Tel: 0118 981 5821
Head: Mrs Shaunagh de Boinville
Age range: 3–8

The Grey House School
Mount Pleasant, Hartley Wintney,
Hampshire RG27 8PW
Tel: 01252 842353
Head: Mrs C E Allen BEd(Cantab)
Age range: 4–11+
Fees: Day £7,365–£8,994

The King's School
Lakesmere House, Allington Lane,
Fair Oak, Eastleigh, Southampton,
Hampshire SO50 7DB
Tel: 023 8060 0986
Head of School: Mrs H
Bowden BA (Hons), PGCE
Age range: 3–16
No. of pupils: 256
Fees: Day £3,900–£6,840

The King's School
Basingstoke Community
Church, Sarum Hill, Basingstoke,
Hampshire RG21 8SR
Tel: 01256 467092
Headteacher: Mr David Robotham
Age range: 7–16
No. of pupils: 172

The Pilgrims' School
3 The Close, Winchester,
Hampshire SO23 9LT
Tel: 01962 854189
Headmaster: Mr Tom Burden
Age range: B4–13
No. of pupils: 250
Fees: Day £17,685 FB £22,335

The Portsmouth Grammar Junior School
High Street, Portsmouth,
Hampshire PO1 2LN
Tel: +44 (0)23 9268 1336
Headmaster: Peter
Hopkinson BA, PGCE
Age range: 4–11
No. of pupils: 398
Fees: Day £8,127–£9,012

The Stroud School
Highwood House, Highwood Lane,
Romsey, Hampshire SO51 9ZH
Tel: 01794 513231
Headmaster: Mr Alastair J
L Dodds MA(Cantab)
Age range: 3–13
Fees: Day £9,060–£14,775

Twyford School
Twyford, Winchester,
Hampshire SO21 1NW
Tel: 01962 712269
Headmaster: Dr S J Bailey
BEd, PhD, FRSA
Age range: 3–13
Fees: Day £4,845–£16,410
WB £20,670

Walhampton
Walhampton, Lymington,
Hampshire SO41 5ZG
Tel: 01590 613 300
Headmaster: Mr Titus Mills
Age range: 2–13
No. of pupils: 353
Fees: Day £8,025–£15,555
FB £20,790

West Hill Park Preparatory School
Titchfield, Fareham,
Hampshire PO14 4BS
Tel: 01329 842356
Headmaster: A P Ramsay
BEd(Hons), MSc
Age range: 2–13
No. of pupils: 288
Fees: Day £8,985–£14,985
FB £13,785–£19,785

Woodhill School, Botley
Brook Lane, Botley, Southampton,
Hampshire SO30 2ER
Tel: 01489 781112
Head Teacher: Mrs M Dacombe
Age range: 3–11
No. of pupils: 100
Fees: Day £2,199–£4,965

Yateley Manor School
51 Reading Road, Yateley,
Hampshire GU46 7UQ
Tel: 01252 405500
Headmaster: Mr R J Williams
MA(Hons)Edinburgh, PGCE Bedford
Age range: 3–13
No. of pupils: 453
Fees: Day £4,500–£12,150

Isle of Wight

Priory School
Beatrice Avenue, Whippingham,
Isle of Wight PO32 6LP
Tel: 01983 861222
Principal: Mr E J Matyjaszek
Age range: 5–18
Fees: Day £3,360–£7,200

Ryde School with Upper Chine
Queen's Road, Ryde, Isle
of Wight PO33 3BE
Tel: 01983 617970
Headmaster: Mr M. A. Waldron MA
Age range: 3–18
No. of pupils: 750 VIth141
Fees: Day £6,225–£11,995 WB
£23,115–£23,505 FB £24,795–£25,185

Kent

Ashford Friars Prep School
Great Chart, Ashford, Kent TN23 3DJ
Tel: 01233 620493
Head: Mr R Yeates BA(Hons)(Exeter)
Age range: 3–11
No. of pupils: 373
Fees: Day £6,414–£11,079

Ashford School
East Hill, Ashford, Kent TN24 8PB
Tel: 01233 739030
Head: Mr M R Buchanan
BSc(Hons), CertEd, NPQH, CPhys
Age range: 3 months–18 years
No. of pupils: 835 VIth170
Fees: Day £8,400–£16,200
WB £28,500 FB £32,400

Beech Grove School
Beech Grove Bruderhof,
Sandwich Road, Nonington,
Dover, Kent CT15 4HH
Tel: 01304 842980
Head: Mr Benjamin Shirky
Age range: 4–14
No. of pupils: 63

Beechwood Sacred Heart
12 Pembury Road, Tunbridge
Wells, Kent TN2 3QD
Tel: 01892 532747
Headmaster: Mr Aaron
Lennon BA(Hons)
Age range: 3–18
No. of pupils: 400 VIth70
Fees: Day £9,060–£15,936
WB £23,460 FB £26,460

Bronte School
Mayfield, 7 Pelham Road,
Gravesend, Kent DA11 0HN
Tel: 01474 533805
Headmaster: Mr R Dyson
Age range: 4–11
No. of pupils: 120
Fees: Day £7,950

Bryony School
Marshall Road, Rainham,
Gillingham, Kent ME8 0AJ
Tel: 01634 231511
Joint Heads: D E and
Mrs M P Edmunds
Age range: 2–11
No. of pupils: 174
Fees: Day £4,551–£5,451

Canterbury Steiner School
Garlinge Green, Chartham,
Canterbury, Kent CT4 5RU
Tel: 01227 738285
Age range: 3–18
Fees: Day £3,246–£4,405.50

Chartfield School
45 Minster Road, Westgate
on Sea, Kent CT8 8DA
Tel: 01843 831716
Head & Proprietor: Miss L P Shipley
Age range: 4–11
No. of pupils: 50
Fees: Day £2,580–£3,000

Combe Bank School
Combe Bank Drive,
Sevenoaks, Kent TN14 6AE
Tel: 01959 563720
Headmistress: Mrs Julie
Tricks BA (Hons), PGCE
Age range: 3–18
No. of pupils: 250

Derwent Lodge School for Girls
Somerhill, Tonbridge, Kent TN11 0NJ
Tel: 01732 352124
Headmistress: Mrs S Michau
MA(Oxon), PGCE
Age range: G7–11
No. of pupils: 134
Fees: Day £12,675

Dover College
Effingham Crescent,
Dover, Kent CT17 9RH
Tel: 01304 205969 Ext:201
Headmaster: Gerry Holden
Age range: 3–18
No. of pupils: 340 VIth100
Fees: Day £6,750–£14,250 WB
£18,900–£22,200 FB £20,700–£27,900

Dulwich Preparatory School
Coursehorn, Cranbrook,
Kent TN17 3NP
Tel: 01580 712179
Headmaster: Mr Paul
David BEd(Hons)
Age range: 3–13
No. of pupils: 535
Fees: Day £4,890–£14,400

Elliott Park School
18-20 Marina Drive, Minster,
Sheerness, Kent ME12 2DP
Tel: 01795 873372
Head: Mr R Barson
Age range: 4–11
No. of pupils: 60
Fees: Day £3,897

Fosse Bank School
Mountains, Noble Tree
Road, Hildenborough,
Tonbridge, Kent TN11 8ND
Tel: 01732 834212
Headmistress: Mrs Lovatt-Young
Age range: 3–11
No. of pupils: 124
Fees: Day £1,560–£10,671

Gad's Hill School
Higham, Rochester,
Medway, Kent ME3 7PA
Tel: 01474 822356
Headmaster: Mr D G Craggs
BSc, MA, NPQH, FCollP, FRSA
Age range: 3–16
No. of pupils: 370
Fees: Day £6,000–£7,600

Haddon Dene School
57 Gladstone Road,
Broadstairs, Kent CT10 2HY
Tel: 01843 861176
Head: Mrs E Rowe
Age range: 3–11
No. of pupils: 200
Fees: Day £4,950–£6,135

Hilden Grange School
62 Dry Hill Park Road,
Tonbridge, Kent TN10 3BX
Tel: 01732 351169
Headmaster: Mr J Withers BA(Hons)
Age range: 3–13
Fees: Day £9,780–£12,950

Hilden Oaks School & Nursery
38 Dry Hill Park Road,
Tonbridge, Kent TN10 3BU
Tel: 01732 353941
Headmistress: Mrs S A Webb
Age range: 0–11 B0–11 G0–11
Fees: Day £7,980–£10,710

Holmewood House School
Langton Green, Tunbridge
Wells, Kent TN3 0EB
Tel: 01892 860006
Headmaster: Mr J D B
Marjoribanks BEd
Age range: 3–13
No. of pupils: 473
Fees: Day £5,900–£16,455

Kent College Nursery, Infant & Junior School
Vernon Holme, Harbledown,
Canterbury, Kent CT2 9AQ
Tel: 01227 762436
Headmaster: Mr A J Carter
Age range: 3–11
No. of pupils: 190
Fees: Day £8,805–£9,615
WB £14,196 FB £18,400

Kent College Pembury
Old Church Road, Pembury,
Tunbridge Wells, Kent TN2 4AX
Tel: +44 (0)1892 822006
Headmistress: Mrs Sally-Anne
Huang MA(Oxon), MSc, PGCE
Age range: G3–18
No. of pupils: 650 VIth102
Fees: Day £7,887–£17,322
FB £21,471–£27,924

King's Preparatory School, Rochester
King Edward Road, Rochester,
Medway, Kent ME1 1UB
Tel: 01634 888577
Headmaster: Mr R Overend
Age range: 4–13
No. of pupils: 228
Fees: Day £7,125–£10,380 FB £16,005

Linton Park School
3 Eccleston Road, Tovil,
Maidstone, Kent ME17 4HT
Tel: 01622 740820
Headteacher: Mr C Allen
Age range: 7–18
No. of pupils: 134

Lorenden Preparatory School
Painter's Forstal, Faversham,
Kent ME13 0EN
Tel: 01795 590030
Headmistress: Mrs R Simmonds
Age range: 3–11
No. of pupils: 158
Fees: Day £7,374–£10,680

Marlborough House School
High Street, Hawkhurst,
Kent TN18 4PY
Tel: 01580 753555
Headmaster: Mr David N
Hopkins MA(Oxon), PGCE
Age range: 2–13
No. of pupils: 334
Fees: Day £2,808–£14,700

Meredale Independent Primary School
Solomon Road, Rainham,
Gillingham, Kent ME8 8EB
Tel: 01634 231405
Headteacher: Miss
Michelle Ingledew
Age range: 3–11
No. of pupils: 53
Fees: Day £5,100

Northbourne Park School
Betteshanger, Deal, Kent CT14 0NW
Tel: 01304 611215/218
Headmaster: Mr Edward Balfour
Age range: 3–13
No. of pupils: 185
Fees: Day £11,400–£13,740 WB
£16,140–£16,140 FB £119,200–£19,200

Rose Hill School
Coniston Avenue, Tunbridge
Wells, Kent TN4 9SY
Tel: 01892 525591
Headmaster: Mr D
Westcombe BA, PGCE
Age range: 3–13
Fees: Day £3,040–£4,130

Russell House School
Station Road, Otford,
Sevenoaks, Kent TN14 5QU
Tel: 01959 522352
Headmistress: Mrs Alison Cooke
Age range: 2–11
Fees: Day £4,650–£9,840

Saint Ronan's School
Water Lane, Hawkhurst,
Kent TN18 5DJ
Tel: 01580 752271
Headmaster: William Trelawny-
Vernon BSc(Hons)
Age range: 3–13
No. of pupils: 300
Fees: Day £6,951–£11,892

Sevenoaks Preparatory School
Godden Green, Sevenoaks,
Kent TN15 0JU
Tel: 01732 762336
Headmaster: Mr Luke Harrison
Age range: 2–13
No. of pupils: 388
Fees: Day £3,552–£11,910

Shernold School
Hill Place, Queens Avenue,
Maidstone, Kent ME16 0ER
Tel: 01622 752868
Headmistress: Mrs L Dack
Age range: 3–11
No. of pupils: 142
Fees: Day £3,525–£4,200

Solefield School
Solefield Road, Sevenoaks,
Kent TN13 1PH
Tel: 01732 452142
Headmaster: Mr D A
Philps BSc(Hons)
Age range: B4–13
No. of pupils: 180
Fees: Day £9,990–£12,060

Somerhill Pre-Prep
Somerhill, Five Oak Green Road,
Tonbridge, Kent TN11 0NJ
Tel: 01732 352124
Headmistress: Mrs J Ruth
Sorensen BEd(Hons), CertEd
Age range: 3–7
No. of pupils: 245

Spring Grove School
Harville Road, Wye,
Ashford, Kent TN25 5EZ
Tel: 01233 812337
Headmaster: Mr Bill Jones
Age range: 2–11
No. of pupils: 194
Fees: Day £2,050–£3,125

St Andrew's School
24-28 Watts Avenue, Rochester,
Medway, Kent ME1 1SA
Tel: 01634 843479
Principal: Mrs J Jabbour BSc
Age range: 3–11
No. of pupils: 367
Fees: Day £6,138–£6,495

St Christopher's School
New Dover Road,
Canterbury, Kent CT1 3DT
Tel: 01227 462960
The Master: Mr D Evans
Age range: 3–11
Fees: Day £7,600

St Edmund's Junior School
St Thomas Hill, Canterbury,
Kent CT2 8HU
Tel: 01227 475600
Master: R G Bacon
BA(Hons)(Durham)
Age range: 3–13
No. of pupils: 230
Fees: Day £6,969–£14,211
WB £18,969 FB £20,817

St Faith's at Ash School
5 The Street, Ash, Canterbury,
Kent CT3 2HH
Tel: 01304 813409
Headmaster: Mr Lawrence Groves
Age range: 2–11
No. of pupils: 225
Fees: Day £6,435–£8,100

St Joseph's Convent Prep School
46 Old Road East, Gravesend, Kent DA12 1NR
Tel: 01474 533012
Head Teacher: Mrs Carola Timney
Age range: 3–11
No. of pupils: 146
Fees: Day £6,655

St Lawrence College
Ramsgate, Kent CT11 7AE
Tel: 01843 572931
Principal: Mr Antony Spencer
Age range: 3–18
No. of pupils: VIth140
Fees: Day £7,047–£17,436 FB £23,640–£31,452

St Michael's Preparatory School
Otford Court, Otford, Sevenoaks, Kent TN14 5SA
Tel: 01959 522137
Headteacher: Mrs Jill Aisher
Age range: 2–13
No. of pupils: 472
Fees: Day £2,064–£12,555

Steephill School
Off Castle Hill, Fawkham, Longfield, Kent DA3 7BG
Tel: 01474 702107
Head: Mrs C Birtwell BSc, MBA, PGCE
Age range: 3–11
No. of pupils: 131
Fees: Day £6,860

Sutton Valence Preparatory School
Underhill, Chart Sutton, Maidstone, Kent ME17 3RF
Tel: 01622 842117
Head: Mr C Gibbs BA(Hons), HDE(1st Class)
Age range: 3–11
No. of pupils: 375
Fees: Day £1,630–£9,135

The Granville School
2 Bradbourne Park Road, Sevenoaks, Kent TN13 3LJ
Tel: 01732 453039
Headmistress: Mrs J Scott BEd(Cantab)
Age range: B3–4 G3–11
No. of pupils: 190
Fees: Day £4,695–£12,120

The Junior King's School, Canterbury
Milner Court, Sturry, Canterbury, Kent CT2 0AY
Tel: 01227 714000
Headmaster: Mr Peter Wells BEd(Hons)
Age range: 3–13
Fees: Day £8,610–£14,610 FB £19,830

The Mead School
16 Frant Road, Tunbridge Wells, Kent TN2 5SN
Tel: 01892 525837
Headmistress: Mrs A Culley CertEd(Oxon)
Age range: 3–11
No. of pupils: 188
Fees: Day £3,900–£9,945

The New Beacon School
Brittains Lane, Sevenoaks, Kent TN13 2PB
Tel: 01732 452131
Headmaster: Mr M Piercy BA(Hons)
Age range: B4–13
No. of pupils: 400
Fees: Day £9,405–£12,135

Walthamstow Hall Pre-Prep and Junior School
Sevenoaks, Kent TN13 3LD
Tel: 01732 451334
Headmistress: Mrs Jill Milner MA(Oxford)
Age range: G2–11
No. of pupils: 218
Fees: Day £1,230–£9,990

Wellesley House
114 Ramsgate Road, Broadstairs, Kent CT10 2DG
Tel: 01843 862991
Headmaster: Mr S T P O'Malley MA(Hons), PGCE
Age range: 7–13
No. of pupils: 133
Fees: Day £14,985–£17,850 FB £22,575

Yardley Court
Somerhill, Five Oak Green Road, Tonbridge, Kent TN11 0NJ
Tel: 01732 352124
Headmaster: J T Coakley MA, BA(Hons), PGCE
Age range: B7–13
No. of pupils: 260
Fees: Day £13,150

Surrey

Aberdour School
Brighton Road, Burgh Heath, Tadworth, Surrey KT20 6AJ
Tel: 01737 354119
Headmaster: Mr Simon Collins
Age range: 2–13
No. of pupils: 255
Fees: Day £3,990–£10,605

ACS Cobham International School
Heywood, Portsmouth Road, Cobham, Surrey KT11 1BL
Tel: +44 (0) 1932 867251
Head of School: Mr A Eysele
Age range: 2–18
No. of pupils: 1460
Fees: Day £10,690–£25,050 FB £36,240–£43,730

ACS Egham International School
Woodlee, London Road, Egham, Surrey TW20 0HS
Tel: +44 (0) 1784 430 800
Head of School: Jeremy Lewis
Age range: 3–18
No. of pupils: 620
Fees: Day £7,010–£23,430

Aldro School
Shackleford, Godalming, Surrey GU8 6AS
Tel: 01483 810266
Headmaster: Mr D W N Aston BA(Hons), PGCE
Age range: B7–13
No. of pupils: 220
Fees: Day £14,610 FB £18,795

Amesbury
Hazel Grove, Hindhead, Surrey GU26 6BL
Tel: 01428 604322
Headmaster: Mr Nigel Taylor MA
Age range: 2–13
No. of pupils: 325
Fees: Day £9,060–£13,875

Barfield School
Runfold, Farnham, Surrey GU10 1PB
Tel: 01252 782271
Head: James Reid
Age range: 2–13
No. of pupils: 280
Fees: Day £5,055–£13,020

Barrow Hills School
Roke Lane, Witley, Godalming, Surrey GU8 5NY
Tel: 01428 683639/682634
Headmaster: Mr M Unsworth BEng, PGCE
Age range: 3–13
No. of pupils: 261
Fees: Day £7,995–£12,720

Belmont Preparatory School
Feldemore, Holmbury St Mary, Dorking, Surrey RH5 6LQ
Tel: 01306 730852
Headmistress: Mrs Helen Skrine BA, PGCE, NPQH, FRSA
Age range: 2–13
No. of pupils: 227
Fees: Day £6,120–£10,428 WB £15,345

Bishopsgate School
Bishopsgate Road, Englefield Green, Egham, Surrey TW20 0YJ
Tel: 01784 432109
Headmaster: Mr Andrew Cowell BEd, CPSE
Age range: 3–13
Fees: Day £4,500–£12,726

Bloo House
The Lodge (Moore Place), Portsmouth Road, Esher, Surrey KT10 9LN
Tel: 01372 477113
Principal: Melissa Carter
Age range: 5–11
Fees: Day £10,500

Bramley School
Chequers Lane, Walton-on-the-Hill, Tadworth, Surrey KT20 7ST
Tel: 01737 812004
Headmistress: Mrs P Burgess
Age range: G3–11
No. of pupils: 110
Fees: Day £3,858–£8,418

Caterham School
Harestone Valley, Caterham, Surrey CR3 6YA
Tel: 01883 343028
Head: Mr C. W. Jones MA(Cantab)
Age range: 11–18
No. of pupils: VIth321

Chinthurst School
Tadworth Street, Tadworth, Surrey KT20 5QZ
Tel: 01737 812011
Headmaster: Mr David Williams BA (Hons), PGCE
Age range: B3–13
No. of pupils: 120
Fees: Day £3,800–£10,650

City of London Freemen's School
Ashtead Park, Ashtead, Surrey KT21 1ET
Tel: 01372 277933
Headmaster: Mr Philip MacDonald MA(Oxon)
Age range: 7–18
No. of pupils: 877 VIth213
Fees: Day £10,872–£14,598 FB £23,238

Claremont Fan Court School
Claremont Drive, Esher,
Surrey KT10 9LY
Tel: 01372 467841
Head of Senior School: Mr
Jonathan Insall-Reid
Age range: 2–18
No. of pupils: 736 VIth90
Fees: Day £4,845–£16,035
(A)(£)(🖊)

Cornerstone School
22 West Hill, Epsom, Surrey KT19 8JD
Tel: 01372 742940
Headmaster: Mr G R Davies BEd
Age range: 5–16

Coworth-Flexlands School
Valley End, Chobham,
Woking, Surrey GU24 8TE
Tel: 01276 855707
Headmistress: Mrs Anne Sweeney
Age range: B3–7 G3–11
No. of pupils: 145
Fees: Day £3,885–£10,185
(🖊)

Cranleigh Preparatory School
Horseshoe Lane, Cranleigh,
Surrey GU8 8QH
Tel: 01483 274199
Headmaster: Mr M T Wilson BSc
Age range: 7–13
No. of pupils: 290
Fees: Day £11,385 FB £14,025

CRANMORE SCHOOL
For further details see p. 69
Epsom Road, West Horsley,
Surrey KT24 6AT
Tel: 01483 280340
Email: admissions@
cranmoreprep.co.uk
Website:
www.cranmoreprep.co.uk
Headmaster: Mr Michael
Connolly BSc, BA, MA, MEd
Age range: 2–13
No. of pupils: 475
(£)(🖊)

Danes Hill School
Leatherhead Road, Oxshott,
Surrey KT22 0JG
Tel: 01372 842509
Headmaster: Mr W Murdock BA
Age range: 3–13
No. of pupils: 872
Fees: Day £1,682–£4,662
(£)(🖊)

Danesfield Manor School
Rydens Avenue, Walton-on-
Thames, Surrey KT12 3JB
Tel: 01932 220930
Principal: Mrs Helen Chalmers
Age range: 2–11
No. of pupils: 250
Fees: Day £7,500
(🖊)

Date Valley School
Mitcham Court, Cricket Green,
Mitcham, Surrey CR4 4LB
Tel: +44 (0)20 8648 4647
Headteacher: Mrs Razina Karim
Age range: 3–11
No. of pupils: 110
Fees: Day £1,869–£3,150
(£)(🖊)

Downsend School
1 Leatherhead Road,
Leatherhead, Surrey KT22 8TJ
Tel: 01372 372197
Headmaster: Floyd Steadman
Age range: 6–13
No. of pupils: 580
Fees: Day £11,640
(🖊)

Downsend School
Ashtead Lodge, 22 Oakfield
Road, Ashtead, Surrey KT21 2RE
Tel: 01372 385439
Head Teacher: Mrs K Barrett
Age range: 2–6
No. of pupils: 66
Fees: Day £2,190–£8,250

Downsend School
Epsom Lodge, 6 Norman Avenue,
Epsom, Surrey KT17 3AB
Tel: 01372 385438
Head Teacher: Miss J Birchall
Age range: 2–6
No. of pupils: 110
Fees: Day £2,325–£11,640
(🖊)

Downsend School
Leatherhead Lodge, Epsom Road,
Leatherhead, Surrey KT22 8ST
Tel: 01372 372123
Headteacher: Mrs Gill Brooks
Age range: 2–6
Fees: Day £6,780–£8,250

Drayton House School
35 Austen Road, Guildford,
Surrey GU1 3NP
Tel: 01483 504707
Headmistress: Mrs J Tyson-Jones
Froebel Cert.Ed. London University
Age range: 3 months–7 years
Fees: Day £4,420–£12,500
(🖊)

Duke of Kent School
Peaslake Road, Ewhurst,
Surrey GU6 7NS
Tel: 01483 277313
Head: Mrs Judith Fremont-Barnes
Age range: 3–16
No. of pupils: 234
Fees: Day £4,860–£14,130 WB
£13,350–£16,770 FB £15,735–£18,855
(🏑)(🏠)(£)(🖊)

Dunottar School
High Trees Road, Reigate,
Surrey RH2 7EL
Tel: 01737 761945
Head: Mrs Rowena Cole
Age range: 11–18
No. of pupils: 200 VIth40
Fees: Day £14,700
(A)(£)

Edgeborough
Frensham, Farnham,
Surrey GU10 3AH
Tel: 01252 792495
Headmaster: Mr C J Davies BA
Age range: 2–13
No. of pupils: 285
Fees: Day £9,105–£14,850
WB £16,752–£18,282
(🏠)(£)(🖊)

Emberhurst School
94 Ember Lane, Esher,
Surrey KT10 8EN
Tel: 020 8398 2933
Headmistress: Mrs P Chadwick BEd
Age range: 2 +–7+
No. of pupils: 70
Fees: Day £2,265–£6,495

Essendene Lodge School
Essendene Road, Caterham,
Surrey CR3 5PB
Tel: 01883 348349
Head Teacher: Mrs J Wermig
Age range: 2–11
No. of pupils: 153
Fees: Day £2,775–£5,550
(£)(🖊)

Ewell Castle School
Church Street, Ewell, Epsom,
Surrey KT17 2AW
Tel: 020 8393 1413
Principal: Peter Harris
Age range: B3–18 G3–11–16–18
No. of pupils: 531
Fees: Day £6,750–£13,020
(A)(£)(🖊)

Feltonfleet School
Cobham, Surrey KT11 1DR
Tel: 01932 862264
Headmaster: Mr P C Ward
Age range: 3–13
No. of pupils: 356
Fees: Day £7,680–£11,250
WB £15,750
(🏠)(£)(🖊)

Focus School - Hindhead Campus
Tilford Road, Hindhead,
Surrey GU26 6SJ
Tel: 01428 601800
Head: Mr S Hardy
Age range: 8–18
No. of pupils: 90

Frensham Heights
Rowledge, Farnham,
Surrey GU10 4EA
Tel: 01252 792561
Headmaster: Mr Andrew
Fisher BA, MEd, FRSA
Age range: 3–18
No. of pupils: 497 VIth105
Fees: Day £5,205–£15,300
FB £19,485–£22,680
(🏑)(A)(🏠)(£)(🖊)

Glenesk School
Ockham Road North, East
Horsley, Surrey KT24 6NS
Tel: 01483 282329
Headmistress: Mrs S Christie-Hall
Age range: 2–7
Fees: Day £1,350–£8,112
(£)(🖊)

Greenacre School for Girls
Sutton Lane, Banstead,
Surrey SM7 3RA
Tel: 01737 352114
Headmistress: Mrs L E Redding
Age range: G3–18
No. of pupils: 320 VIth30
Fees: Day £8,898–£15,282
(🏑)(A)(£)(🖊)

Greenfield
Brooklyn Road, Woking,
Surrey GU22 7TP
Tel: 01483 772525
Headmistress: Mrs Tania Botting BEd
Age range: 3–11
No. of pupils: 179
Fees: Day £4,284–£9,450
(£)(🖊)

Guildford High School
London Road, Guildford,
Surrey GU1 1SJ
Tel: 01483 561440
Headmistress: Mrs F J
Boulton BSc, MA
Age range: G4–18
No. of pupils: 980 VIth160
Fees: Day £9,591–£15,564
(🏑)(A)(£)

Hall Grove School
London Road, Bagshot,
Surrey GU19 5HZ
Tel: 01276 473059
Headmaster: Mr A R
Graham BSc, PGCE
Age range: 3–13
Fees: Day £8,880–£12,480
(🏠)

Halstead Preparatory School
Woodham Rise, Woking,
Surrey GU21 4EE
Tel: 01483 772682
Headmistress: Mrs P Austin
Age range: G3–11
No. of pupils: 220
Fees: Day £2,673–£12,162
(🏑)(£)(🖊)

Hampton Court House
Hampton Court Road, East
Molesey, Surrey KT8 9BS
Tel: 020 8943 0889
Headmistress: Lady
Houstoun-Boswall
Age range: 3–16
No. of pupils: VIth8
Fees: Day £7,842–£10,017
(£)

Haslemere Preparatory School
The Heights, Hill Road,
Haslemere, Surrey GU27 2JP
Tel: 01428 642350
Head: Mr P Wenham
MA(Cantab), PGCE
Age range: B3–13 G3–4
No. of pupils: 191
Fees: Day £2,199–£3,145
(🏑)(£)(🖊)

Hawley Place School
Fernhill Road, Blackwater,
Camberley, Surrey GU17 9HU
Tel: 01276 32028
Head of School: Mr Michael Stone
Age range: B2–11 G2–16
No. of pupils: 370
Fees: Day £4,446–£11,400

Hazelwood School
Wolf's Hill, Limpsfield,
Oxted, Surrey RH8 0QU
Tel: 01883 712194
Head: Mrs Maxine Shaw
Age range: 2–13
No. of pupils: 399
Fees: Day £3,585–£11,100

Hoe Bridge School
Hoe Place, Old Woking Road,
Woking, Surrey GU22 8JE
Tel: 01483 760018 & 01483
772194
Head: Mr N Arkell BSc
Age range: 2–14
Fees: Day £5,355–£14,080

International School of London (ISL) Surrey
Old Woking Road, Woking,
Surrey GU22 8HY
Tel: +44 (0)1483 750409
**Campus Principal & Head of
Secondary:** Richard Parker
Age range: 2–18 years
No. of pupils: 252
Fees: Day £17,700–£21,900

Kingswood House School
56 West Hill, Epsom, Surrey KT19 8LG
Tel: 01372 723590
Headmaster: Mr Peter R
Brooks MA, BEd(Hons)
Age range: B3–13 G3–7
No. of pupils: 210
Fees: Day £7,440–£9,825

Lanesborough
Maori Road, Guildford,
Surrey GU1 2EL
Tel: 01483 880650
Head: Mrs Clare Turnbull BA(Hons)
Age range: B3–13
No. of pupils: 350
Fees: Day £7,437–£10,026

Lingfield Notre Dame School
Lingfield, Surrey RH7 6PH
Tel: 01342 833176
Headmaster: Mr R Bool
Age range: 2–18
No. of pupils: 886 VIth120
Fees: Day £8,900–£12,000

Longacre School
Shamley Green, Guildford,
Surrey GU5 0NQ
Tel: 01483 893225
Headmistress: Ms Alexia
Bracewell MA, BA(Hons), QTS
Age range: 2–11
No. of pupils: 237

Lyndhurst School
36 The Avenue, Camberley,
Surrey GU15 3NE
Tel: 01276 22895
Head: Mr A Rudkin BEd(Hons)
Age range: 2–11
Fees: Day £9,690–£11,655

Manor House School
Manor House Lane, Little Bookham,
Leatherhead, Surrey KT23 4EN
Tel: 01372 458538
Headmistress: Miss Zara Axton
Age range: G2–16
No. of pupils: 360
Fees: Day £750–£4,070

Maple House School
23 Parchmore Road, Thornton
Heath, Surrey CR7 8LY
Tel: 020 8653 1827
Headteacher: Mrs Pauline Khoo
Age range: 5–10
No. of pupils: 97

Micklefield School
10/12 Somers Road, Reigate,
Surrey RH2 9DU
Tel: 01737 242615
Headmistress: Mrs L Rose
BEd(Hons), CertEd, Dip PC
Age range: 3–11
No. of pupils: 272
Fees: Day £2,565–£9,030

MILBOURNE LODGE SCHOOL
For further details see p. 72
Arbrook Lane, Esher,
Surrey KT10 9EG
Tel: 01372 462737
Email: registrar@
milbournelodge.co.uk
Website:
www.milbournelodge.co.uk
Head: Mrs Judy Waite
Age range: 4–13
No. of pupils: 236
Fees: Day £10,845–£13,500

NOTRE DAME SCHOOL
For further details see p. 73
Cobham, Surrey KT11 1HA
Tel: 01932 869990
Website: www.notredame.co.uk
Principal: Mr David Plummer
B.Ed. (Hons.), Dip HE, FRSA
Age range: 2–18
No. of pupils: 600

Oakhyrst Grange School
160 Stanstead Road,
Caterham, Surrey CR3 6AF
Tel: 01883 343344
Headmaster: Mr A Gear
Age range: 4–11
No. of pupils: 142
Fees: Day £1,107–£2,450

Parkside School
The Manor, Stoke d'Abernon,
Cobham, Surrey KT11 3PX
Tel: 01932 862749
Headmaster: Mr David
Aylward BEd(Hons), MA
Age range: B2–13 G2–4
No. of pupils: 382
Fees: Day £1,089–£13,350

Priory Preparatory School
Bolters Lane, Banstead,
Surrey SM7 2AJ
Tel: 01737 366920
Headmaster: Graham D
Malcom MA, BEd, FRSA
Age range: B2–13
No. of pupils: 200
Fees: Day £4,650–£10,350

Redehall Preparatory School
Redehall Road, Smallfield,
Horley, Surrey RH6 9QL
Tel: 01342 842987
Headmistress: Mrs J Wright
Age range: 3–11
Fees: Day £1,620

Reigate St Mary's Prep & Choir School
Chart Lane, Reigate,
Surrey RH2 7RN
Tel: 01737 244880
Headmaster: Mr Marcus
Culverwell MA
Age range: 3–11
No. of pupils: 280

Ripley Court School
Rose Lane, Ripley, Surrey GU23 6NE
Tel: 01483 225217
Headmaster: Mr A J Gough
Age range: 3–13
No. of pupils: 281
Fees: Day £8,745–£12,960

Rowan Preparatory School
6 Fitzalan Road, Claygate,
Esher, Surrey KT10 0LX
Tel: 01372 462627
Headteacher: Mrs Susan Clarke
Age range: G2–11
No. of pupils: 322
Fees: Day £10,098–£13,395

Rydes Hill Preparatory School
Rydes Hill House, Aldershot Road,
Guildford, Surrey GU2 8BP
Tel: 01483 563160
Headmistress: Mrs Stephanie
Bell MA(Oxon)
Age range: B3–7 G3–11
No. of pupils: 200
Fees: Day £897–£3,771

Shrewsbury Lodge School
22 Milbourne Lane, Esher,
Surrey KT10 9EA
Tel: 01372 462781
Head: Mrs Gill Hope
Age range: 3–7
Fees: Day £2,475–£3,945

St Catherine's School
Bramley, Guildford, Surrey GU5 0DF
Tel: 01483 893363
Headmistress: Mrs A M
Phillips MA(Cantab)
Age range: G4–18
No. of pupils: 900
Fees: Day £7,695–£15,660 FB £25,770

St Christopher's School
6 Downs Road, Epsom,
Surrey KT18 5HE
Tel: 01372 721807
Headteacher: Mrs A C
Thackray MA, BA(Hons)
Age range: 3–7
No. of pupils: 137
Fees: Day £1,250–£2,450

St Edmund's School
Portsmouth Road, Hindhead,
Surrey GU26 6BH
Tel: 01428 604808
Headmaster: Mr A J Walliker
MA(Cantab), MBA, PGCE
Age range: 2–13
Fees: Day £2,160–£13,842

St George's Junior School
Thames Street, Weybridge,
Surrey KT13 8NL
Tel: 01932 839400
Head Master: Mr Antony Hudson
Age range: 3–11 years
No. of pupils: 647
Fees: Day £4,680–£12,120

St Hilary's School
Holloway Hill, Godalming,
Surrey GU7 1RZ
Tel: 01483 416551
Headmistress: Mrs Jane
Whittingham BEdCert,
ProfPracSpLD
Age range: B2–7 G2–11
No. of pupils: 155
Fees: Day £9,375–£13,800

St Ives School
Three Gates Lane, Haslemere,
Surrey GU27 2ES
Tel: 01428 643734
Headteacher: Mrs S E
Cattaneo CertEd
Age range: B3–4 G3–11
No. of pupils: 149
Fees: Day £6,600–£9,225

St Teresa's Effingham (Preparatory School)
Effingham, Surrey RH5 6ST
Tel: 01372 453456
Headmaster: Mr. Mike Farmer
Age range: B2–4 G2–11
No. of pupils: 100
Fees: Day £735–£11,235
WB £19,845 FB £21,780

St. Andrew's School
Church Hill House, Horsell,
Woking, Surrey GU21 4QW
Tel: 01483 760943
Headmaster: Mr A Perks
Age range: 3–13
No. of pupils: 303
Fees: Day £3,492–£13,710

Surbiton Preparatory School
3 Avenue Elmers, Surbiton,
Surrey KT6 4SP
Tel: 020 8390 6640
**Head of Surbiton High, Junior
Girls' & Bo:** Ms C Bufton BA(Hons)
Age range: B4–11
No. of pupils: 135
Fees: Day £6,783–£9,246

TASIS The American School in England
Coldharbour Lane, Thorpe,
Surrey TW20 8TE
Tel: +44 (0)1932 582316
Head: Dr Mindy Hong
Age range: 3–18
No. of pupils: 740
Fees: Day £6,810–£22,070
FB £38,350

The Hawthorns School
Pendell Court, Bletchingley,
Redhill, Surrey RH1 4QJ
Tel: 01883 743048
Headmaster: Mr A E Floyd
BSc(Hons), PGCE
Age range: 2–13
No. of pupils: 535
Fees: Day £1,920–£12,600

The Royal School, Haslemere
Farnham Lane, Haslemere,
Surrey GU27 1BE
Tel: 01428 603052
Principal: Mrs Anne Lynch
BEd, PGCE, FRSA
Age range: B6 weeks–16
years G6 weeks–18 years
No. of pupils: 500
Fees: Day £3,026–£5,619 WB
£7,741–£8,290 FB £8,893–£9,442

Tormead School
27 Cranley Road, Guildford,
Surrey GU1 2JD
Tel: 01483 575101
Headmistress: Mrs Christina Foord
Age range: G4–18
No. of pupils: 760 VIth120
Fees: Day £5,520–£11,565

Warlingham Park School
Chelsham Common,
Warlingham, Surrey CR6 9PB
Tel: 01883 626844
Headmaster: Mr M R Donald BSc
Age range: 3–11
No. of pupils: 110
Fees: Day £3,660–£7,410

Weston Green School
Weston Green Road, Thames
Ditton, Surrey KT7 0JN
Tel: 020 8398 2778
Head: Mrs Lucia Harvey CertEd
Age range: 4–8
Fees: Day £4,574–£7,800

Westward Preparatory School
47 Hersham Road, Walton-
on-Thames, Surrey KT12 1LE
Tel: 01932 220911
Headmistress: Mrs P
Robertson CertEd
Age range: 3–12
No. of pupils: 140
Fees: Day £4,560–£5,655

Woodcote House School
Snows Ride, Windlesham,
Surrey GU20 6PF
Tel: 01276 472115
Headmaster: Mr Henry Knight
Age range: B7–13
No. of pupils: 100
Fees: Day £14,025 FB £18,900

Yehudi Menuhin School
Stoke Road, Stoke d'Abernon,
Cobham, Surrey KT11 3QQ
Tel: 01932 864739
Headmaster: Dr. Richard J
Hillier MA(Cantab), PhD
Age range: 7–19
No. of pupils: 80 VIth36
Fees: FB £41,928

West Sussex

Ardingly College Preparatory School
Haywards Heath, West
Sussex RH17 6SQ
Tel: 01444 893200
Headmaster: Mr Chris Calvey BEd
Age range: 2–13
Fees: Day £5,925–£13,950

Brambletye
Brambletye, East Grinstead,
West Sussex RH19 3PD
Tel: 01342 321004
Headmaster: Will Brooks
Age range: 2–13
No. of pupils: 280
Fees: Day £16,500 FB £22,800

Burgess Hill School for Girls
Keymer Road, Burgess Hill,
West Sussex RH15 0EG
Tel: 01444 241050
Headmistress: Mrs Kathryn
Bell BSc (Hons), PGCE
Age range: B2–4 G2–18
No. of pupils: 530 VIth93
Fees: Day £7,020–£15,300
FB £26,220–£27,000

Conifers School
Egmont Road, Midhurst,
West Sussex GU29 9BG
Tel: 01730 813243
Headmistress: Mrs Emma Smyth
Age range: 2–13
No. of pupils: 104
Fees: Day £6,030–£8,400

Copthorne Prep School
Effingham Lane, Copthorne,
West Sussex RH10 3HR
Tel: 01342 712311
Headmaster: Mr C Jones
Age range: 2–13
No. of pupils: 366
Fees: Day £7,785–£13,185
WB £15,030

Cottesmore School
Buchan Hill, Pease Pottage,
West Sussex RH11 9AU
Tel: 01293 520648
Head: T F Rogerson
Age range: 4–13
No. of pupils: 150
Fees: Day £4,800–£12,600
WB £16,875 FB £18,750

Cumnor House School
Danehill, Haywards Heath,
West Sussex RH17 7HT
Tel: 01825 790347
Headmaster: C St J Heinrich BA
Age range: 4–13
No. of pupils: 368
Fees: Day £8,100–£18,210 FB £18,210

Dorset House School
The Manor, Church Lane, Bury,
Pulborough, West Sussex RH20 1PB
Tel: 01798 831456
Headmaster: R C M
Brown MA, PGCE
Age range: 3–13
No. of pupils: 135
Fees: Day £7,290–£14,595
WB £15,810–£17,685

Farlington Preparatory School
Strood Park, Horsham,
West Sussex RH12 3PN
Tel: 01403 282566
Prep Headmistress: Ms
Frances Mwale
Age range: G3–11
No. of pupils: 150
Fees: Day £6,975–£12,915
WB £21,780 FB £22,770

Great Ballard School
Eartham, Chichester,
West Sussex PO18 0LR
Tel: 01243 814236
Head: Mr Richard Evans
Age range: 2–13
No. of pupils: 125
Fees: Day £7,800–£13,650
WB £15,000 FB £21,000

Great Walstead School
East Mascalls Lane,
Lindfield, Haywards Heath,
West Sussex RH16 2QL
Tel: 01444 483528
Headmaster: Mr C Baty
NPQH, BEd(Waikato NZ)
Age range: 2–13
No. of pupils: 421
Fees: Day £7,500–£14,475

Handcross Park School
Handcross, Haywards Heath,
West Sussex RH17 6HF
Tel: 01444 400526
Headmaster: Mr Graeme
Owton BEd(Hons)
Age range: 2–13
No. of pupils: 339
Fees: Day £2,860–£5,640 WB
£4,750–£6,610 FB £5,340–£7,200

HURSTPIERPOINT COLLEGE PREP SCHOOL
For further details see p. 70
Hurstpierpoint, West Sussex BN6 9JS
Tel: 01273 834975
Email: hurstprep@hppc.co.uk
Website: www.hppc.co.uk
Head: Mr I D Pattison BSc
Age range: 4–13
No. of pupils: 360

Lancing College Preparatory School at Worthing
Broadwater Road, Worthing, West Sussex BN14 8HU
Tel: 01903 201123
Head of School: Mrs Heather Beeby
Age range: 2–13
No. of pupils: 177
Fees: Day £540–£8,400
(£)

Lavant House
West Lavant, Chichester, West Sussex PO18 9AB
Tel: 01243 527211
Headteacher: Mrs Nicola Walker BSC (Hons), MEdm NPQH, MBA, PGCE
Age range: G4–18
No. of pupils: Vlth20

Oakwood School
Chichester, West Sussex PO18 9AN
Tel: 01243 575209
Headteacher: Mrs Gill Proctor
Age range: 3–11
No. of pupils: 247
Fees: Day £2,760–£8,880
(£)

Our Lady of Sion School
Gratwicke Road, Worthing, West Sussex BN11 4BL
Tel: 01903 204063
Headmaster: Mr M Scullion MA, BEd
Age range: 2–18
No. of pupils: 528 Vlth55
Fees: Day £5,715–£9,150
(A)(£)

Pennthorpe School
Church Street, Horsham, West Sussex RH12 3HJ
Tel: 01403 822391
Headmaster: Mr Matthew King BA(Hons)
Age range: 2–13
No. of pupils: 362
Fees: Day £1,392–£12,690
(£)

Seaford College
Lavington Park, Petworth, West Sussex GU28 0NB
Tel: 01798 867392
Headmaster: J P Green MA BA
Age range: 6–18
No. of pupils: 690 Vlth173
Fees: Day £9,930–£19,380 WB £19,320–£26,130 FB £29,985

Shoreham College
St Julians Lane, Shoreham-by-Sea, West Sussex BN43 6YW
Tel: 01273 592681
Headmaster: Mr R Taylor-West
Age range: 3–16 years
No. of pupils: 375
Fees: Day £8,550–£13,350
(£)

Sompting Abbotts Preparatory School for Boys and Girls
Church Lane, Sompting, West Sussex BN15 0AZ
Tel: 01903 235960
Principal: Mrs P M Sinclair
Age range: 2–13
No. of pupils: 185
Fees: Day £7,860–£10,095

Tavistock & Summerhill School
Summerhill Lane, Lindfield, Haywards Heath, West Sussex RH16 1RP
Tel: 01444 450256
Headmaster: Mr Andrew Giles MEd, BSc, PGCE
Age range: 3–13
No. of pupils: 150
Fees: Day £5,700–£10,350
(£)

The Prebendal School
54 West Street, Chichester, West Sussex PO19 1RT
Tel: 01243 772220
Head Master: Mr T R Cannell
Age range: 3–13
No. of pupils: 200
Fees: Day £7,500–£14,250 WB £18,450 FB £19,350
(£)

The Towers Convent School
Convent of the Blessed Sacrement, Henfield Road, Upper Beeding, Steyning, West Sussex BN44 3TF
Tel: 01903 812185
Headmistress: Mrs Clare Trelfa
Age range: B2–8 G2–16
No. of pupils: 320
Fees: Day £7,320–£10,200

Westbourne House School
Shopwyke, Chichester, West Sussex PO20 2BH
Tel: 01243 782739
Headmaster: Mr Martin Barker
Age range: 2.5–13 years
No. of pupils: 458
Fees: Day £9,360–£15,840 FB £19,410
(£)

Willow Tree Montessori School
Charlwood House, Charlwood Road, Lowfield Heath, Crawley, West Sussex RH11 0QA
Tel: 01293 820721
Headmistress: Mrs G Kerfante MontDip
Age range: 1–8
Fees: Day £2,310–£2,700

Windlesham House School
Washington, Pulborough, West Sussex RH20 4AY
Tel: 01903 874700
Headmaster: Mr Richard Foster BEd(Hons)
Age range: 4–13
No. of pupils: 350
(£)

South-West

KEY TO SYMBOLS

- (†) *Boys' school*
- (‡) *Girls' school*
- (🌐) *International school*
- (16) *Tutorial or sixth form college*
- (A) *A levels*
- (🏫) *Boarding accommodation*
- (£) *Bursaries*
- (IB) *International Baccalaureate*
- (✎) *Learning support*
- (16) *Entrance at 16+*
- (💼) *Vocational qualifications*
- (IAPS) *Independent Association of Prep Schools*
- (HMC) *The Headmasters' & Headmistresses' Conference*
- (ISA) *Independent Schools Association*
- (GSA) *Girls' School Association*
- (BSA) *Boarding Schools' Association*
- (S) *Society of Heads*

Unless otherwise indicated, all schools are coeducational day schools. Single-sex and boarding schools will be indicated by the relevant icon.

Cornwall

Polwhele House School
Truro, Cornwall TR4 9AE
Tel: 01872 273011
Headmaster: Mr Alex McCullough
Age range: 3–13
No. of pupils: 100
Fees: Day £1,350–£10,845
WB £10,929–£14,865

Roselyon School
St Blazey Road, Par,
Cornwall PL24 2HZ
Tel: 01726 812110
Head Teacher: Hilary Mann
Age range: 2–11
No. of pupils: 103
Fees: Day £504–£8,142

St Joseph's School
15 St Stephen's Hill, Launceston,
Cornwall PL15 8HN
Tel: 01566 772580
Head Teacher: Mrs Sue Rowe
Age range: 3–16
No. of pupils: 226
Fees: Day £4,566–£8,475

St Petroc's School
Ocean View Road, Bude,
Cornwall EX23 8NJ
Tel: 01288 352876
Headmaster: D. J. W. Thornburn
Age range: 0–11
Fees: Day £4,950–£7,335

St Piran's School
Trelissick Road, Hayle,
Cornwall TR27 4HY
Tel: 01736 752612
Headteacher: Mrs Carol de
Labat BEd(Hons), CertEd
Age range: 3–16
Fees: Day £2,823–£12,480

The Valley Nursery
Trevowah Road, Crantock,
Newquay, Cornwall TR8 5RU
Tel: 01637 830680
Principal: Mrs Gail P Wilson
Age range: 3 months–5 years
Fees: Day £1,098–£2,700

Truro High School for Girls
Falmouth Road, Truro,
Cornwall TR1 2HU
Tel: 01872 272830
Head: Caroline Pascoe
Age range: B3–5 G3–18
No. of pupils: 432 VIth60
Fees: Day £7,254–£10,890 WB
£19,755–£20,460 FB £19,998–£20,703

Truro School
Trennick Lane, Truro,
Cornwall TR1 1TH
Tel: 01872 272763
Headmaster: Mr A S Gordon-
Brown BCom, MSc, CA (SA)
Age range: 3–18
No. of pupils: 751 VIth200

Devon

Abbey School
Hampton Court, St Marychurch,
Torquay, Devon TQ1 4PR
Tel: 01803 327868
Principal: Mrs S J Greinig
Age range: 0–11
Fees: Day £673.20–£7,200

**Blundell's Preparatory
School**
Milestones House, Blundell's
Road, Tiverton, Devon EX16 4NA
Tel: 01884 252393
Head Master: Mr Andrew
Southgate BA Ed (Hons)
Age range: 3–11
No. of pupils: 220
Fees: Day £1,591–£11,100
WB £18,720 FB £20,775

Bramdean School
Richmond Lodge, Homefield Road,
Heavitree, Exeter, Devon EX1 2QR
Tel: 01392 273387
Head: D Stoneman NAHT
Age range: 3–18
No. of pupils: 180 VIth12
Fees: Day £4,740–£7,875

Emmanuel School
36-38 Blackboy Road,
Exeter, Devon EX4 6SZ
Tel: 01392 258150
Principal: Mr John Parker
Age range: 3–16
No. of pupils: 26
Fees: Day £2,988

**EXETER CATHEDRAL
SCHOOL**
For further details see p. 75
The Chantry, Palace Gate,
Exeter, Devon EX1 1HX
Tel: 01392 255298
Email: admissions@exetercs.org
Website: www.exetercs.org
Headmaster: James
Featherstone
Age range: 3–13
No. of pupils: 275
Fees: Day £6,519–£10,872
FB £16,683–£17,658

Exeter School
Victoria Park Road, Exeter,
Devon EX2 4NS
Tel: 01392 273679
Headmaster: Mr R Griffin
Age range: 7–18
No. of pupils: 931 VIth209
Fees: Day £10,185–£11,295

Fletewood School
88 North Road East,
Plymouth, Devon PL4 6AN
Tel: 01752 663782
Headmaster: J Martin
Age range: 3–11
Fees: Day £3,975

King's School
Hartley Road, Mannamead,
Plymouth, Devon PL3 5LW
Tel: 01752 771789
Headteacher: Mrs Jane Lee
Age range: 3–11
No. of pupils: 142
Fees: Day £4,980–£5,730

KINGSLEY SCHOOL
For further details see p. 76
Northdown Road, Bideford,
Devon EX39 3LY
Tel: 01237 426200
Email: admissions@
kingsleyschoolbideford.co.uk
Website: www.kingsleyschool
bideford.co.uk
Headmaster: Mr Simon
Woolcott BSc ARCS
Age range: 0–18
No. of pupils: 395
Fees: Day £1,870–£3,180
WB £5,410 FB £6,870

Magdalen Court School
Mulberry House, Victoria Park
Road, Exeter, Devon EX2 4NU
Tel: 01392 494919
Head: Mr Jeremy Bushrod
Age range: 0–18+
No. of pupils: 150 VIth20
Fees: Day £1,800–£8,250

Park School
Park Road, Dartington,
Totnes, Devon TQ9 6EQ
Tel: 01803 864588
Teacher-in-charge:
Amanda Bellamy
Age range: 3–12
Fees: Day £4,518–£6,738

Plantings School
33 Old Park Road, Peverell,
Plymouth, Devon PL3 4PY
Tel: 01752 265171
Headmistress: Miss D J
Webber CertEd
Age range: 3–16
No. of pupils: 12
Fees: Day £1,200–£1,440

**Plymouth College
Preparatory School**
St Dunstan's Abbey, The Millfields,
Plymouth, Devon PL1 3JL
Tel: 01752 201352
Headmaster: Chris Gatherer
Age range: 3–11
No. of pupils: 310
Fees: Day £1,867–£6,000

Rudolf Steiner School
Hood Manor, Buckfastleigh Road,
Dartington, Totnes, Devon TQ9 6AB
Tel: 01803 762528
Education Manager: Ms Gillian Mills
Age range: 3–16
No. of pupils: 307
Fees: Day £2,397–£3,978

Shebbear College
Shebbear, Beaworthy,
Devon EX21 5HJ
Tel: 01409 282000
Headmaster: Mr S. D.
Weale MA (Oxon)
Age range: 3–18
No. of pupils: 350 VIth54
Fees: Day £7,185–£11,400 WB
£12,390–£17,190 FB £15,990–£22,245

**St Christopher's
Preparatory School**
Mount Barton, Staverton,
Devon TQ9 6PF
Tel: 01803 762202
Headmistress: Victoria Kennington
Age range: 3–11
No. of pupils: 100
Fees: Day £3,600–£5,565

St John's International School
Broadway, Sidmouth,
Devon EX10 8RG
Tel: 01395 513984
Headmaster: Mr Simon Larter
Age range: 2–18
No. of pupils: 197 VIth5
Fees: Day £6,495–£10,215 WB
£12,141 FB £15,570–£19,200

St Peter's School
Harefield, Lympstone,
Exmouth, Devon EX8 5AU
Tel: 01395 272148
Headmaster: N Neeson
NPQH, BEd(Hons)
Age range: 3–13
No. of pupils: 275
Fees: Day £6,042–£10,350
WB £15,580
(symbols)

St Wilfrid's School
25 St David's Hill, Exeter,
Devon EX4 4DA
Tel: 01392 276171
Headmistress: Mrs Alexandra E
M MacDonald-Dent DPhyEd
Age range: 5–16
Fees: Day £2,085–£3,060
(£)

Stover School
Newton Abbot, Devon TQ12 6QG
Tel: 01626 354505
Principal: Mrs Sue Bradley
BSc, CBiol, MSB
Age range: 3–18
No. of pupils: 423 VIth67
Fees: Day £6,879–£10,695 WB
£15,183–£21,894 FB £16,575–£20,850
(symbols)

The Maynard School
Denmark Road, Exeter,
Devon EX1 1SJ
Tel: 01392 273417
Headmistress: Ms B Hughes
Age range: G7–18
No. of pupils: VIth80
Fees: Day £8,790–£10,992
(symbols)

The New School
The Avenue, Exminster,
Exeter, Devon EX6 8AT
Tel: 01392 496122
Headmistress: Miss M
Taylor BA(Hons), PGCE
Age range: 3–7
No. of pupils: 61
Fees: Day £690–£5,430
(symbol)

Tower House School
Fisher Street, Paignton,
Devon TQ4 5EW
Tel: 01803 557077
Headteacher: Mrs A
Jordan BA, HDE
Age range: 2–16
Fees: Day £6,552–£9,576
(£)

Trinity School
Buckeridge Road, Teignmouth,
Devon TQ14 8LY
Tel: 01626 774138
Headmaster: Mr Tim Waters
Age range: 4–11
No. of pupils: 110
(symbols)

West Buckland School
Barnstaple, Devon EX32 0SX
Tel: 01598 760281
Headmaster: J Vick MA(Cantab)
Age range: 3–18
No. of pupils: VIth135
Fees: Day £2,280–£4,250 WB
£6,760–£7,880 FB £6,760–£7,880
(symbols)

Dorset

**Bournemouth
Collegiate School**
St Osmunds Road, Parkstone,
Poole, Dorset BH14 9JY
Tel: 01202 742626
Head Teacher: Mrs Mercer
Age range: 2–16
No. of pupils: 301
Fees: Day £2,925–£9,225
(£)

Buckholme Towers School
18 Commercial Road, Lower
Parkstone, Poole, Dorset BH14 0JW
Tel: 01202 742871
Headteacher: Mr I Robertson
Age range: 3–12
No. of pupils: 104
Fees: Day £863–£1,819
(symbol)

Castle Court School
Knoll Lane, Corfe Mullen,
Wimborne, Dorset BH21 3RF
Tel: 01202 694438
Headmaster: Mr Richard Stevenson
Age range: 2–13
No. of pupils: 307
Fees: Day £1,350–£12,945
(symbols)

**Clayesmore
Preparatory School**
Iwerne Minster, Blandford
Forum, Dorset DT11 8PH
Tel: 01747 813203
Head of Prep: Mr R Geffen
Age range: 3–13
Fees: Day £8,187–£16,650
FB £20,454–£22,419
(symbols)

Dumpton School
Deans Grove House, Deans Grove,
Wimborne, Dorset BH21 7AF
Tel: 01202 883818
Headmaster: A W Browning
BSc(Hons), MA(Ed), PGCE
Age range: 2.5–13
No. of pupils: 355
Fees: Day £8,025–£14,379
(symbols)

Hanford School
Child Okeford, Blandford
Forum, Dorset DT11 8HL
Tel: 01258 860219
Headmaster: Mr N S Mackay
Age range: G7–13
Fees: Day £16,500 FB £19,950
(symbols)

Knighton House School
Durweston, Blandford
Forum, Dorset DT11 0PY
Tel: 01258 452065
Headmistress: Ms Alison Tremewan
Age range: B2–7 G2–13
No. of pupils: 128
Fees: Day £6,786–£13,410
WB £17,850 FB £17,850
(symbols)

**Leweston Preparatory
School**
Leweston, Sherborne,
Dorset DT9 6EN
Tel: 01963 210790
Headteacher: Mrs M Allen
Age range: 2–11
No. of pupils: 84
Fees: Day £7,485–£10,695
WB £13,695 FB £15,855
(symbols)

Park School
45-49 Queens Park, South Drive,
Bournemouth, Dorset BH8 9BJ
Tel: 01202 396640
Headmaster: Mr Andrew
D. Edwards
Age range: 2–11
No. of pupils: 273
Fees: Day £5,100–£7,140
(symbols)

Port Regis
Motcombe Park, Shaftesbury,
Dorset SP7 9QA
Tel: 01747 857800
Headmaster: B H Dunhill BA(Hons)
(London), PGCE(Sussex)
Age range: 3–13
No. of pupils: 324
Fees: Day £6,300–£15,105
WB £19,395 FB £19,395
(symbols)

**Sherborne Preparatory
School**
Acreman Street, Sherborne,
Dorset DT9 3NY
Tel: 01935 812097
Headmaster: Mr Nick Folland
Bsc (Hons), MIAPS, MISI
Age range: 2–13
No. of pupils: 258
Fees: Day £7,305–£13,515 WB
£18,495–£19,350 FB £18,495–£19,350
(symbols)

St Martin's School
15 Stokewood Road,
Bournemouth, Dorset BH3 7NA
Tel: 01202 292011
Headteacher: Sue Martin BSc(Hons)
Age range: 4–11 years
No. of pupils: 100
Fees: Day £4,485–£6,996

St Mary's School
Shaftesbury, Dorset SP7 9LP
Tel: 01747 852416
Headmaster: Mr Richard James
BMus(Hons)(London), ARCM
Age range: G11–18
No. of pupils: 275 VIth91
Fees: Day £17,220–£19,335
FB £24,960–£28,050
(symbols)

St Thomas Garnet's School
Parkwood Road, Boscombe,
Bournemouth, Dorset BH5 2BH
Tel: 01202 420172
Headteacher: Mrs Sarah Breeze
Age range: 3–11
Fees: Day £5,580–£7,800

**Sunninghill
Preparatory School**
South Court, South Walks,
Dorchester, Dorset DT1 1EB
Tel: 01305 262306
Headmaster: Mr Andrew Roberts-
Wray BA(Hons) Dunelm, PGCE
Age range: 3–13
(symbols)

Talbot Heath
Rothesay Road, Bournemouth,
Dorset BH4 9NJ
Tel: 01202 761881
Head: Mrs A Holloway MA, PGCE
Age range: G3–18
No. of pupils: 535 VIth80
Fees: Day £5,658–£12,539
WB £21,032 FB £21,950
(symbols)

**Talbot House
Preparatory School**
8 Firs Glen Road, Bournemouth,
Dorset BH9 2LR
Tel: 01202 510348
Headteacher: Mrs Emma Haworth
Age range: 3–11
Fees: Day £1,182–£2,279

Yarrells Preparatory School
Yarrells House, Upton,
Poole, Dorset BH16 5EU
Tel: 01202 622229
Headmistress: Mrs
Charlotte Oosthizen
Age range: 2–13
No. of pupils: 212
Fees: Day £1,642–£3,365
(symbols)

Somerset

All Hallows Preparatory School
Cranmore Hall, Shepton Mallet, Somerset BA4 4SF
Tel: 01749 881600
Head: Ms A M Lee MA,BA,LTCL,PGCE
Age range: 3–13
No. of pupils: 300
🏫£

Chard School
Fore Street, Chard, Somerset TA20 1QA
Tel: 01460 63234
Head of School: Mrs Sarah Graham
Age range: 2–11
No. of pupils: 100
Fees: Day £4,545–£5,400
£🖉

Chilton Cantelo School
Chilton Cantelo, Yeovil, Somerset BA22 8BG
Tel: 01935 850555
Headmistress: Mrs Verity White
Age range: 3–18
No. of pupils: 229 VIth20
Fees: Day £5,995–£12,885 WB £13,500–£18,285 FB £18,060–£23,985
🌐A🏫£🖉

Hazlegrove
Hazlegrove, Sparkford, Yeovil, Somerset BA22 7JA
Tel: 01963 442606/440314
Headmaster: Mr Richard Fenwick MA
Age range: 2–13
No. of pupils: 381
Fees: Day £7,287–£14,772 WB £16,566–£21,138 FB £16,566–£21,138
🏫£🖉

King's Hall School
Kingston Road, Taunton, Somerset TA2 8AA
Tel: 01823 285920
Headmaster: Mr Justin Chippendale
Age range: 3–13
Fees: Day £4,350–£11,520 FB £13,110–£17,040
🏫£🖉

Millfield Preparatory School
Edgarley Hall, Glastonbury, Somerset BA6 8LD
Tel: 01458 832446
Headmistress: Mrs S Shayler
Age range: 2–13
No. of pupils: 453
Fees: Day £2,575–£5,660 WB £8,300 FB £8,300
🏫£🖉

Perrott Hill
North Perrott, Crewkerne, Somerset TA18 7SL
Tel: 01460 72051
Headteacher: Mr R Morse BEd
Age range: 3–13
No. of pupils: 204
Fees: Day £5,265–£13,755 WB £14,835 FB £18,345
🏫£🖉

Queen's College
Trull Road, Taunton, Somerset TA1 4QS
Tel: 01823 272559
Headmaster: Mr Christopher J Alcock BSc, FRSG, FRSA
Age range: 3–18
No. of pupils: 784 VIth150
Fees: Day £5,250–£14,700 FB £10,605–£23,400
🌐A🏫£🖉

Springmead Preparatory School & Nursery
Castle Corner, Beckington, Frome, Somerset BA11 6TA
Tel: 01373 831555
Principal: Ms Madeleine Taylor
Age range: 2–11
No. of pupils: 105
Fees: Day £5,445–£6,051
🖉

Sunny Hill Prep School
Sunny Hill, Bruton, Somerset BA10 0NT
Tel: 01749 814 427
Head: Mrs Helen Snow BEd
Age range: B2–7 G2–11
No. of pupils: 68
Fees: Day £4,650–£9,600 WB £15,750–£16,050 FB £16,905–£17,205
🚶🏃🏫£🖉

Taunton Preparatory School
Staplegrove Road, Taunton, Somerset TA2 6AE
Tel: 01823 703305
Headmaster: Duncan Sinclair
Age range: 0–13
No. of pupils: 418
Fees: Day £6,195–£13,395 FB £12,030–£21,795
🏫£🖉

The Park School
The Park, Yeovil, Somerset BA20 1DH
Tel: 01935 423514
Head: Mrs J Huntington ARAM GRSM LRAM CPSEd
Age range: 3–18+
No. of pupils: VIth30
Fees: Day £4,350–£8,640 WB £14,385–£15,405 FB £15,750–£17,550
🌐A🏫£🖉

Wellington Prep School
South Street, Wellington, Somerset TA21 8NT
Tel: 01823 668700
Headmaster: Adam Gibson
Age range: 3–11
Fees: Day £5,685–£10,350 WB £16,521 FB £21,036
🖉

Wellington School
South Street, Wellington, Somerset TA21 8NT
Tel: 01823 668800
Headmaster: Henry Price MA (Oxon)
Age range: 3–18
No. of pupils: VIth165
Fees: Day £12,459–£13,659 FB £25,668–£28,185
🌐A🏫£🖉

Wells Cathedral Junior School
8 New Street, Wells, Somerset BA5 2LQ
Tel: 01749 834400
Headteacher: Mr N M Wilson BA, PGCE
Age range: 3–11
No. of pupils: 150
Fees: Day £6,054–£11,265 WB £15,951 FB £19,545
🏫£🖉

WELLS CATHEDRAL SCHOOL
For further details see p. 77
The Liberty, Wells, Somerset BA5 2ST
Tel: 01749 834200
Email: admissions@wells-cathedral-school.com
Website: www.wells-cathedral-school.com
Head: Mrs Elizabeth Cairncross
Age range: 3–18
No. of pupils: 730
Fees: Day £6,999–£17,223 FB £23,196–£28,824
🌐A🏫£🖉

West Midlands

KEY TO SYMBOLS

(†) Boys' school
(♀) Girls' school
(🌐) International school
(16) Tutorial or sixth form college
(A) A levels
(🏫) Boarding accommodation
(£) Bursaries
(IB) International Baccalaureate
(✎) Learning support
(16) Entrance at 16+
(💼) Vocational qualifications
(IAPS) Independent Association of Prep Schools
(HMC) The Headmasters' & Headmistresses' Conference
(ISA) Independent Schools Association
(GSA) Girls' School Association
(BSA) Boarding Schools' Association
(S) Society of Heads

Unless otherwise indicated, all schools are coeducational day schools. Single-sex and boarding schools will be indicated by the relevant icon.

Herefordshire

Hereford Cathedral Junior School
28 Castle Street, Hereford,
Herefordshire HR1 2NW
Tel: 01432 363511
Headmaster: Mr T C
Wheeler MA, BA, PGCE
Age range: 3–11
Fees: Day £7,200–£8,937
£ ✏

Hereford Waldorf School
Much Dewchurch, Hereford,
Herefordshire HR2 8DL
Tel: 01981 540221
Age range: 3–16
✏

Lucton School
Lucton, Leominster,
Herefordshire HR6 9PN
Tel: 01568 782000
Headmistress: Mrs Gill Thorne MA
Age range: 7–19
No. of pupils: 348 VIth53
Fees: Day £6,285–£12,330 WB
£19,845–£23,430 FB £27,180
🌐 A 🏛 £ ✏

St Richard's School
Bredenbury Court, Bromyard,
Herefordshire HR7 4TD
Tel: 01885 482491
Head: Mr N S Cheesman BEd(Hons)
Age range: 3–13
No. of pupils: 142
Fees: Day £4,710–£12,555
WB £17,295 FB £18,660
🏛 £ ✏

Shropshire

Adcote School for Girls
Little Ness, Shrewsbury,
Shropshire SY4 2JY
Tel: 01939 260202
Headmaster: Mr Gary Wright
Age range: G4–18
No. of pupils: 280
Fees: Day £4,635–£13,320 WB
£15,495–£18,645 FB £17,160–£24,325
🏃 🌐 A 🏛 £ ✏

Bedstone College
Bedstone, Bucknell,
Shropshire SY7 0BG
Tel: 01547 530303
Headmaster: Mr M S
Symonds BSc, PGCE
Age range: 3–18
No. of pupils: VIth34
Fees: Day £3,960–£11,550
FB £13,800–£20,955
🌐 A 🏛 £ ✏

Birchfield School
Albrighton, Wolverhampton,
Shropshire WV7 3AF
Tel: 01902 372534
Headmaster: Mr H Myott
Age range: B4–13 G4–12
No. of pupils: 145
Fees: Day £5,995–£12,420
WB £17,565
🏛 £ ✏

Castle House School
Chetwynd End, Newport,
Shropshire TF10 7JE
Tel: 01952 811035
Headmaster: Mr M Crewe-
Read BSc Econ, PGCE
Age range: 2–11
No. of pupils: 91
Fees: Day £6,330–£7,275
£ ✏

Ellesmere College
Ellesmere, Shropshire SY12 9AB
Tel: 01691 622321
Head: Mr B J Wignall
MA, FRSA, MCMI
Age range: 7–18
No. of pupils: VIth161
Fees: Day £9,756–£15,975 WB
£20,079–£20,646 FB £21,564–£26,955
🌐 A 🏛 £ IB ✏

MOOR PARK
For further details see p. 79
Ludlow, Shropshire SY8 4DZ
Tel: 01584 872342
Email: head@moorpark.org.uk
Website: www.moorpark.org.uk
Headmaster: Mr Charles
G O'B Minogue
Age range: 3–13 years
No. of pupils: 226
Fees: Day £6,930–£15,465
FB £18,990–£22,785
🏛 £ ✏

Moreton Hall
Weston Rhyn, Oswestry,
Shropshire SY11 3EW
Tel: 01691 773671
Head: Jonathan Forster
BA, PGCE, FRSA
Age range: B3–11 G3–18
No. of pupils: 400
🏃 🌐 A 🏛 £ ✏

Oswestry School
Upper Brook Street, Oswestry,
Shropshire SY11 2TL
Tel: 01691 655711
Headmaster: Mr Douglas
Robb MA, MEd
Age range: 4–19
No. of pupils: VIth92
Fees: Day £7,305–£13,140 WB
£17,610–£21,390 FB £20,085–£23,385
🌐 A 🏛 £ ✏

Packwood Haugh School
Ruyton XI Towns, Shrewsbury,
Shropshire SY4 1HX
Tel: 01939 260217
Headmaster: Clive Smith-
Langridge BA (Hons), PGCE
Age range: 4–13
No. of pupils: 210
Fees: Day £7,710–£16,680 FB £20,970
🏛 £ ✏

Prestfelde Preparatory School
London Road, Shrewsbury,
Shropshire SY2 6NZ
Tel: 01743 245400
Headmaster: Mr M C Groome
Age range: 3–13
No. of pupils: 275
Fees: Day £4,020–£12,825
WB £16,500
🏛 £ ✏

Shrewsbury High School GDST
32 Town Walls, Shrewsbury,
Shropshire SY1 1TN
Tel: 01743 494000
Headmaster: Mr M Getty
BA(Hons), NPQH
Age range: B3–13 G3–18
No. of pupils: VIth120
Fees: Day £8,049–£11,082
🏃 🌐 A £ ✏

St Winefride's Convent School
Belmont, Shrewsbury,
Shropshire SY1 1TE
Tel: 01743 369883
Headmistress: Sister M
Felicity CertEd, BA(Hons)
Age range: 3–11
No. of pupils: 178
Fees: Day £4,035–£4,260
✏

The Old Hall School
Stanley Road, Wellington,
Shropshire TF1 3LB
Tel: 01952 223117
Headmaster: Martin Stott
Age range: 4–11
No. of pupils: 239
Fees: Day £7,605–£11,775
£ ✏

White House School
Heath Road, Whitchurch,
Shropshire SY13 2AA
Tel: 01948 662730
Headmistress: Mrs H M Clarke
Age range: 3–11
Fees: Day £3,900
✏

Staffordshire

Abbots Bromley School
High Street, Abbots Bromley,
Rugeley, Staffordshire WS15 3BW
Tel: 01283 840232
Executive Head: Mrs Victoria
Musgrave BA M Ed
Age range: B3–11 & 15–18 G3–18
No. of pupils: 198
Fees: Day £4,518–£15,357 WB
£17,040–£21,552 FB £20,904–£25,725
🌐 A 🏛 £ ✏

Abbotsholme School
Rocester, Uttoxeter,
Staffordshire ST14 5BS
Tel: 01889 590217
Headmaster: Mr Steve Fairclough
Age range: 2–18
No. of pupils: 310 VIth55
Fees: Day £8,490–£20,715 WB
£16,545–£25,470 FB £22,625–£30,420
🌐 A 🏛 £

Chase Grammar School
Lyncroft House, St John's Road,
Cannock, Staffordshire WS11 0UR
Tel: 01543 501800
Principal: Mr Mark Ellse
Age range: 11–18
No. of pupils: 219 VIth9
Fees: Day £2,940–£10,092 FB £13,320
🌐 A 🏛 £

Copsewood Primary School
Verulam Road, Stafford,
Staffordshire ST16 3EA
Tel: 01785 258482
Head: Mr J Spicer
Age range: 7–11
No. of pupils: 20

Denstone College Preparatory School
Smallwood Manor, Uttoxeter, Staffordshire ST14 8NS
Tel: 01889 562083
Headmaster: Mr M Harrison
Age range: 2–11
No. of pupils: 146
Fees: Day £2,346–£10,125

Edenhurst Preparatory School
Westlands Avenue, Newcastle-under-Lyme, Staffordshire ST5 2PU
Tel: 01782 619348
Headmaster: N H F Copestick BSc, CertEd
Age range: 3 months–11 years
Fees: Day £7,780–£9,335

Lichfield Cathedral School
The Palace, The Close, Lichfield, Staffordshire WS13 7LH
Tel: 01543 306170
Head: Mrs Susan E Hannam BA (Hons) MA PGCE
Age range: 3–18 years
No. of pupils: 426
Fees: Day £1,795–£5,960

Newcastle-under-Lyme School
Mount Pleasant, Newcastle-under-Lyme, Staffordshire ST5 1DB
Tel: 01782 631197
Headmaster: N A Rugg
Age range: 3–18
No. of pupils: 953 VIth200
Fees: Day £7,916–£10,877

St Bede's School
Bishton Hall, Wolseley Bridge, Stafford, Staffordshire ST17 0XN
Tel: 01889 881277
Headmaster: Mr Charlie Northcote
Age range: 3–13
No. of pupils: 75
Fees: Day £6,000–£9,900 WB £12,000 FB £12,000

St Dominic's Priory School Stone
21 Station Road, Stone, Staffordshire ST15 8EN
Tel: +44 (0)1785 814181
Headteacher: Mrs Patricia Adamson
Age range: B3 months–11 G3 months–18
No. of pupils: 320 VIth40
Fees: Day £6,522–£10,242

St Joseph's Preparatory School
London Road, Trent Vale, Stoke-on-Trent, Staffordshire ST4 5NT
Tel: 01782 417533
Head: Mrs S D Hutchinson
Age range: 3–11
Fees: Day £1,460–£1,930

St. Dominic's Brewood
32 Bargate Street, Brewood, Staffordshire ST19 9BA
Tel: 01902 850248
Headteacher: Mr Harvey R J Trump MA, NPQH
Age range: B3–11 years G3–18 years
No. of pupils: 198 VIth31
Fees: Day £6,015–£11,625 FB £21,500–£21,500

Vernon Lodge Preparatory School
School Lane, Stretton, Brewood, Staffordshire ST19 9LJ
Tel: 01902 850568
Headteacher: Mrs P Sills BEd, CertEd, RSA, CertSpLd
Age range: 2–11
No. of pupils: 78
Fees: Day £5,685–£6,720

Yarlet School
Yarlet, Stafford, Staffordshire ST18 9SU
Tel: 01785 286568
Headmaster: Mr I Raybould BEd(Hons)
Age range: 2–13
No. of pupils: 169
Fees: Day £2,305–£3,865

Warwickshire

Arnold Lodge School
15-17 Kenilworth Road, Leamington Spa, Warwickshire CV32 5TW
Tel: 01926 778050
Headmaster: David Williams
Age range: 3–16
No. of pupils: 252
Fees: Day £6,960–£9,540

Bilton Grange
Dunchurch, Rugby, Warwickshire CV22 6QU
Tel: 01788 810217
Headmaster: Mr Alex Osiatynski MA Oxon PGCE
Age range: 4–13
No. of pupils: 321

Crackley Hall School
St Joseph's Park, Kenilworth, Warwickshire CV8 2FT
Tel: 01926 514444
Headmaster: Mr R Duigan
Age range: 2–11
No. of pupils: 233
Fees: Day £7,836–£8,274

Emscote House School
46 Warwick Place, Leamington Spa, Warwickshire CV32 5DE
Tel: 01926 425067
Headmistress: Mrs G J Andrews CertEd, BEd
Age range: 2–8
No. of pupils: 47
Fees: Day £6,450

Milverton House School
Holman Way, Park Street, Attleborough, Warwickshire CV11 4EL
Tel: 024 7664 1722
Head Teacher: Mr O Pipe
Age range: 0–11
No. of pupils: 275
Fees: Day £3,400–£3,800

Stratford Preparatory School
Church House, Old Town, Stratford-upon-Avon, Warwickshire CV37 6BG
Tel: 01789 297993
Headmaster: Mr N Musk MA, BA(Jt Hons), PGCE
Age range: 2–11
Fees: Day £1,300–£8,625

The Crescent School
Bawnmore Road, Bilton, Rugby, Warwickshire CV22 7QH
Tel: 01788 521595
Headteacher: Mr Huw Marshall
Age range: 3–11
No. of pupils: 171
Fees: Day £6,990–£7,560

The Croft Preparatory School
Alveston Hill, Loxley Road, Stratford-upon-Avon, Warwickshire CV37 7RL
Tel: 01789 293795
Headmaster: Mr Marcus Cook
Age range: 2–11
No. of pupils: 425
Fees: Day £1,560–£10,800

The Kingsley School
Beauchamp Avenue, Leamington Spa, Warwickshire CV32 5RD
Tel: 01926 425127
Headteacher: Ms Heather Owens
Age range: B3–7 G3–18
No. of pupils: 333 VIth61
Fees: Day £6,990–£11,460

Twycross House Pre-Preparatory School
The Hollies, The Green, Atherstone, Warwickshire CV9 3PQ
Tel: 01827 880725
Joint Heads: Mr S D Assinder BA & Mrs R T Assinder BEd
Age range: 4–8
Fees: Day £6,000

Twycross House School
Main Road, Twycross, Atherstone, Warwickshire CV9 3QA
Tel: 01827 880651
Headmaster: Mr S D Assinder
Age range: 8–18
Fees: Day £5,775–£6,750

Warwick Preparatory School
Bridge Field, Banbury Road, Warwick, Warwickshire CV34 6PL
Tel: 01926 491545
Headmaster: Mr M Turner BA(Hons), PCGE, NPQH
Age range: B3–7 G3–11
No. of pupils: 438
Fees: Day £3,393–£8,670

Warwick School
Myton Road, Warwick, Warwickshire CV34 6PP
Tel: 01926 776400
Head Master: Mr A R Lock MA (Oxon)
Age range: B7–18
No. of pupils: 1214 VIth249
Fees: Day £8,505–£10,935 WB £21,870 FB £23,337

West Midlands

Al-Ameen Primary School
Stanfield House, 447 Warwick Way, Birmingham, West Midlands B11 2JR
Tel: 0121 706 3322
Officer in Charge: Mrs Shefa Malik
Age range: 3–11
No. of pupils: 22

Al-Hijrah School
Cherrywood Centre, Burbidge Road, Bordesley Green, Birmingham, West Midlands B9 4US
Tel: 0121 7737979
Headteacher: Mohammad Abdul Karim Saqib
Age range: 5–10
No. of pupils: 306

Bablake Junior School
Coundon Road, Coventry, West Midlands CV1 4AU
Tel: 024 7627 1260
Head: Neil Price
Age range: 3–11
Fees: Day £5,770–£7,230
(£)(✏)

Bablake PrePrep
8 Park Road, Coventry, West Midlands CV1 2LH
Tel: 024 7622 1677
Headmistress: Mrs F P Ward CertEd
Age range: 3–8
Fees: Day £2,070–£2,220

Birmingham Muslim School
Bisley Works, Golden Hillock Road, Sparkbrook, Birmingham, West Midlands B11 2PY
Tel: 0121 7668129
Principal: Ms A Abdrabba
Age range: 4–10
No. of pupils: 90

Childfirst Day Nursery Solihull
Cooks Lane, Kingshurst, Solihull, West Midlands B37 6NZ
Tel: 0121 788 8148

Coventry Muslim School
643 Foleshill Road, Coventry, West Midlands CV6 5JQ
Tel: 024 7626 1803
Head: Mrs Ashique
Age range: G5–16
No. of pupils: 97
Fees: Day £1,300
(♟)

Edgbaston High School for Girls
Westbourne Road, Edgbaston, Birmingham, West Midlands B15 3TS
Tel: 0121 454 5831
Head: Dr Ruth A Weeks BSc, PhD
Age range: G2–18
No. of pupils: 950 VIth104
Fees: Day £6,501–£10,005
(♟)(A)(£)(✏)

Elmfield Rudolf Steiner School
14 Love Lane, Stourbridge, West Midlands DY8 2EA
Tel: 01384 394633
College of Teachers: Education Admin
Age range: 3–17
No. of pupils: VIth100
Fees: Day £3,240–£6,290
(£)(✏)

Emmanuel School (Walsall)
36 Wolverhampton Road, Walsall, West Midlands WS2 8PR
Tel: 01922 635810
Head Teacher: Mr Jonathan Swain BA PGCE
Age range: 3–16
No. of pupils: 82
Fees: Day £558–£7,200

Eversfield Preparatory School
Warwick Road, Solihull, West Midlands B91 1AT
Tel: 0121 705 0354
Headmaster: Mr R A Yates BA, PGCE, LPSH
Age range: 2–11
Fees: Day £4,337–£9,066
(£)(✏)

Hallfield School
48 Church Road, Edgbaston, Birmingham, West Midlands B15 3SJ
Tel: 0121 454 1496
Headmaster: Mr R Outwin-Flinders
Age range: 3 months–11 years
Fees: Day £8,019–£11,220
(✏)

Hamd House Preparatory School
730 Bordesley Green, Birmingham, West Midlands B9 5PQ
Tel: +44 (0) 121 771 3030
Headteacher: Mr S Ali
Age range: 3–11
No. of pupils: 206

Highclare School
10 Sutton Road, Erdington, Birmingham, West Midlands B23 6QL
Tel: 0121 373 7400
Head: Dr Richard Luker
Age range: B1–12 G1–18
No. of pupils: 638 VIth28
Fees: Day £3,990–£9,330
(A)(£)(✏)

Hydesville Tower School
25 Broadway North, Walsall, West Midlands WS1 2QG
Tel: 01922 624374
Headmaster: Mr Andrew McGinnes
Age range: 2–16
No. of pupils: 338
Fees: Day £5,445–£9,480
(£)

KING HENRY VIII PREPARATORY SCHOOL *For further details see p. 78*
Kenilworth Road, Coventry, West Midlands CV3 6PT
Tel: 024 7627 1307
Email: swallows@khps.co.uk
Website: www.khps.co.uk
Headteacher: Mrs Gillian Bowser
Age range: 3–11
Fees: Day £8,052–£8,580
(£)(✏)

Kingswood School
St James Place, Shirley, Solihull, West Midlands B90 2BA
Tel: 0121 744 7883
Headmaster: Mr Rob Luckham BSc(Hons), PGCE
Age range: 2–11
No. of pupils: 66
Fees: Day £5,586–£6,264
(£)(✏)

Lambs Christian School
113 Soho Hill, Hockley, Birmingham, West Midlands B19 1AY
Tel: 0121 5543790
Headteacher: Mrs Patricia Ekhuenelo
Age range: 3–11
No. of pupils: 43

Mayfield Preparatory School
Sutton Road, Walsall, West Midlands WS1 2PD
Tel: 01922 624107
Headmaster: Mr Matthew Draper
Age range: 2–11
No. of pupils: 206
Fees: Day £4,545–£7,575
(✏)

Newbridge Preparatory School
51 Newbridge Crescent, Tettenhall, Wolverhampton, West Midlands WV6 0LH
Tel: 01902 751088
Headmistress: Mrs Sarah Fisher
Age range: B3–4 G3–11
No. of pupils: 148
Fees: Day £4,215–£6,408
(♟)(✏)

Norfolk House School
4 Norfolk Road, Edgbaston, Birmingham, West Midlands B15 3PS
Tel: 0121 454 7021
Headmistress: Mrs Sarah Morris BA (Hons), PGCE
Age range: 3–11
No. of pupils: 146
Fees: Day £6,420–£8,391

Pattison College
86-90 Binley Road, Coventry, West Midlands CV3 1FQ
Tel: 024 7645 5031
Principal: Mrs E.A.P. McConnell B.Ed. (Hons)
Age range: 3–16
No. of pupils: VIth16
Fees: Day £4,050–£5,160

Priory School
39 Sir Harry's Road, Edgbaston, Birmingham, West Midlands B15 2UR
Tel: 0121 440 4103
Headmaster: Mr J Cramb
Age range: 6 months–18 years
No. of pupils: 438 VIth23
Fees: Day £2,705–£4,085
(A)(£)(✏)

Rosslyn School
1597 Stratford Road, Hall Green, Birmingham, West Midlands B28 9JB
Tel: 0121 744 2743
Principal: Mrs Jane Scott
Age range: 2–11
Fees: Day £2,000–£3,900
(✏)

Ruckleigh School
17 Lode Lane, Solihull, West Midlands B91 2AB
Tel: 0121 705 2773
Headmistress: Mrs Barbara Forster
Age range: 3–11
Fees: Day £2,549–£7,404
(✏)

Saint Martin's School
Malvern Hall, Brueton Avenue, Solihull, West Midlands B91 3EN
Tel: 0121 705 1265
Headmistress: Mrs J Carwithen BSc, MA, PGCE
Age range: G3–18
No. of pupils: 430 VIth40
Fees: Day £7,335–£10,095
(♟)(A)(£)(✏)

Salafi Independent School
472 Coventry Road, Birmingham, West Midlands B10 0UG
Tel: 0121 7724567
Headteacher: Abdul Moxin
Age range: 5–11
No. of pupils: 159

Solihull School
Warwick Road, Solihull, West Midlands B91 3DJ
Tel: 0121 705 0958
Headmaster: Mr David E J J Lloyd
Age range: 7–18
No. of pupils: 1013 VIth279
Fees: Day £8,673–£10,590
(A)(£)(✏)

St George's School, Edgbaston
31 Calthorpe Road, Birmingham, West Midlands B15 1RX
Tel: 0121 625 0398
Headmaster: Sir Robert Dowling Kt
Age range: 2–18
No. of pupils: 368 VIth48
Fees: Day £4,965–£9,765
(A)(£)(✏)

Tettenhall College
Wood Road, Tettenhall, Wolverhampton, West Midlands WV6 8QX
Tel: 01902 751119
Head: Mr D C Williams
Age range: 2–18
No. of pupils: VIth66
Fees: Day £7,002–£13,284 WB £15,156–£20,541 FB £19,044–£25,518
(♞)(A)(♟)(£)(✏)

The Blue Coat School
Somerset Road, Edgbaston,
Birmingham, West Midlands B17 0HR
Tel: 0121 410 6800
Headmaster: Mr A D J
Browning MA(Cantab)
Age range: 2–11
Fees: Day £7,050–£10,845

The Davenport Lodge School
21 Davenport Road, Coventry,
West Midlands CV5 6QA
Tel: 024 7667 5051
Headteacher: Mrs M
D Martin BPhilEd
Age range: 6weeks–8 years
No. of pupils: 97
Fees: Day £5,910

The Shrubbery School
Walmley Ash Road, Walmley, Sutton
Coldfield, West Midlands B76 1HY
Tel: 0121 351 1582
Head Teacher: Hilary Atkins
Age range: 3–11
Fees: Day £1,542–£3,093

West House School
24 St James's Road,
Edgbaston, Birmingham,
West Midlands B15 2NX
Tel: 0121 440 4097
Headmaster: Mr A M J
Lyttle BA(Hons), PGCE
Age range: B1–11 G1–4
No. of pupils: 290
Fees: Day £1,024–£3,333

Worcestershire

Abberley Hall
Abberley Hall, Worcester,
Worcestershire WR6 6DD
Tel: 01299 896275
Headmaster: Mr Will Lockett
Age range: 2–13
Fees: Day £7,200–£15,495 FB £19,440

Bowbrook House School
Peopleton, Pershore,
Worcestershire WR10 2EE
Tel: 01905 841242
Headteacher: Mr C D
Allen BSc(Hons)
Age range: 3–16
Fees: Day £3,480–£6,450

Bromsgrove Preparatory School
Old Station Road, Bromsgrove,
Worcestershire B60 2BU
Tel: 01527 579600
Headmaster: P Lee-Smith
Age range: 7–13
Fees: Day £7,860–£10,245 WB
£10,260–£13,245 FB £15,600–£19,350

Bromsgrove Pre-preparatory & Nursery School
Avoncroft House, Hanbury Road,
Bromsgrove, Worcestershire B60 4JS
Tel: 01527 873007
Headmistress: Mrs Susan
Pickering BPhil(Ed), CertEd
Age range: 2–7
Fees: Day £2,490–£4,800

Cambian New Elizabethan School
Quarry Bank, Hartlebury,
Kidderminster,
Worcestershire DY11 7TE
Tel: 01299 250258
Headteacher: Craig Moreton
BA (Hons), PGCE, NPQH
Age range: 4–16
No. of pupils: 21
Fees: Day £3,000–£7,500

Dodderhill School
Crutch Lane, Droitwich,
Worcestershire WR9 0BE
Tel: 01905 778290
Headmistress: Mrs C H M Awston
Age range: B3–9 G3–16
No. of pupils: 220
Fees: Day £7,500–£9,750

Heathfield School
Wolverley Road, Kidderminster,
Worcestershire DY10 3QE
Tel: 01562 850 204
Head: Roger Brierly BEd
Age range: 0–16
Fees: Day £6,036–£10,005

King's Hawford
Worcester, Worcestershire WR3 7SE
Tel: 01905 451292
Headmaster: Mr J Turner
Age range: 2–11
No. of pupils: 357
Fees: Day £5,150–£9,585

King's St Alban's School
Mill Street, Worcester,
Worcestershire WR1 2NJ
Tel: 01905 354906
Headmaster: Mr I R Griffin
BA (Hons) QTS
Age range: 4–11
No. of pupils: 216
Fees: Day £5,904–£10,305

Madresfield Early Years Centre
Hayswood Farm, Madresfield,
Malvern, Worcestershire WR13 5AA
Tel: 01684 574378
Head: Mrs A Bennett
Age range: 1–8
No. of pupils: 216
Fees: Day £5,800–£6,500

Moffats School
Kinlet Hall, Kinlet, Bewdley,
Worcestershire DY12 3AY
Tel: 01299 841230
Head: Mrs R McCarthy MA (Oxon)
Age range: 3–13
No. of pupils: 60
Fees: Day £6,480–£10,260 FB £17,850

RGS Springfield
Springfield, Britannia Square,
Worcester, Worcestershire WR1 3DL
Tel: 01905 24999
Headmistress: Laura Brown
Age range: 2–11
Fees: Day £1,870–£3,226

RGS The Grange
The Grange, Grange Lane, Claines,
Worcester, Worcestershire WR1 1HP
Tel: 01905 451205
Headmaster: Gareth Hughes
Age range: 2–11
Fees: Day £1,992–£3,186

River School
Oakfield House, Droitwich Road,
Worcester, Worcestershire WR3 7ST
Tel: 01905 457047
Principal: Mr Richard Wood
Age range: 5–16
Fees: Day £4,140

The Downs Malvern
Colwall, Malvern,
Worcestershire WR13 6EY
Tel: 01684 544100
Headmaster: Mr Alastair Cook
Age range: 3–13
Fees: Day £5,793–£13,908
FB £13,968–£18,408

The Elms
Colwall, Malvern,
Worcestershire WR13 6EF
Tel: 01684 540344
Headmaster: Mr A J L Thomas
Age range: 3–13
No. of pupils: 200
Fees: Day £6,720–£17,052
FB £17,880–£18,870

The Knoll School
33 Manor Avenue, Kidderminster,
Worcestershire DY11 6EA
Tel: 01562 822622
Head of School: Mr N J
Humphreys BEd(Hons)
Age range: 3 months–11 years
No. of pupils: 125
Fees: Day £1,796–£2,731

Winterfold House
Chaddesley Corbett,
Kidderminster,
Worcestershire DY10 4PL
Tel: 01562 777234
Headmaster: Mr W Ibbetson-Price BA, MA, NPQH
Age range: 6 weeks–13 years
Fees: Day £6,360–£10,680

Yorkshire & Humberside

KEY TO SYMBOLS

- (†) Boys' school
- (♀) Girls' school
- (🌐) International school
- (16¹) Tutorial or sixth form college
- (A) A levels
- (🏛) Boarding accommodation
- (£) Bursaries
- (IB) International Baccalaureate
- (✎) Learning support
- (16⁺) Entrance at 16+
- (💼) Vocational qualifications
- (IAPS) Independent Association of Prep Schools
- (HMC) The Headmasters' & Headmistresses' Conference
- (ISA) Independent Schools Association
- (GSA) Girls' School Association
- (BSA) Boarding Schools' Association
- (S) Society of Heads

Unless otherwise indicated, all schools are coeducational day schools. Single-sex and boarding schools will be indicated by the relevant icon.

East Riding of Yorkshire

Froebel House School
5 Marlborough Avenue,
Kingston upon Hull, East
Riding of Yorkshire HU5 3JP
Tel: 01482 342272
Headmistress: Mrs L A
Roberts CertEd, BA(Ed)
Age range: 4–11
No. of pupils: 120
Fees: Day £4,080

Hessle Mount School
Jenny Brough Lane, Hessle, East
Riding of Yorkshire HU13 0JZ
Tel: 01482 643371
Headmistress: Mrs C Cutting
Age range: 3–8
No. of pupils: 155
Fees: Day £3,300–£3,525

Hull Collegiate School
Tranby Croft, Anlaby, Kingston
upon Hull, East Riding of
Yorkshire HU10 7EH
Tel: 01482 657016
Headteacher: Mrs Rebecca Glover
Age range: 2–18
No. of pupils: Vlth109
Fees: Day £4,740–£10,926
Ⓐ Ⓔ ✎

Hymers College
Hymers Avenue, Kingston upon Hull,
East Riding of Yorkshire HU3 1LW
Tel: 01482 343555
Headmaster: Mr D Elstone
Age range: 8–18
No. of pupils: 977 Vlth215
Fees: Day £7,443–£8,946
Ⓐ Ⓔ

North Yorkshire

Ashville College
Green Lane, Harrogate,
North Yorkshire HG2 9JP
Tel: 01423 566358
Headmaster: D M Lauder
Age range: 3–18
No. of pupils: Vlth152
Fees: Day £7,650–£13,225
FB £16,400–£26,575
🌐 Ⓐ 🏛 Ⓔ ✎

Aysgarth School
Newton le Willows, Bedale,
North Yorkshire DL8 1TF
Tel: 01677 450240
Head of School: Rob Morse
No. of pupils: 200
Fees: Day £5,865 WB
£880–£1,165 FB £7,635
👤 🏛 Ⓔ ✎

Bootham Junior School
Rawcliffe Lane, York, North
Yorkshire YO30 6NP
Tel: 01904 655021
Head: Mrs Helen Todd
Age range: 3–11
Fees: Day £6,390–£9,285
✎

Botton Village School
Danby, Whitby, North
Yorkshire YO21 2NJ
Tel: 01287 661 206
Age range: 4–14

Brackenfield School
128 Duchy Road, Harrogate,
North Yorkshire HG1 2HE
Tel: 01423 508558
Headteacher: Ms Patricia Sowa
Age range: 2–11
No. of pupils: 179
Fees: Day £2,065–£2,230
✎

Chapter House Preparatory School
Thorpe Underwood Hall, Ouseburn,
York, North Yorkshire YO26 9SZ
Tel: 01423 333330
Head Teacher: Mrs
Karen Kilkenny BSc
Age range: 3–10
No. of pupils: 122
Fees: Day £4,518–£6,144
FB £20,250–£20,904
🏛 Ⓔ ✎

Clifton School and Nursery
York, North Yorkshire YO30 6AB
Tel: 01904 527361
Head: Philip Hardy BA (Hons) PGCE
Age range: 3–8
No. of pupils: 199
Fees: Day £7,200–£7,620

Cundall Manor School
Helperby, York, North
Yorkshire YO61 2RW
Tel: 01423 360200
Joint Heads: Mrs Amanda Kirby
BA (Hons) PGCE, NPQH & Mr
John Sample BSc (Hons) PGCE
Age range: 2–16
No. of pupils: 350
Fees: Day £8,985–£14,415
WB £18,975
🏛 Ⓔ ✎

Fyling Hall School
Robin Hood's Bay, Whitby,
North Yorkshire YO22 4QD
Tel: 01947 880353
Headmaster: Mr. Steven Allen
Age range: 4–18
No. of pupils: Vlth54
Fees: Day £6,552–£8,736 WB
£15,288–£17,784 FB £15,912–£19,032
🌐 Ⓐ 🏛 Ⓔ ✎

Giggleswick Junior School
Mill Lane, Giggleswick, Settle,
North Yorkshire BD24 0DG
Tel: 01729 893100
Headmaster: Mr. James Mundell
Age range: 3–11 (boarding from 9)
No. of pupils: 75
Fees: Day £3,912 FB £6,515
🏛 Ⓔ ✎

Highfield Prep School
Clarence Drive, Harrogate,
North Yorkshire HG1 2QG
Tel: 01423 504 543
Headmistress: Rachel Colbourn
Age range: 4–10
No. of pupils: 216
Fees: Day £6,090–£6,600

Pocklington Montessori School
Bielby Lane, Pocklington, York,
North Yorkshire YO42 1NT
Tel: 01759 305436
Headmistress/Owner: Ms Rosie
Pressland DipComEd(Dist),
DipMontEd(Dist)
Age range: 0–8
No. of pupils: 300
Fees: Day £1,550
✎

POCKLINGTON PREP SCHOOL
For further details see p. 81
West Green, Pocklington, York,
North Yorkshire YO42 2NH
Tel: 01759 321228
Email: enquiry@
pocklingtonprepschool.com
Website:
www.pocklingtonschool.com
Headmaster: Mr I D Wright
BSc(Hons), PGCE, NPQH
Age range: 4–11
No. of pupils: 218
Fees: Day £7,080–£11,106
WB £18,975 FB £20,439
🏛 Ⓔ ✎

Queen Ethelburga's Collegiate Foundation
Thorpe Underwood Hall, Ouseburn,
York, North Yorkshire YO26 9SS
Tel: 01423 33 33 30
Principal: Steven Jandrell BA
Age range: 3–19
No. of pupils: 1605 Vlth610
Fees: Day £7,785–£14,985
🌐 Ⓐ 🏛 Ⓔ ✎

Queen Mary's School
Baldersby Park, Topcliffe, Thirsk,
North Yorkshire YO7 3BZ
Tel: 01845 575000
Head: Mr Robert
McKenzie Johnston
Age range: B3–8 G3–16
No. of pupils: 235
Fees: Day £5,445–£13,050
FB £14,400–£16,995
👤 🌐 🏛 Ⓔ ✎

Read School
Drax, Selby, North Yorkshire YO8 8NL
Tel: 01757 618248
Headmaster: J A
Sweetman BSc, PhD
Age range: 3–18
No. of pupils: Vlth36
Fees: Day £6,480–£9,180 WB
£15,447–£17,748 FB £17,295–£19,800
🌐 Ⓐ 🏛 Ⓔ ✎

Scarborough College
Filey Road, Scarborough,
North Yorkshire YO11 3BA
Tel: +44 (0)1723 360620
Head of School: Isobel Nixon
Age range: 3–18
No. of pupils: 450
Fees: Day £5,580–£9,360
FB £16,140–£17,340
🌐 Ⓐ 🏛 Ⓔ IB ✎

St Martins Ampleforth
Gilling Castle, Gilling East, York,
North Yorkshire YO62 4HP
Tel: 01439 766600
Headmaster: Mr M O'Donnell
Age range: 3–13 years
No. of pupils: 164
Fees: Day £7,578–£14,046 FB £21,132
🏛 Ⓔ ✎

St Olave's School
Clifton, York, North
Yorkshire YO30 6AB
Tel: 01904 527416
The Master: Mr A Falconer
Age range: 8–13
No. of pupils: 338
Fees: Day £10,530–£12,435
FB £19,440–£21,435
🏛 Ⓔ ✎

Terrington Hall
Terrington, York, North
Yorkshire YO60 6PR
Tel: 01653 648227
Headmaster: Mr. Stephen
Mulryne B.Ed (Hons) Liverpool
Age range: 3–13
No. of pupils: 150
🏛 Ⓔ ✎

The Minster School
Deangate, York, North
Yorkshire YO1 7JA
Tel: 0844 939 0000
Headmaster: Mr A Donaldson
Age range: 3–13
Fees: Day £4,674–£7,188
✎

Tregelles
Junior Department, The Mount School, Dalton Terrace, York, North Yorkshire YO24 4DD
Tel: 01904 667513
Head: Mr Martyn Andrews BSc(Hons), PGCE
Age range: 3–11
Fees: Day £1,710–£2,280

Wharfedale Montessori School
Bolton Abbey, Skipton, North Yorkshire BD23 6AN
Tel: 01756 710452
Headmistress/Principal: Mrs Jane Lord
Age range: 2–12
Fees: Day £6,225

York Steiner School
Danesmead, Fulford Cross, York, North Yorkshire YO10 4PB
Tel: 01904 654983
Administrator: Maurice Dobie
Age range: 3–14
No. of pupils: 197
Fees: Day £728–£4,800

North-East Lincolnshire

Montessori School
Station Road, Stallingborough, North-East Lincolnshire DN41 8AJ
Tel: 01472 886000
Headteacher: Ms Theresa Ellerby
Age range: 4–11
No. of pupils: 21

St James' School
22 Bargate, Grimsby, North-East Lincolnshire DN34 4SY
Tel: 01472 503260
Headteacher: Mrs S M Isaac BA, PGCE
Age range: 2–18
No. of pupils: 238 VIth25
Fees: Day £4,605–£11,067 WB £11,775–£17,367 FB £13,125–£18,717

St Martin's Preparatory School
63 Bargate, Grimsby, North-East Lincolnshire DN34 5AA
Tel: 01472 878907
Headmaster: Mr S Thompson BEd
Age range: 2–11
Fees: Day £4,620–£5,790

South Yorkshire

Ashdell Preparatory School
266 Fulwood Road, Sheffield, South Yorkshire S10 3BL
Tel: 0114 266 3835
Headteacher: Mrs Anne Camm
Age range: B3–4 G3–11
No. of pupils: 130
Fees: Day £8,985–£9,600

Bethany School
Finlay Street, Sheffield, South Yorkshire S3 7PS
Tel: 0114 272 6994
Headteacher: K Walze
Age range: 4–16
No. of pupils: 76

Birkdale School
Oakholme Road, Sheffield, South Yorkshire S10 3DH
Tel: 0114 2668409
Head Master: Dr Paul Owen
Age range: B4–18 G16–18
No. of pupils: VIth200
Fees: Day £7,716–£11,052

Handsworth Christian School
231 Handsworth Road, Handsworth, Sheffield, South Yorkshire S13 9BJ
Tel: 0114 2430276
Headteacher: Mrs Pauline Elizabeth Arnott
Age range: 4–16
No. of pupils: 148
Fees: Day £2,340

Hill House School
6th Avenue, Auckley, Doncaster, South Yorkshire DN9 3GG
Tel: +44 (0)1302 776300
Principal: David Holland
Age range: 2 3–16
Fees: Day £6,150–£879

Hope House School Barnsley
Hope House, Blucher Street, Barnsley, South Yorkshire S70 1AP
Tel: 01226 211011
Headteacher: Mr G J Barnes
Age range: 4–16
No. of pupils: 79
Fees: Day £3,300–£4,980

Mylnhurst Preparatory School & Nursery
Button Hill, Woodholm Road, Ecclesall, Sheffield, South Yorkshire S11 9HJ
Tel: 0114 2361411
Headmaster: Christopher Emmott BSc(Hons), PGCE
Age range: 3–11
No. of pupils: 185
Fees: Day £7,575

Sheffield High School GDST
10 Rutland Park, Sheffield, South Yorkshire S10 2PE
Tel: 0114 266 0324
Headmistress: Mrs Dunsford BA
Age range: G4–18
No. of pupils: 1020
Fees: Day £6,912–£9,531

Sycamore Hall Preparatory School
1 Hall Flat Lane, Balby, Doncaster, South Yorkshire DN4 8PT
Tel: 01302 856800
Headmistress: Miss J Spencer
Age range: 3–11
Fees: Day £1,650

Westbourne School
Westbourne Road, Sheffield, South Yorkshire S10 2QT
Tel: 0114 2660374
Headmaster: Mr John B Hicks MEd
Age range: 4–16
No. of pupils: 338
Fees: Day £2,550–£3,590

West Yorkshire

Ackworth School
Pontefract Road, Ackworth, nr. Pontefract, West Yorkshire WF7 7LT
Tel: 01977 611401
Head: Mr. Anton Maree BA Rhodes (HDE)
Age range: 2–18
No. of pupils: 480 VIth91
Fees: Day £8,050–£10,441 FB £24,150–£31,323

Al Mumin Primary School
15-17 Spring Gardens, Bradford, West Yorkshire BD1 3EJ
Tel: 01274 733150
Headteacher: Mr M M Azam
Age range: 3–10
No. of pupils: 102

Al-Furqan Preparatory School
Drill Hall House, Bath Street, Dewsbury, West Yorkshire WF13 2JR
Tel: 01924 453 661
Headteacher: Mr Ahmad Farook Raja
Age range: 5–11
No. of pupils: 139

Bradford Christian School
Livingstone Road, Bolton Woods, Bradford, West Yorkshire BD2 1BT
Tel: 01274 532649
Headmaster: P J Moon BEd(Hons)
Age range: 4–16
Fees: Day £1,236–£2,532

Bradford Grammar School
Keighley Road, Bradford,
West Yorkshire BD9 4JP
Tel: 01274 553702
Headmaster: Mr Kevin Riley BA, MEd
Age range: 6–18
No. of pupils: VIth266
Ⓐ Ⓔ ⦿

Bronte House School
Apperley Bridge, Bradford,
West Yorkshire BD10 0NR
Tel: 0113 2502811
Headmaster: Simon W Dunn
Age range: 2–11
No. of pupils: 300
Fees: Day £7,500–£900
WB £17,000 FB £18,000
⬛ Ⓔ ⦿

Crystal Gardens
38-40 Greaves Street, Bradford,
West Yorkshire BD5 7PE
Tel: 01274 575400
Headteacher: Muhammad
Abdur Raqeeb
Age range: 5–11
No. of pupils: 20

Dale House Independent School
Ruby Street, Carlinghow, Batley,
West Yorkshire WF17 8HL
Tel: 01924 422215
Headmistress: Mrs S M G
Fletcher BA, CertEd
Age range: 2–11
No. of pupils: 100
Ⓔ ⦿

Darul Uloom Dawatul Imaan
Harry Street, Off Wakefield Road,
Bradford, West Yorkshire BD4 9PH
Tel: 01274 402233
Principal: Mr Mohamed Bilal Lorgat
Age range: B11–13
No. of pupils: 112
⬥

FULNECK JUNIOR SCHOOL
For further details see p. 80
Fulneck, Pudsey, Leeds,
West Yorkshire LS28 8DS
Tel: 0113 257 0235
Email: enquiries@
fulneckschool.co.uk
Website:
www.fulneckschool.co.uk
Head of Junior School:
Mr Chris Bouckley
Age range: 3–11
(boarding from age 9)
No. of pupils: 128

Gateways School
Harewood, Leeds, West
Yorkshire LS17 9LE
Tel: 0113 2886345
Headmistress: Dr Tracy Johnson
Age range: B2–11 G2–18
No. of pupils: 394 VIth48
Fees: Day £7,110–11,820
⬥ Ⓐ Ⓔ ⦿

Ghyll Royd School
Greystone Manor, Ilkley
Road, Burley in Wharfedale,
West Yorkshire LS29 7HW
Tel: 01943 865575
Headteacher: Mrs Irene Connor
Age range: B2–11
No. of pupils: 100
Fees: Day £1,560–£5,577
⬥ Ⓔ ⦿

Hipperholme Grammar Junior School
45 Wakefield Road, Lightcliffe,
Halifax, West Yorkshire HX3 8AQ
Tel: 01422 201330
Headteacher: Mrs Louise Reynolds
Age range: 3–11
No. of pupils: 131
Fees: Day £3,250–£7,845
Ⓔ ⦿

Hipperholme Grammar School
Bramley Lane, Hipperholme,
Halifax, West Yorkshire HX3 8JE
Tel: 01422 202256
Headmaster: Mr Jack
D Williams BSc
Age range: 3–18
No. of pupils: VIth41
Fees: Day £8,646–£10,800
Ⓐ Ⓔ ⦿

Huddersfield Grammar School
Royds Mount, Luck Lane,
Marsh, Huddersfield, West
Yorkshire HD1 4QX
Tel: 01484 424549
Headmaster: Mr Tim Hoyle
Age range: 3–16
No. of pupils: 400
Fees: Day £6,300–£8,000
Ⓔ

Inglebrook Preparatory School
Northgate Close, Pontefract,
West Yorkshire WF8 1JL
Tel: 01977 700120
Head: Mrs J S Bellamy
Age range: 2–11
No. of pupils: 114
Fees: Day £1,656–£3,252

Islamic Tarbiyah Preparatory School
Ambler Street, Bradford,
West Yorkshire BD8 8AW
Tel: 01274 490462
Headteacher: Mr S A Nawaz
Age range: 5–10
No. of pupils: 123

Lady Lane Park Preparatory School
Lady Lane, Bingley, West
Yorkshire BD16 4AP
Tel: 01274 551168
Headmistress: Mrs Gill Wilson
Age range: 2–11
No. of pupils: 171
Fees: Day £7,479
⦿

Leeds Menorah School
393 Street Lane, Leeds,
West Yorkshire LS17 6HQ
Tel: 0113 268 3390
Headteacher: Rabbi J Refson
Age range: 5–16
No. of pupils: 55

Madni Muslim Girls High School
Thornie Bank, Off Scarborough
St, Savile Town, Dewsbury,
West Yorkshire WF12 9AX
Tel: 01924 520720
Headmistress: Mrs S A Mirza
Age range: G3–18
No. of pupils: 250
⬥ Ⓐ

Mill Cottage Montessori School
Wakefield Road, Brighouse,
West Yorkshire HD6 4HA
Tel: 01484 400500
Principal: Ailsa Nevile
Age range: 0–11

Moorfield School
Wharfedale Lodge, 11
Ben Rhydding Road, Ilkley,
West Yorkshire LS29 8RL
Tel: 01943 607285
Headmistress: Mrs Jessica Crossley
Age range: 3–11
Fees: Day £7,980
Ⓔ ⦿

Moorlands School
Foxhill, Weetwood Lane, Leeds,
West Yorkshire LS16 5PF
Tel: 0113 2785286
Headmaster: Mr J Davies
Age range: 2.2–13
No. of pupils: 197
Fees: Day £7,491–£8,379
Ⓔ ⦿

Mount School
3 Binham Road, Edgerton,
Huddersfield, West
Yorkshire HD2 2AP
Tel: 01484 426432
Headteacher: Janet Brook
Age range: 3–11
Fees: Day £6,075
⦿

Netherleigh & Rossefield School
Parsons Road, Heaton, Bradford,
West Yorkshire BD9 4AY
Tel: 01274 543162
Headteacher: Mrs R M Midgley
Age range: 3–11
No. of pupils: 110
Fees: Day £2,880–£5,115

Paradise Primary School
1 Bretton Street, Dewsbury,
West Yorkshire WF12 9BB
Tel: 01924 439803
Headteacher: Mr Rashid Kola
Age range: 5–11
No. of pupils: 121

Queen Elizabeth Grammar School (Junior School)
158 Northgate, Wakefield,
West Yorkshire WF1 3QY
Tel: 01924 373821
Head: Mrs L A Gray
Age range: B7–11
No. of pupils: 261
Fees: Day £6,207–£6,558
⬥ Ⓔ

Queenswood School
Queen Street, Morley, Leeds,
West Yorkshire LS27 9EB
Tel: 0113 2534033
Headteacher: Mrs J A Tanner
MMus, BA, FTCL, ARCO
Age range: 4–11
Fees: Day £3,885–£4,275

Rastrick Independent School
Ogden Lane, Rastrick, Brighouse,
West Yorkshire HD6 3HF
Tel: 01484 400344
Headmistress: Mrs S A Vaughey
Age range: 0–16
No. of pupils: 200
Fees: Day £5,985–£8,760
Ⓐ Ⓔ ⦿

Richmond House School
170 Otley Road, Leeds,
West Yorkshire LS16 5LG
Tel: 0113 2752670
Headmistress: Mrs J E Disley
Age range: 3–12
No. of pupils: 211
Fees: Day £1,980–£7,725
Ⓔ ⦿

Rishworth School
Rishworth, Halifax, West
Yorkshire HX6 4QA
Tel: 01422 822217
Headmaster: Mr. A S Gloag
Age range: 3–18
No. of pupils: 600 VIth90
Fees: Day £4,905–£9,585 WB
£15,285–£16,725 FB £16,830–£18,360
⬥ Ⓐ ⬛ Ⓔ ⦿

Silcoates School
Wrenthorpe, Wakefield,
West Yorkshire WF2 0PD
Tel: 01924 291614
Headmaster: Darryl S Wideman
Age range: 7–18
No. of pupils: 768
Fees: Day £6,618–£11,181
Ⓐ Ⓔ

St Hilda's School
Dovecote Lane, Horbury,
Wakefield, West Yorkshire WF4 6BB
Tel: 01924 260706
Headmistress: Mrs J L Sharpe
Age range: B0–7 G0–11
No. of pupils: 127
Fees: Day £4,722–£4,944
⦿

Sunny Hill House School

Wrenthorpe Lane, Wrenthorpe,
Wakefield, West Yorkshire WF2 0QB
Tel: 01924 291717
Headmistress: Mrs H K
Cushing CertEd, MA
Age range: 2–7
No. of pupils: 116
Fees: Day £5,256

The Branch Christian School

Dewsbury Revival Centre,
West Park Street, Dewsbury,
West Yorkshire WF13 4LA
Tel: +44 (0)1924 452511
Headteacher: R Ward
Age range: 3–16
No. of pupils: 26

THE FROEBELIAN SCHOOL
For further details see p. 82
Clarence Road, Horsforth,
Leeds, West Yorkshire LS18 4LB
Tel: 0113 2583047
Email: admissions@
froebelian.co.uk
Website: www.froebelian.com
Head Teacher: Mrs Catherine
Dodds B.Ed (Hons), PGCE
Age range: 3–11
No. of pupils: 185
Fees: Day £4,590–£6,850

The Gleddings School

Birdcage Lane, Savile Park,
Halifax, West Yorkshire HX3 0JB
Tel: 01422 354605
School Director: Mrs P J Wilson CBE
Age range: 3–11
No. of pupils: 191
Fees: Day £3,555–£5,910

The Grammar School at Leeds

Alwoodley Gates, Harrogate Road,
Leeds, West Yorkshire LS17 8GS
Tel: 0113 2291552
Principal and CEO: Mr
Michael Gibbons
Age range: 3–18
No. of pupils: 2120 VIth418
Fees: Day £7,723–£11,282

Wakefield Girls' High School (Junior School)

2 St John's Square, Wakefield,
West Yorkshire WF1 2QX
Tel: 01924 374577
Headmistress: Daphne
Cawthorne BEd
Age range: B3–7 G3–11
No. of pupils: 493
Fees: Day £6,609–£7,212

Wakefield Independent School

The Nostell Centre, Doncaster
Road, Nostell, Wakefield,
West Yorkshire WF4 1QG
Tel: 01924 865757
Headmistress: Mrs K E Caryl
Age range: 2.5–16
No. of pupils: 190
Fees: Day £4,590–£6,375

West Cliffe Montessori School & Nursery

33, Barlow Road, access
Belgrave Road, Keighley,
West Yorkshire BD21 2TA
Tel: 01535 609797
Principal: Mrs T Bisby
Age range: 0–8
No. of pupils: 42

Westville House Preparatory School

Carter's Lane, Middleton, Ilkley,
West Yorkshire LS29 0DQ
Tel: 01943 608053
Headteacher: Mrs R James
BSc(Hons), PGCE
Age range: 3–11
Fees: Day £4,545–£7,875

Northern Ireland

KEY TO SYMBOLS

- 🧍 Boys' school
- 🧍 Girls' school
- 🌐 International school
- 16 Tutorial or sixth form college
- Ⓐ A levels
- 🛏 Boarding accommodation
- £ Bursaries
- IB International Baccalaureate
- ✒ Learning support
- 16 Entrance at 16+
- ⚙ Vocational qualifications
- (IAPS) Independent Association of Prep Schools
- (HMC) The Headmasters' & Headmistresses' Conference
- (ISA) Independent Schools Association
- (GSA) Girls' School Association
- (BSA) Boarding Schools' Association
- Ⓢ Society of Heads

Unless otherwise indicated, all schools are coeducational day schools. Single-sex and boarding schools will be indicated by the relevant icon.

County Antrim

Campbell College Junior School
Belmont Road, Belfast,
County Antrim BT4 2ND
Tel: 028 9076 3076
Head: Mrs H M Rowan
Age range: B3–11 G3–4
Fees: Day £3,484–£3,740

Inchmarlo
Cranmore Park, Belfast,
County Antrim BT9 6JR
Tel: 028 9038 1454
Head of School: Mr A Smyth

Methodist College
1 Malone Road, Belfast,
County Antrim BT9 6BY
Tel: 028 9020 5205
Principal: J Scott W Naismith
Age range: 4–19
No. of pupils: 2307 VIth548
Fees: Day £130–£3,425

Victoria College Belfast
Cranmore Park, Belfast,
County Antrim BT9 6JA
Tel: 028 9066 1506
Principal: Ms Patricia Slevin
Age range: G5–18
No. of pupils: 1070 VIth224
Fees: Day £432 WB £10,500
FB £10,500–£17,100

County Down

Holywood Rudolf Steiner School
Saralies House, 34 Croft Road,
Holywood, County Down BT18 0PR
Tel: 028 9042 8029
Administrator: Edward Galloway
Age range: 3–17
No. of pupils: 120
Fees: Day £3,447

Rockport School
Craigavad, Holywood,
County Down BT18 0DD
Tel: 028 9042 8372
Headmaster: Mr George Vance
Age range: 3–18
No. of pupils: 200
Fees: Day £5,640–£12,360 WB
£12,720–£16,470 FB £16,770–£20,460

Scotland

KEY TO SYMBOLS

(♂) *Boys' school*

(♀) *Girls' school*

(🌐) *International school*

(16) *Tutorial or sixth form college*

(A) *A levels*

(🏫) *Boarding accommodation*

(£) *Bursaries*

(IB) *International Baccalaureate*

(✐) *Learning support*

(16•) *Entrance at 16+*

(🎓) *Vocational qualifications*

(IAPS) *Independent Association of Prep Schools*

(HMC) *The Headmasters' & Headmistresses' Conference*

(ISA) *Independent Schools Association*

(GSA) *Girls' School Association*

(BSA) *Boarding Schools' Association*

(S) *Society of Heads*

Unless otherwise indicated, all schools are coeducational day schools. Single-sex and boarding schools will be indicated by the relevant icon.

Aberdeen

Albyn School
17-23 Queen's Road,
Aberdeen AB15 4PB
Tel: 01224 322408
Headmaster: Ian E Long
AKC, PhD, FRGS, FRSA
Age range: B2–14 G2–18
No. of pupils: 675 VIth57
Fees: Day £3,500–£9,785
(£)(✐)

Robert Gordon's College
Schoolhill, Aberdeen AB10 1FE
Tel: 01224 646346
Head of College: Mr Hugh
Ouston MA, DipEd
Age range: 4–18
No. of pupils: 1573 VIth350
Fees: Day £5,949–£9,264
(£)(✐)

**St Margaret's
School for Girls**
17 Albyn Place, Aberdeen AB10 1RU
Tel: 01224 584466
Headmistress: Miss A Tomlinson
MTheol (Hons), PGCE
Age range: B3–5 years G3–18 years
No. of pupils: 417 VIth35
Fees: Day £7,071–£11,202
(♟)(£)(✐)

Aberdeenshire

**International School
of Aberdeen**
Pitfodels House, North Deeside
Road, Pitfodels, Cults, Aberdeen,
Aberdeenshire AB15 9PN
Tel: 01224 730300
Director: Dr D A Hovde
Age range: 3–18
No. of pupils: VIth64
Fees: Day £18,235–£20,420
(🌐)(£)(IB)(✐)

Angus

Lathallan School
Brotherton Castle, Johnshaven,
Montrose, Angus DD10 0HN
Tel: 01561 362220
Headmaster: Mr R Toley
Age range: 0–18
No. of pupils: 220
Fees: Day £9,000–£14,500
(♟)(£)(✐)

Argyll & Bute

Lomond School
10 Stafford Street, Helensburgh,
Argyll & Bute G84 9JX
Tel: 01436 672476
Principal: Mrs Johanna Urquhart
Age range: 3–18
No. of pupils: VIth50
Fees: Day £4,470–£9,120 FB £20,030
(🌐)(♟)(£)(✐)

Borders

St Mary's Prep School
Abbey Park, Melrose,
Borders TD6 9LN
Tel: 01896 822517
Headmaster: Mr Liam Harvey
Age range: 2–13
Fees: Day £8,700–£11,550
WB £14,250
(♟)(£)(✐)

Clackmannanshire

Dollar Academy
Dollar, Clackmannanshire FK14 7DU
Tel: 01259 742511
Rector: Mr David Knapman Mphil
Age range: 5–18
No. of pupils: 1200 VIth142
Fees: Day £7,974–£10,665 WB
£20,637–£23,328 FB £21,978–£24,669

Dundee

High School of Dundee
Euclid Crescent, Dundee DD1 1HU
Tel: 01382 202921
Rector: Dr John Halliday
Age range: 5–18
No. of pupils: 1019 VIth99
Fees: Day £6,930–£9,840

East Lothian

Belhaven Hill
Dunbar, East Lothian EH42 1NN
Tel: 01368 862785
Headmaster: I K MacAskill BEd
Age range: 8–13
No. of pupils: 122
Fees: Day £14,325 FB £20,655

Loretto Junior School
North Esk Lodge, 1 North
High Street, Musselburgh,
East Lothian EH21 6JA
Tel: 0131 653 4570
Headmaster: Richard Selley BEd
Age range: 3–12
No. of pupils: 200
Fees: Day £6,210–£11,550
FB £13,500–£15,000

The Compass School
West Road, Haddington,
East Lothian EH41 3RD
Tel: 01620 822642
Headmaster: Mr Mark
Becher MA(Hons), PGCE
Age range: 4–12
No. of pupils: 120
Fees: Day £6,685–£7,755

Edinburgh

Cargilfield School
45 Gamekeeper's Road,
Edinburgh EH4 1PU
Tel: 0131 336 2207
Headmaster: Mr. Robert Taylor
Age range: 3–13
No. of pupils: 325
Fees: Day £4,080–£11,850
WB £14,400 FB £15,000

Clifton Hall
Newbridge, Edinburgh EH28 8LQ
Tel: 0131 333 1359
Headmaster: Mr R Grant
Age range: 3–18
No. of pupils: 299 VIth8
Fees: Day £1,500–£9,500

Edinburgh Steiner School
60 Spylaw Road,
Edinburgh EH10 5BR
Tel: 0131 337 3410
Age range: 3–18
Fees: Day £3,756–£7,860

**Fettes College
Preparatory School**
East Fettes Avenue,
Edinburgh EH4 1QZ
Tel: 0131 332 2976
Headmaster: Mr A A Edwards
Age range: 7–13
No. of pupils: 169
Fees: Day £11,331 FB £17,739

George Heriot's School
Lauriston Place, Edinburgh EH3 9EQ
Tel: 0131 229 7263
Principal: Mr Gareth E Doodes MA
Age range: 4–18
No. of pupils: 1641 VIth352
Fees: Day £6,867–£10,299

George Watson's College
Colinton Road, Edinburgh EH10 5EG
Tel: 0131 446 6000
Principal: Mr Melvyn Roffe
Age range: 3–18
No. of pupils: 2336
Fees: Day £4,260–£10,983

**MERCHISTON
CASTLE SCHOOL**
For further details see p. 84
294 Colinton Road,
Edinburgh EH13 0PU
Tel: 0131 312 2201
Email: admissions@
merchiston.co.uk
Website: www.merchiston.co.uk
Headmaster: Mr A R Hunter BA
Age range: B7–18
No. of pupils: 460
Fees: Day £12,525–£20,190
FB £17,545–£27,465

St George's School for Girls
Garscube Terrace,
Edinburgh EH12 6BG
Tel: 0131 311 8000
Head: Ms Anne Everest BA(Hons)
Age range: B2–5 years G2–18 years
Fees: Day £7,785–£12,645 FB £26,630

St Mary's Music School
Coates Hall, 25 Grosvenor
Crescent, Edinburgh EH12 5EL
Tel: 0131 538 7766
Headteacher: Mrs Jennifer
Rimer BMus(Hons), LRAM,
DipEd, Hon ARAM
Age range: 9–19
No. of pupils: VIth17

The Edinburgh Academy
42 Henderson Row,
Edinburgh EH3 5BL
Tel: 0131 556 4603
Rector: Marco Longmore
Age range: 2–18
No. of pupils: 992 VIth93
Fees: Day £8,860–£14,960

**The Mary Erskine &
Stewart's Melville
Junior School**
Queensferry Road,
Edinburgh EH4 3EZ
Tel: 0131 311 1111
Headmaster: Mr Bryan Lewis
Age range: 3–11
No. of pupils: 1218
Fees: Day £5,574–£7,218 WB
£14,628–£14,814 FB £15,051–£15,237

Fife

St Leonards School
St Andrews, Fife KY16 9QJ
Tel: 01334 472126
Headmaster: Dr Michael Carslaw
Age range: 5–19
No. of pupils: VIth138
Fees: Day £8,259–£11,388
FB £27,114–£27,114
🌍 🎓 £ IB ✐

Glasgow

Belmont House School
Sandringham Avenue, Newton
Mearns, Glasgow G77 5DU
Tel: 0141 639 2922
Principal: Mr Melvyn D Shanks
BSc, DipEd, MInstP, CPhys, SQH
Age range: 3–18
No. of pupils: 300
Fees: Day £5,976–£11,316
£ ✐

Craigholme School
72 St Andrews Drive, Pollokshields,
Glasgow G41 4HS
Tel: 0141 427 0375
Principal: Ms Gillian C K
Stobo BSc, MSc, DipEd
Age range: B3–5 G3–18
No. of pupils: 442 VIth30
Fees: Day £4,137–£9,735
🎓 £ ✐

Fernhill School
Fernbrae Avenue, Burnside,
Rutherglen, Glasgow G73 4SG
Tel: 0141 634 2674
Headteacher: Mrs Jacqueline
Sexton BSc, PGCE
Age range: B4–11 G4–18
No. of pupils: 300 VIth16
Fees: Day £7,470–£8,976
🎓 £ ✐

**Hutchesons'
Grammar School**
21 Beaton Road, Glasgow G41 4NW
Tel: 0141 423 2933
Rector: Dr Kenneth M
Greig MA, PhD
Age range: 5–18
No. of pupils: 1650 VIth151
Fees: Day £7,427–£9,473
Ⓐ £ ✐

St Aloysius' College
45 Hill Street, Glasgow G3 6RJ
Tel: 0141 332 3190
Headmaster: Mr J E Stoer BA
Age range: 3–18
No. of pupils: 1289 VIth81
Fees: Day £6,804–£9,009
Ⓐ £ ✐

The Glasgow Academy
Colebrooke Street, Kelvinbridge,
Glasgow G12 8HE
Tel: 0141 334 8558
Rector: Mr Peter Brodie MA, MA(Ed)
Age range: 3–18
No. of pupils: 1148 VIth221
Fees: Day £3,255–£9,645
£ ✐

**The Glasgow
Academy Dairsie**
54 Newlands Road, Newlands,
Glasgow G43 2JG
Tel: 0141 632 0736
Headmistress: Mrs Shona McKnight
Age range: 3–9
No. of pupils: 74
Fees: Day £2,730–£5,505

**The Glasgow Academy,
Milngavie**
Mugdock Road, Milngavie,
Glasgow G62 8NP
Tel: +44 (0)1419 563758
Head of School: Miss JA McMorran
Fees: Day £3,540–£8,025

**The High School
of Glasgow**
637 Crow Road, Glasgow G13 1PL
Tel: 0141 954 9628
Rector: Colin D R Mair
Age range: 3–18
No. of pupils: 1042 VIth201
Fees: Day £3,321–£10,236
£ ✐

The Kelvinside Academy
33 Kirklee Road, Glasgow G12 0SW
Tel: 0141 357 3376
Rector: Mrs Lesley Douglas
Age range: 3–18
No. of pupils: 640 VIth73
Fees: Day £2,313–£8,895
Ⓐ £ ✐

Moray

GORDONSTOUN
For further details see p. 83
Elgin, Moray IV30 5RF
Tel: 01343 837829
Email: admissions@
gordonstoun.org.uk
Website:
www.gordonstoun.org.uk
Principal: Mr Simon Reid BA
Age range: 7–18
No. of pupils: 104
Fees: Day £13,176 WB
£21,429 FB £21,429
🌍 Ⓐ 🎓 £ ✐

Moray Steiner School
Drumduan, Clovenside Road,
Forres, Moray IV36 2RD
Tel: 01309 676300
Age range: 3–16

Perth & Kinross

Ardvreck School
Gwydyr Road, Crieff, Perth
& Kinross PH7 4EX
Tel: 01764 653112
Headmaster: Richard Harvey
Age range: 3–13
No. of pupils: 150
Fees: Day £12,537 FB £18,840

**Craigclowan
Preparatory School**
Edinburgh Road, Perth,
Perth & Kinross PH2 8PS
Tel: 01738 626310
Interim Co-Heads: Liz
Henderson & Patrick Borderie
Age range: 3–13
Fees: Day £11,130

KILGRASTON SCHOOL
For further details see p. 86
Bridge of Earn, Perth, Perth
& Kinross PH2 9BQ
Tel: 01738 812257
Email: headoffice@
kilgraston.com
Website: www.kilgraston.com
Headmistress: Mrs.
Dorothy MacGinty
Age range: B3–5 G3–18
No. of pupils: 285 VIth60
Fees: Day £8,985–£16,305
FB £21,285–£27,855

Morrison's Academy
Crieff, Perth & Kinross PH7 3AN
Tel: 01764 653885
Principal: Simon Pengelley BA(Hons)
Age range: 3–18
No. of pupils: VIth51
Fees: Day £7,161–£10,839

Renfrewshire

**Cedars School of
Excellence**
31 Ardgowan Square, Greenock,
Renfrewshire PA16 8NJ
Tel: 01475 723905
Headteacher: Mrs Alison Speirs
Age range: 5–16
No. of pupils: 95
Fees: Day £3,400–£5,000

St Columba's School
Duchal Road, Kilmacolm,
Renfrewshire PA13 4AU
Tel: 01505 872238
Head of School: Mr D Girdwood
DL, BSc, MEd, SQH
Age range: 3–18
No. of pupils: 731 VIth106
Fees: Day £2,490–£9,780

South Ayrshire

Wellington School
Carleton Turrets, Ayr, South
Ayrshire KA7 2XH
Tel: 01292 269321
Head: Mr R M Parlour BSc(Hons), BA,
PGCE(Oxon), MMBA, FIAP, FRSA
Age range: 3–18
No. of pupils: VIth45
Fees: Day £5,304–£10,407

South Lanarkshire

Hamilton College
Bothwell Road, Hamilton,
South Lanarkshire ML3 0AY
Tel: 01698 282700
Principal: Ms Margaret Clarke
Age range: 3–18
No. of pupils: VIth49
Fees: Day £6,450–£8,574

Stirling

Beaconhurst School
52 Kenilworth Road, Bridge
of Allan, Stirling FK9 4RR
Tel: 01786 832146
Headmaster: Mr Iain
Kilpatrick BA, MEd, FRSA
Age range: 3–18
No. of pupils: 403
Fees: Day £6,474–£8,706

Wales

KEY TO SYMBOLS

- (†) Boys' school
- (♀) Girls' school
- (🌐) International school
- (16+) Tutorial or sixth form college
- (A) A levels
- (🏠) Boarding accommodation
- (£) Bursaries
- (IB) International Baccalaureate
- (✎) Learning support
- (16+) Entrance at 16+
- (🎓) Vocational qualifications
- (IAPS) Independent Association of Prep Schools
- (HMC) The Headmasters' & Headmistresses' Conference
- (ISA) Independent Schools Association
- (GSA) Girls' School Association
- (BSA) Boarding Schools' Association
- (S) Society of Heads

*Unless otherwise indicated, all schools are
coeducational day schools. Single-sex and boarding
schools will be indicated by the relevant icon.*

Carmarthenshire

St Michael's School
Bryn, Llanelli, Carmarthenshire
SA14 9TU
Tel: 01554 820325
Head of School: Mr Alun Millington
Age range: 3–18
No. of pupils: 420 VIth80
Fees: Day £4,179–£7,968 FB £18,250
Ⓐ Ⓐ 🏛

Clwyd

**Rydal Penrhos
Preparatory School**
Pwllycrochan Avenue, Colwyn
Bay, Clwyd LL29 7BP
Tel: 01492 530381
Headmaster: Mr Roger McDuff
Age range: 2.5–11
No. of pupils: 180
Fees: Day £2,250–£2,990
🏛 ✎

Denbighshire

Fairholme School
The Mount, Mount Road, St
Asaph, Denbighshire LL17 0DH
Tel: 01745 583505
Principal: Mrs E Perkins MA(Oxon)
Age range: 3–11
No. of pupils: 110
Fees: Day £6,000–£6,600

Ruthin School
Ruthin, Denbighshire LL15 1EE
Tel: 01824 702543
Headmaster: Mr T J Belfield
Age range: 3–18
No. of pupils: 240 VIth41
Fees: Day £5,550–£10,320
WB £13,965 FB £16,755
Ⓐ Ⓐ 🏛 £

Glamorgan

**Howell's School,
Llandaff GDST**
Cardiff Road, Llandaff, Cardiff,
Glamorgan CF5 2YD
Tel: 029 2056 2019
Principal: Mrs Sally Davis
Age range: 16–18 G3–18
No. of pupils: 798 VIth200
Fees: Day £7,652–£12,993
Ⓐ Ⓐ £ ✎

Kings Monkton School
6 West Grove, Cardiff,
Glamorgan CF24 3XL
Tel: 02920 482 854
Principal: Mr Paul Norton
Age range: 2–18
No. of pupils: 236
Ⓐ £ ✎

Oakleigh House School
38 Penlan Crescent, Uplands,
Swansea, Glamorgan SA2 0RL
Tel: 01792 298537
Headmistress: Mrs R Ferriman
BA(Hons)Ed, MEd
Age range: 2–11
Fees: Day £5,550–£6,570
£ ✎

St Clare's School
Newton, Porthcawl,
Glamorgan CF36 5NR
Tel: 01656 782509
Headteacher: Mrs C M Barnard
Age range: 3–18
No. of pupils: 298 VIth45
Fees: Day £4,080–£7,665
Ⓐ

St John's College, Cardiff
College Green, Old St Mellons,
Cardiff, Glamorgan CF3 5YX
Tel: 029 2077 8936
Headmaster: Dr D J Neville
MA(Cantab), BSc, MusD,
FRSA, AWACM, PGCE
Age range: 3–18
No. of pupils: 485
Fees: Day £6,760–£13,300
Ⓐ £ ✎

**The Cathedral
School, Llandaff**
Llandaff, Cardiff,
Glamorgan CF5 2YH
Tel: 029 2056 3179
Headmaster: Mr P L Gray
MA(Cantab), ARCO, PGCE
Age range: 3–16
Fees: Day £5,625–£8,175
£

Westbourne School
Hickman Road, Penarth,
Glamorgan CF64 2AJ
Tel: 029 2070 5705
Head of School: Mr K W
Underhill MA(Ed)
Age range: 3–18
No. of pupils: 162
Fees: Day £6,450–£11,700
FB £23,350–£25,850
Ⓐ 🏛 £ Ⓘ🅱 ✎

Gwynedd

Hillgrove School
5 Ffriddoedd Road, Bangor,
Gwynedd LL57 2TW
Tel: 01248 353568
Heads: Mr J G Porter & Mrs S Porter
Age range: 3–16
No. of pupils: 155
Fees: Day £2,475–£4,200

St Gerard's School
Ffriddoedd Road, Bangor,
Gwynedd LL57 2EL
Tel: 01248 351656
Headteacher: Miss Anne
Parkinson BA(Hons)
Age range: 3–18
No. of pupils: VIth25
Fees: Day £5,790–£8,760
(A) (£)

Monmouthshire

Haberdashers' Agincourt School
Dixton Lane, Monmouth,
Monmouthshire NP25 3SY
Tel: 01600 713970
Head: Mrs E Thomas
Age range: 3–7
No. of pupils: 124
Fees: Day £2,574–£4,134

Haberdashers' Monmouth School for Girls
Hereford Road, Monmouth,
Monmouthshire NP25 5XT
Tel: 01600 711104
Head: Mrs H Davy MA(Oxon)
Age range: G7–18
No. of pupils: 582 VIth156
Fees: Day £9,537–£12,141
FB £18,171–£23,112

Monmouth School
Almshouse Street, Monmouth,
Monmouthshire NP25 3XP
Tel: 01600 710433
Headmaster: Dr. Andrew J
Daniel BSc, MEd, PhD
Age range: B7–18
No. of pupils: 685 VIth207
Fees: Day £9,951–£14,187
FB £18,717–£27,255

Rougemont School
Llantarnam Hall,
Malpas Road, Newport,
Monmouthshire NP20 6QB
Tel: 01633 820800
Headmaster: Mr Robert Carnevale
Age range: 3–18
No. of pupils: 700 VIth111
Fees: Day £5,880–£9,240
(A) (£) (pen)

St John's-on-the-Hill
Tutshill, Chepstow,
Monmouthshire NP16 7LE
Tel: 01291 622045
Headmaster: Mr N Folland BSc
Age range: 3 months–13 years
No. of pupils: 362
Fees: Day £7,005–£11,565
WB £16,275 FB £16,275

Pembrokeshire

Nant-y-Cwm Steiner School
Llanycefn, Clunderwen,
Pembrokeshire SA66 7QJ
Tel: 01437 563 640
Age range: 0–14

Redhill Preparatory School
The Garth, St David's
Road, Haverfordwest,
Pembrokeshire SA61 2UR
Tel: 01437 762472
Principal: Mrs Lovegrove
Age range: 0–11
Fees: Day £4,950–£5,100
(£) (pen)

Appendix

Glossary of abbreviations

AEB	Associated Examining Board for the General Certificate of Education
AGBIS	Association of Governing Bodies of Independent Schools
ASCL	Association of School & College Leaders
BA	Bachelor of Arts
BAC	British Accreditation Council for Independent Further and Higher Education
BEd	Bachelor of Education
BSA	Boarding Schools' Association
BSc	Bachelor of Science
BTEC	Range of work-related, practical programmes leading to qualifications equivalent to GCSEs and A levels awarded by Edexcel
Cantab	Cambridge University
CertEd	Certificate of Education
DipEd	Diploma of Education
Edexcel	GCSE Examining group, incorporating Business and Technology Education Council (BTEC) and University of London Examinations and Assessment Council (ULEAC)
EFL	English as a Foreign Language
ESL	English as a Second Language
FRSA	Fellow of the Royal Society of Arts
GCSE	General Certificate of Secondary Education
GDST	Girls' Day School Trust
GNVQ	General National Vocational Qualifications
GSVQ	General Scottish Vocational Qualifications
GSA	Girls' Schools Association
HMC	Headmasters' and Headmistresses' Conference
HMCJ	Headmasters' and Headmistresses' Conference Junior Schools
IAPS	Independent Association of Prep Schools
IB	International Baccalaureate
ISA	Independent Schools Association
ISBA	Independent Schools' Bursars' Association
ISC	Independent Schools Council
ISEB	Independent Schools Examination Board
ITEC	International Examination Council
LA	Local Authority (formerly LEA - Local Educational Authority)
MA	Master of Arts
MEd	Master of Education
MLitt	Master of Letters
MMI	Maria Montessori Institute
MSc	Master of Science
NAGC	National Association for Gifted Children
NAHT	National Association of Head Teachers
NAIS	National Association of Independent Schools
NVQ	National Vocational Qualifications
OCR	Oxford, Cambridge and RSA Examinations
Oxon	Oxford University
PGCE	Post Graduate Certificate in Education
PhD	Doctor of Philosophy
QCA	Qualifications and Curriculum Authority
RSIS	The Round Square Schools
SATIPS	Support & Training in Prep Schools
SCIS	Scottish Council of Independent Schools
SEN	Special Educational Needs
SoH	Society of Heads
SQA	Scottish Qualifications Authority

Index

Index

C

Index

G

H

Index

M

N

O

Index

Index

U

V